THE BOOK OF
A MORMON:

The Real Life and Strange Times of an LDS missionary
Scott D. Miller and Mark A. Hubble

ISBN 978-0-9966624-1-3

Cover and Interior Design: Annabel Brandon

To Karen, for loving me
To my son Michael, for being
To Mark, for enduring friendship
To Vin, for listening

CONTENTS

ACKNOWLEDGEMENTS

We want to express deep appreciation to our colleagues and friends who volunteered to read and comment on earlier versions of this manuscript. Their critique, advice and enthusiasm inspired us to continue. The book is better for their efforts. In alphabetical order, we thank: Chris Beukema, John and Renee Dalton, John Dehlin, Karen Donahey, Jaime Freedman, Jean Hubble, Day Irmiter, Kirk Kinsey, Douglas Miller, Lynn D. Johnson, Melody Rognan, Rich Simon, Jeff St. John, and Sara Stech. Any flaws or shortcomings are entirely our own. Finally, we are grateful to Paul Lamb, at Howard Morhaim Literary Agency, for his heartfelt encouragement.

DISCLAIMER

All of the events related in this book are true. Characters have been created and events rearranged in order to tell the story in a compelling and coherent fashion as well as protect the identity of real people and places. With the exception of Elder Scott Miller and his immediate family, any resemblance of the characters to actual people, living or dead, is purely coincidental.

THREE YEARS ON:

A PREFACE TO THE 2018 EDITION

"You live life looking forward, you understand life looking back."

Soren Kierkegaard

In the bedroom I shared with my younger brother growing up, we had a double dresser with a bookcase. The top drawer, on the right-hand side, just under the complete set of the *Childcraft Encyclopedia*, was mine. Into it, I put everything that mattered to me as a kid. My mother called it, "Scott's Junk Drawer." The contents remained undisturbed after I left for college and were there when I returned from my mission for the Church of Jesus Christ of Latter-day Saints. In the years that followed, when I came home for a visit, I'd sometimes open that drawer. *One day*, I'd say to myself, *I've gotta clean this out.*

Much later, after both my parents had died, and the task of preparing their home for sale fell to me and my two brothers, I went through the drawer one last time. The same bits and pieces were there, as they had been for more than three decades. Empty plastic shell casings from my *Johnny Eagle US Army Lieutenant* toy pistol. A set of purple clackers – a toy later banned because they were prone to shatter, sending shards of sharp acrylic flying everywhere. A chrome-plated peace sign, four inches in diameter, I'd worn on a chain during seventh grade. And, a bright, red personal diary in simulated leather, complete with lock and key.

Holding each item brought back strong memories. The Christmas I'd received the toy gun. The time I used my allowance to purchase the clackers at a weekend swap meet. The Rexall drug store where I'd first seen the journal. *Why hadn't I thrown out this stuff a long time ago?* The pistol had been missing for years, along with the tips to the plastic bullets. At most, I played with those clackers for a week or two after buying them. And the journal? I'd never even made a single entry. Not to mention all the other junk –scraps of paper, empty boxes, a collection of small springs from old ballpoint pens, a bag of shattered windshield glass, and much more.

I remember sitting there for a few moments and then, picking up the drawer, dumping the contents into a large, heavy duty trash bag – one of the many my brothers and I would fill that day. I did not feel sad or happy, wistful or resolved. Neither have I, in the time since, experienced a moment's indecision, thinking my actions rash or wishing I'd kept one particular item or another. I didn't need those things any longer. In a word, I felt complete.

Curiously, the same feeling accompanies me now as I write the forward to the second, revised and newly edited, *The Book of a Mormon: The Real Life and Strange Times of an LDS Missionary.* It wasn't always that way. For decades following my mission experience, I kept a "junk drawer" of sorts – boxes of books, papers, letters, and other ephemera I carted around with me from California to Utah and back, then on to Milwaukee, where I took my first job, and finally to Chicago where I live today. Every so often –especially when I was moving – I'd open the boxes and think, *Why am I keeping this stuff?* Then, I'd dutifully haul all of it to my new home where it would wind up in the back of a closet.

Although I didn't know it at the time, writing and publishing the story of my two-year mission would foster another experience of completion. Disparate memories formed into a story, the arc of which offered a perspective on my life that, until then, had proven elusive. The response of readers was especially gratifying. Reviews posted on Amazon and other sites were overwhelmingly positive. Non-Mormons frequently mentioned being helped to understand the faith. Former missionaries wrote they felt affirmed and validated by the stories shared. Several of those I'd served with reached out to me. Some were still active, committed members. Others, like me, no longer participated. Ultimately, the book won a prize -- The Brodie for "Best LDS Nonfiction."

A handful took umbrage, questioning my motives and even the truthfulness of my account. The raw language and matter-of-fact description of masturbation and other sexual situations apparently did not ring true to them. "No missionary uses such words," one reader asserted. Another, thinking they had found an inconsistency in the story's timeline, openly questioned whether I, or anything in the book, could be trusted. What can be said? In the first instance, the person obviously had never met or spoke with me during my mission. As it is, I *did* use such language. Regarding the claimed "inconsistency," I offered no response as several other readers published reviews affirming the accuracy of my account.

Between the first and present edition, nothing substantive has changed. My friend, co-author, and colleague, Mark Hubble, and I met writer and editor, Day Irmiter, who kindly offered to run through the volume, correcting errors and making suggestions to improve readability. We owe her a great deal of gratitude. Thanks to her, the book is much stronger. Of course, no biography, including this one, contains every detail of a person's life or experience. That said, what is included is sufficient to tell the story, and is true. In fact, I found that the telling was in no small way healing.

Scott D. Miller

Chicago, Illinois (USA)

September 10, 2018

INTRODUCTION

"I don't blame anyone for not believing my history. If I had not experienced what I have, I would not believe it myself."

Joseph Smith (1844)
First Prophet, Seer, and Revelator
Church of Jesus Christ of Latter Day Saints

"Polygamy." That's what most say when asked what they know about Mormons or the Mormon Church. Some mention the flamboyant, Tony Award winning Broadway play, *The Book of Mormon*. Others have visited Salt Lake City, heard the Tabernacle Choir, or seen those huge, imposing temples off the interstate. You can't miss them. Tall spires of blistering white marble topped by some big golden guy, blowing a horn.

Do *you* know any Mormons?

They know you: where you live, your religious affiliation, and family history. They keep records. Lots of records. Last count 3.5 billion images on microfilm, microfiche, and digital media, all buried in a granite vault deep in the Wasatch Mountains near Church headquarters.

Don't worry. There's nothing nefarious taking place. It's not about invading your privacy or stealing your identity. The Mormons are on a mission. They want to save your soul—yours, and every man, woman, and child on Earth. For that to happen, you have to join their church, the only true church. It *is* the only way to get into Heaven.

A good chance exists many of your family members are already Mormon. And, they are in remarkable company. Elvis Presley, Princess Diana, Pope John Paul II, and even Adolf Hitler were baptized into the faith, posthumously. That's right. What you don't do in life, Mormons will take care of for you in death.

The Church is frantic. Time is running out. These are the "Latter Days." Jesus is coming back and this time he means business. Everyone that can be saved, must be saved, NOW!

No doubt exists—members are bound and determined to make you one of them. It's been that way since the Church was established in 1830. That year, its founder, the young American Prophet Joseph Smith, dispatched the first missionaries. Around the world they went. To date, millions have served. Millions! Tens of thousands are out today, their ranks recently surging to 80,000 when Church leaders lowered the age of eligibility from 19 to 18.

Most are boys, some girls. They always travel in pairs. If they haven't already, they are coming to knock on a door near you. Always smiling and polite, you can't mistake them for anyone else. They are instantly recognizable in their blue suits and black name tags. Not home? No worries. They'll "friend" you on Facebook, or send you a Tweet. A whole division, housed in Dilbert-like cubicles, trolls the web on a daily basis, answering questions and offering live chat. You can't hide.

I know. I was one of them. This is my story. Had I not gone through the experience myself, spent two years in a foreign country doing my best to bring new members into the fold, I honestly would not believe a word of what follows. And yet, it's true. Every last bit.

Don't get me wrong. If you are hoping to find some juicy piece of debauchery—ritualized sexual abuse of young children or bodies in the basement—you are going to be disappointed. I wasn't buggered by a member of the clergy, and no one I knew had more than one wife.

Sure, that kind of stuff gets headlines—and if I had wanted to write a screed, there is plenty to rant about in the history, current practices and politics of the Church, including:

- Joseph Smith sent young men on missions and then secretly married their wives while they were away;

- Brigham Young, the man who became the Church's second leader following the murder of Smith, continued the practice, taking at least 55 women as wives, some of them as young as 15;

- For more than a century, and long after the passing of civil rights legislation, the Church continued to practice segregation, banning people of

African ancestry from full participation and refusing them the rights and privileges available to white members;

- Mormons are deeply involved in national law enforcement and intelligence agencies. Two prominent members were responsible for crafting and sanctioning guidelines for the use of torture on suspected terrorists;

- Very recently, church leaders orchestrated a massive, secret, and successful campaign to pass a constitutional amendment in the State of California denying gay people the right to marry in the State.

As unsettling as these facts are, their tabloidesque nature distracts attention from a much bigger story. Of course, it is human nature. A stream of sensational stories, of misconduct and abuse of power, leads many to dismiss Mormonism out of hand. Parody only adds fuel to this fire. Not only are these people corrupt, they are silly. Watch the "All about Mormons" episode on *Southpark* or take in the Broadway play. Why would anyone take them seriously? No reasonable person would. They're kooks.

For all that, few would be so cavalier if they knew what takes place on a Mormon mission. The experience irrevocably changed me. Everything I grew up believing about what most matters in life—family, faith, and friendship—was turned upside down. Actually, it was ripped away. I was no longer an innocent. One day, I was a regular kid like everyone else. On Sundays, I went to church. On weekends, I was surfing the sunny shores of Southern California. The next, I was marching lockstep in service to an organization I quickly discovered I knew very little about and which, to my complete dismay, cared nothing about me, the other young men with whom I served, or the people I'd been sent to save.

For many years following my mission, I wondered, "How could this have happened?" "How could I be so blind?" I had a hard time explaining to myself why I went, why I stayed, and justifying what I did for two years. At some point, I decided it was best a story forgotten, to put it out of my mind, regard it as a lapse in judgement, never to be shared or revealed.

Who would care anyway? Certainly not Mormons. Members refer to missionary service as "the best two years" of a man's life. As soon as little boys are out of diapers, they learn the Sunday school song, *I Hope they Call Me on a Mission* ("When I have grown a foot or two. I hope by then I will be ready. To teach and preach and work as missionaries do ...”). Think otherwise and you are unworthy in the sight of God.

And non-Mormons? The public? The people church members refer to as, “Gentiles?” Why would they be interested? To them, we are just a bunch of whackjobs, that group of wingnuts holed up in Utah.

Despite the apparent differences between Mormons and Gentiles, they are very much alike. Both are ignorant of and, sadly, indifferent toward what happens to the thousands of kids shipped out each year to serve as missionaries. In the name of Christ, these young people are told, who you are, what you feel, and what happens to you, does not matter. You have one job and one job alone: obey, submit, do what you are told, whatever the cost.

No one who goes through such an experience merits scorn or ridicule, much less disinterest. They deserve our empathy. This is what I hope to achieve by revealing the real life and strange times of my own mission experience.

Scott D. Miller

Chicago, Illinois (USA)

https://www.facebook.com/pages/
The-Book-of-a-Mormon/1442562596072686

1

THE ARRIVAL

∾

"The question is asked: Should every young man fill a mission? And the answer of the Church is yes, and the answer of the LORD is yes."

Spencer W. Kimball
12th Prophet , Seer, and Revelator
Church of Jesus Christ of Latter Day Saints
(*Ensign*, May 1974, p. 86)

∾

I don't remember getting off the plane. It had been a long journey, my first out of the country. *SAS* went on strike shortly after our departure from the U.S., leaving us stranded for hours and hours in Copenhagen without currency, contacts, or a clue of how we would reach our final destination. Somehow, we eventually made it to Göteborg (pronounced, "you-tah-bore-ē"), Sweden's second largest municipality, and the place that would be my HQ for the next two years.

I do recall the seemingly endless trip from Landvetter Airport into town. Nothing was as I expected. Beyond the yellow-tinged lamps lighting the expressway, the landscape was flat, cold, and featureless, more barren tundra than winter wonderland. *Where are the mountains, the Alps?* I asked myself. *Majestic vistas? Snow swept valleys? Saint Bernard dogs and brown cows? And hey, what about the people, where are they? You know, tow-headed men in lederhosen and buxom women in clogs?* Looking back now, I was more than naïve. Call me Ishmael? Hardly. Call me Rube.

What a sight we made. We were squeezed together in a Mercedes, not the luxury vehicle I knew from the highways of southern California, but an old utility van refitted for transporting stripling crusaders to the front. Our driver was a tall, imposing figure with bulging blue eyes and thin, angular features. Other than the machine gun toting customs officials, he had been the only person at the airport.

"Thorsson heter jag," (Thorsson is my name) he declared in perfect Swedish and then greeted each of us with a prolonged, bone-crushing handshake and penetrating stare. Those eyes. In that moment, it was as though he read my innermost thoughts, instantly measured my moral worth, and found me wanting. I had no idea how powerful a role this man would play in my life over the next two years, controlling every aspect—when I went to bed, how long I slept, when I woke, what I ate, what I read, and where and with whom I lived.

On the ride, no one spoke a word. Physically, mentally, and emotionally spent, conversation proved too much of a challenge. The gung ho spirit, muted. The only sound to be heard was the rhythmic thumping of the tires hitting breaks in the pavement. A witness to our silence, unfamiliar with how fatigued we were, might be tempted to say, "This is one disciplined bunch of 19-year-olds." That impression would have been supported by our appearance, particularly our shared attire, the uniform of our calling: blue suit straight off the rack at Sears, Van Huesen white dress shirt, conservative tie, dark Gold Toe® brand socks, and black lace-up wingtips.

Truth is, we *were* a disciplined bunch, mightily in fact, having just graduated from our flagship bootcamp of the soul. Two months of rigorous preparation at the Language Training Mission (LTM) in Provo, Utah. The goal was to ensure our hands were clean, our hearts pure, and our spirits contrite. To forge one mind and commitment to the only cause that mattered. For us, the newly arrived in this land of the midnight sun, Vikings, and ABBA, the charge was clear: "att frälsa Svenska folket" (to save the Swedish people [pronounced, "aht frail-sah Sven-ska foal-khet"]). Soldiers of the restored covenant of the Christ, we were the Mormon missionaries.

~

Four months earlier, going on a mission had seemed like such a good idea. Now, with wingtips on the ground, a voice in my head screamed, *What were you thinking?* Hang up your surfboard, leave your friends and family, cut your hair, put off college, and for the next two years swear off anything that would remotely be considered fun by most 19-year olds. No TV or radio. No dating (actually, no contact with girls in any form beyond a handshake). No music (apart from the *Mormon Tabernacle Choir*). No magazines (except those published by the Church). No books (save the *Bible* and *Book of Mormon*). No car. No leisure time. No time alone whatsoever. All this, and you have the added joy of paying for it by yourself. No one I knew in my family had ever gone on a mission. Siblings, parents, aunts, uncles, cousins, grandparents. Not a missionary among them, but Mormons all, with roots extending back to the earliest days of the Church. My ancestors in Wales, Scotland, Denmark, Sweden, and Iceland, sacrificed everything, leaving their homes, possessions, work, friends and relatives, to join the rest of the faithful in the United States. Many perished along the way.

Within days of their arrival in Missouri, and following an arduous three month long voyage by steamship, my great-great-grandmother Mary Bowen and six month old daughter, Ann, succumbed to cholera. Her husband, David, was heartbroken. He was also penniless, having been cheated out of wages promised for work aboard ship by Orson Pratt, a revered figure among Mormons. Pratt was a close confidant of Joseph Smith, the charismatic and controversial founder of the Church, and a member of the Quorum of Twelve Apostles, a group analogous to the original Disciples of Christ. Despite his many misfortunes, my great-great-grandfather pushed on. With his two and a half year old son, Morgan, he traveled first to Council Bluffs, Iowa, and then eventually by Schuttler wagon to Salt Lake City, Utah.

My father never even considered going on a mission. It really wasn't a choice. World War II was raging. His older brother Bill, fighting in Belgium, had been wounded in the Battle of Bastogne. Feeling compelled to serve, Dad, at 17, enlisted in the Navy, forging my grandparents' signature on the required letter of consent. In San Diego, California, he trained as a corpsman at the Hospital Corp School. After being assigned to the Fleet Marine

Force, he was transferred to Camp Pendleton to complete his schooling. From there, he joined the invasion forces headed for Okinawa, destined to be the bloodiest battle of the Pacific War. Later, when MacArthur accepted the surrender of the Japanese on the deck of the USS Missouri, my father was there. Back in the States, he tended to the wounded returning from Europe and the Pacific as they were transported on troop trains to their homes and hospitals across the country.

Dad married Mom on a weekend pass. Her family's sacrifices for and affiliation with the Church were no less notable. In fact, the only missionary among our ancestors, Zerah Pulsifer, was her great-great-great grandfather. He joined in 1831, only one year after the Church was formed. History places him at every major event in the early days of the Faith: when the Mormons were driven from Missouri, when Joseph Smith was attacked and killed by a mob in Illinois, and when Brigham Young ascended to the leadership of the Church and ordered the migration westward. Among his many converts was Wilford Woodruff, the man who would become the fourth president and prophet of the Mormon religion—best known for his *1890 Manifesto* prohibiting the practice of polygamy, a decision that opened the door to statehood for the Utah Territory.

Growing up, I knew little of my family's rich heritage. It was not something we talked about. Some start or join organizations celebrating their pedigree and connection to important historical events or people. The Daughters of the American Revolution and the Society of the Descendants of the Founding Fathers are good examples. Not us. We were just an average American family living in Glendora, California, a suburb of Los Angeles. Mom, Dad, older brother Doug, younger brother Marc and me.

By the time I was born, my father was an elementary school principal; my mother, like most women at the time, a homemaker. We attended public schools, lived and were active in a community that was religiously diverse. For us, being a Mormon simply meant that we attended a different church on Sundays than our neighbors, one who happened to be Lutheran, the other Catholic. As far as I knew, no one knew about or cared that my family was Mormon. Unlike my forbearers, the Church was a part of our lives, *not* our whole life.

∽

When the van came to an abrupt stop, so ended my reverie and brief trip down memory lane. I had no idea where we were. Wiping the frost from the window, I peered outside. Grey, stone, five-story buildings lined the dimly lit street on both sides. Still no people. According to my watch, it was eight o'clock back home in California. Or was that the time in Provo, Utah? AM or PM? The hour was completely lost on me. Clearly it was late here.

The snow crunched under our feet as we exited and made our way around to the back of the van. Outside, I reacted immediately to the biting cold. On reflex, I hunched over and grabbed my arms, finding my unlined, London Fog raincoat—a goodbye gift from my parents—wholly inadequate for the climate. "Is this where we are staying," I asked to no one in particular. Immediately, I felt a hand on the back of my neck, squeezing. Hard. Vice-like. I turned in response to the pain, thinking one of my fellow missionaries was horsing around, only to find Thorsson glaring at me.

"Svenska, Äldste Miller," (Swedish, Elder Miller), he directed, using the formal title given to all missionaries, and then repeated slowly for the rest to hear, "*Prata Svenska*" (Speak Swedish).

Had I been able to say what I wanted in Swedish, I would have. From the outset of our training at the LTM (Language Training Mission), we had been encouraged to speak the language as much as possible. It was a recommendation that made perfect sense to me. Notwithstanding eight weeks of intensive training, and receiving top scores on their standardized language tests, my command of Swedish was both elementary and severely limited. I could count to a hundred, ask for directions to the nearest toilet, and deliver a ten minute monologue on the Mormon plan of salvation.

Thorsson continued in Swedish, "In the Sweden-Gothenburg mission, *all* missionaries are required to speak the language one hundred percent of the time."

All the time? I wondered.

Then, as though confirming his Kreskin-like abilities to know what I was thinking, he added, again in Swedish, "And that means that you speak Swedish full time, when you are proselytizing *and* when you are home alone with your companion."

Feeling singled out, embarrassed, and already on the wrong side of the man presumably in charge, I froze, saying nothing. Not a bright beginning for someone who had been in the country less than an hour and had two years to go. Stealing a quick glance at the others, I concluded they shared my discomfort. All were giving considerable attention to their feet, except Elder O'Leary of course.

"Ja visst!" (Yes, indeed) he said immediately, standing almost at attention while vigorously nodding in the affirmative. I was not surprised. The diminutive, red-haired, freckle-faced Idahoan was the most ardent among us. The first out of bed in the morning. The first on his knees to pray for guidance. The first to publicly affirm his faith.

All of us had been instructed to sit by a stranger on the flight over and strike up a conversation about the Church, to begin our efforts to bring people into the fold the moment we boarded the plane. While the rest of us were pinned to our seats simmering in apprehension, O'Leary went from row to row introducing himself, shaking hands, and passing out leaflets.

His piety was only matched by his prowess in the martial arts. At the end of most days back in Provo at the LTM, O'Leary would treat us to demonstrations of what he claimed were Ninjitsu fighting stances. What did I know? All I could do was recount episodes of the TV series, *Kung Fu*. He was Kwai Chang Kane in the flesh, capable of impressive kicks and flurries of punches accompanied by Bruce Lee-like glares and guttural screeches. I watched in awe, uncertain of whether he was someone to emulate or best regard as a showboating jerk. Judging by the leaders' response, it was the former. Early on, O'Leary was appointed *Il Duce* of our band of brothers.

Taking our silence for understanding, Thorsson turned, opened the doors at the rear of the van, and while motioning toward our bags said, "Come Elders, follow me."

I waited behind several others to retrieve my luggage. O'Leary, true to form, headed up the line. All that I owned and was permitted to have for the next two years was crammed into two grey, Samsonite® hard cover bags. As we made our way to the door of a nearby building I struggled to keep my footing, the leather soles of my new shoes having all the gripping power of a pair of waxed skis.

The entry way of the building was as dark as everything else I had experienced in Sweden so far—the only illumination coming from a flickering red orb no larger than a nickel. Light filled the stairwell when Thorsson reached out and tapped what in actuality was a switch. A loud ticking ensued.

"We're going to the top floor," he said. When no one moved, he continued, "Skynda på, Äldsta, vi har bråttom. Ljuset skall släckas om en minut" (Hurry up, Elders, we are in a hurry, the lights will go out automatically in a minute).

The ticking continued, speeding up with each passing second.

As the group inched towards the accordion gate of an old-fashioned, freight elevator, Thorsson stepped in front of us.

"The easy way is not *our* way, Elders" he said, pointing to the stairs.

Turning toward the winding, spiral staircase, we began our ascent to the fifth floor, hurriedly arranging ourselves in single file to negotiate the surprisingly narrow steps. Mustering what was left of my strength, I lifted my bags and began the climb, determined not to be left in the dark.

The names on the doors at each floor read like a Swedish phonebook: Svensson, Larsson, Nilsson, Johansson, Andersson, Persson, Ericsson. Here, everyone was a son of someone else. By the time I reached the landing, this son of Paul and Darlene Miller was winded, and the timer was beating with the tempo of a snare drum. I had just enough time to glimpse the sign on the door before the lights went out:

Jesu Kristi Kyrka av Sista Dagars Heliga
Sverige Göteborg Missionskontor

(THE CHURCH OF JESUS CHRIST OF LATTER DAY SAINTS)
(SWEDEN GOTHENBURG MISSION OFFICE)

OK, I thought, *so this isn't a hotel. At least I know where I am, and as long as there is a bed in there, I'll be happy.*

By this time, my arms felt like rubber bands, and I was convinced that the contents of my bags had been replaced with cannon balls. That is when the door opened, instantly filling the stairwell with a glaring fluorescent light.

"Stig på! Välkommen till Sverige, Äldsta!" (Enter! Welcome to Sweden, Elders) a voice exclaimed.

As we made our way through the door, the figure shook our hands and smiled broadly, his bright white teeth gleaming in the light.

"God dag, Äldste Miller" (Good day, Elder Miller), he said.

"God dag," I mechanically replied, at the same time thinking, *How in the world did this guy know my name?* Then, my tired mind reminded me we all had name tags pinned to our left lapels. We had been wearing them since the very first day at the LTM. A conspicuous black, plastic plate with our rank, last name, and affiliation engraved in bold, white letters.

"Drop your bags there," he added, pointing to a small room on my left.

Turning to comply, I looked around and realized I had walked into an anthill. The office was teeming with activity, a blur of blue and white. Young men in suits were frantically but silently typing, filing, and mimeographing—shuttling back and forth with unyielding purpose between their desks and the various rooms in the office.

I stopped midstride, astonished by what I was seeing. *Don't these people ever sleep?! Are we going to work all day and all night? According to the clock on their wall, it's three AM! These people are nuts.*

Suddenly, a favorite passage from *Alice in Wonderland*—a book read to me again and again by my parents—popped in my head:

"I don't want to go among mad people," Alice says.
"Oh, you can't help that," the Cheshire Cat responds, "we're all mad here. I'm mad. You're mad."
"How do you know I'm mad?" asks Alice.
"You must be," the Cat retorts, "or you wouldn't have come here."

My stomach muscles sharply contracted, sending a tingling feeling from the pit of my stomach to the top of my head, the sensation identical to looking over the edge of a precipice without a guardrail. I steadied myself, looked back over my shoulder, catching a last glimpse as the door closed on the rabbit hole.

"Skynda på, Äldste Miller" (Hurry Up, Elder Miller) a voice commanded, "it's late, and we have a lot to do."

After depositing my bags, I was directed, along with everyone else, through a set of double doors and into an oval shaped room. A massive oak desk greeted us, in front of which were eight metal folding chairs. On the desk, a carved wood name plate sat in a metal holder. It read, "Oscar Thorsson, President, Sweden Gothenburg Mission." *I was right. He is the man in charge.*

The President sat behind the desk perched on the edge of a black, leather chair, his hands steepled in anticipation.

"Brethren, let us pray," were the first words he uttered once the group had assembled. He stood, coming around to the front of his desk and kneeled.

Familiar with this drill, we followed. A fervent prayer—surprisingly in English—ensued.

> "Our kind, dear *Father in Heaven*," he began, "we meet Thee on bended knee, grateful for the many blessings Thou hast bestowed on us. At this time, O Lord, we give special thanks, for safely delivering your faithful followers to this benighted land. We beseech Thee, O Lord, to enter their hearts, make their spirits contrite, and strengthen their will to resist all temptation. In Your infinite wisdom, You have made us Your chosen people, sent us to *this* earth during these latter days to teach the restored Gospel of Jesus Christ as revealed through the Prophet Joseph Smith. We recognize that where much is given, much is expected and humbly accept, *Heavenly Father,* the great responsibility You place upon us. We recognize, Father, that our worthiness is all that stands between the delivery of Your children in Sweden and darkness. Look upon these young men, dear Lord, free them from all worldly distractions, let them commit, without reservation, body, mind, and spirit to the work. Make them tireless. In the face of trials and tribulation, sustain them in the knowledge that true joy and happiness only comes through personal sacrifice and absolute obedience to Your commandments and the leaders of this Church and mission …".

I couldn't tell if God was getting the message, but I certainly was. Thorsson was not one for subtlety. His words banged around in my head like billiard balls. I was a missionary. God's emissary. For the next two years, I was charged with nothing less than saving *every* Swede I met. What's more, success came down to me. My devotion. My worthiness. Up to this moment, I had somehow managed to avoid what my commitment meant, what I would be called upon to do. *Geez,* I thought, *I hope the Second Coming is soon, tomorrow even. I'm just a kid from Southern California, let HIM do it. And what in the heck does benighted mean?*

Unsure if Thorsson had finished or was about to continue, I opened my eyes just enough to sneak a peek. All heads remained bowed—except Cary

Wells, one of my closest friends from the LTM. I could see he was staring at me. When our eyes met, he rolled his with obvious contempt. I knew what he would say, "This guy is one piece of work."

In the two months we had known each other, I had come to look up to Cary, to depend on his ability to cut through any pretense and hear what was really being said. He possessed a quiet confidence that contrasted sharply with the swaggering bombast of O'Leary. I trusted him, knew he would have my back.

Cary was born and raised in New Haven, Connecticut. His father was a surgical oncologist at the Yale School of Medicine, his mother an English Professor. The family had been members of the Church from its earliest days. In fact, a long dead relative was one of the original "Eight Witnesses"— an esteemed group among Mormons. According to Joseph Smith, an Angel named Moroni directed him to a spot near his home where a set of gold plates lay buried. On the plates were engravings, a record of God's dealings with ancient inhabitants of the American continent. *The Book of Mormon*, members believe, is Smith's inspired translation of these writings. The eight were one of two groups besides Joseph Smith who claimed both to have seen *and* handled the plates. To this day, their testimony appears in the opening pages of every printed copy of the book.

I gave a quick smile of acknowledgement and then we both looked at Ken Arnold. Ordinarily, Elders are paired off and called "companions." Two by two, they go out to preach, convert, and baptize. We were three owing to the odd number of missionaries that entered our LTM class.

Ken was from Logan, Utah. Raised on a farm, his body showed the effect of hard work—big biceps and rock solid abs. He had a curious habit of keeping his right eye clenched tightly shut whenever he spoke. Even though we weren't supposed to use nicknames, we started calling him Popeye soon after we met. He was a hard guy not to like, down to earth, folksy and fearless. Despite our differences, we grew tight, the others in time referring to us as "The Three Musketeers."

That's when Thorsson resumed, "We humbly ask these things, O Heavenly Father, in the name of Our Lord and Savior, Jesus Christ, amen." Having concluded the prayer, he stood and so did we.

"Take your seats," he began. Sitting on the edge of his desk, he paused, searching our faces.

"This is an important time for the people of Sweden. After decades of living in sin and iniquity, a great opportunity is now before them. In July of this year, one of *the* Twelve Apostles, Thomas S. Monson, under the direction of our Prophet Spencer W. Kimball, rededicated this land to missionary work, hallowing the ground you walk on now and invoking the powers of Heaven to soften the hearts of those you meet. I am here to help you succeed. *We* are here to help you succeed. On my right is Elder Pierce, my left, Elder Payne, my current assistants."

I looked at the two men. Everything about them screamed veteran: their age, worn attire, steely composure, and unchanging beatific smile. One, Pierce, "Mr. Hurry-Up," I had already encountered at the door. The other was new to me. Whether or not we had met before mattered little. I *knew* who these two were: *Assistants to the President*. Despite this seemingly unimpressive title, Pierce and Payne occupied the top two leadership positions in the mission after Thorsson.

AP's are the elite among missionaries; a select few awarded a battlefield promotion for extraordinary performance. All of us knew, understood, and had been instructed to respect the chain of command. It was the same in every mission. At the top was the President. He was followed by Assistants to the President, Zone Leaders, District Leaders, Area Leaders, and at the bottom, Junior Companions, the new recruits, just like me.

"You have your *Missionary Handbook*," Thorsson continued, and then ordered, "Take them out."

I reached inside the breast pocket of my suit jacket, fumbling to find the small, three by five inch, vinyl covered booklet we had been given our first day at the LTM. The thirty-nine pages, known to Elders as the "White Bible," laid out our general orders, code of conduct and field objectives. Early on, we had been told to read the manual daily, carry it with us near our hearts at all times, and commit its contents to memory.

I was still searching my pockets when I noticed the indefatigable O'Leary proudly holding up his copy for all to see.

"Elders Pierce and Payne are handing out two items. First, the *Sweden Göteborg Mission Handbook Supplement*. Second, two 'Baptismal Goal' cards. Elders, you have one and only one purpose here: cry repentance unto this people. Apostle Monson has paved the way for you. And, as the Lord said through the Prophet Joseph Smith, 'How great will be your joy if you should bring many souls unto me."

I looked at the card with a mixture of surprise and worry. In bold letters, it asked me to commit to baptizing a specific number of people and enter that number into an empty box, followed by my signature.

"You have been given two cards. Why?" Thorsson asked rhetorically, his voice rising with emphasis, "because we have found that most missionaries lack the faith necessary to set goals befitting the level of trust God has placed in them."

Silence followed.

"Remember the words of our Lord and Savior Jesus Christ" he abruptly continued, "'Many are called, but few are chosen.' So, let His Spirit inform you as you complete and sign your card."

Others busily wrote. I had no idea what number to enter. One, two, five, a hundred, one thousand? Word at the LTM had it that most baptized none. *Pretty discouraging but, if true, why are we being asked to do this?*

Apparently, the Spirit took a fast look at me and decided to move on to better prospects. Retrieving the pen from my shirt pocket I pretended to write.

"Your 'Baptismal Goal' card should be inserted into your *Handbook* directly behind your *Certificate of Ordination* as a missionary," Elder Pierce interjected, showing the appropriate placement with his worn copy.

"Precis," (Exactly) added Elder Payne in Swedish.

I did as instructed, dutifully placing the two *empty* forms behind my laminated certificate, the official document identifying me as a "Duly Ordained Minister of the Gospel," with the serial number 95722.

Walking to the wall directly behind us, Elder Payne added, "You should review the progress you make toward your goal at your 'Weekly Companionship Inventory Meeting.'" Once he was sure we were looking at him, he pointed to a chart listing the various zones within our mission. For the most part, these areas of operation shared the name of the county in which they were located, known in Swedish as "kommuner" (pronounced, comb-moon-erh).

"Every time you bring someone to the fold through the sacrament of baptism, your zone gets credit on this chart. Each month the chart is reproduced in our mission newsletter, *The Harvester*. That way, you can see how your zone is doing in comparison to others."

At this point, as though on cue, Elders Pierce and Payne returned to their flanking positions at the President's desk.

Thorsson thanked them both before removing a copy of the *White Bible* from his jacket pocket, clenching it between his right thumb and forefinger. Standing, he raised it to eye level, and began shaking it, "Elders, I promise you will reach your baptismal goal if you heed, without reservation, the guidelines laid out in this book."

Dropping his right hand, he reached behind him, and with his left grabbed a copy of the *Sweden Göteborg Mission Handbook Supplement*. This, too, he brought to eye level and shook vigorously.

"To the divinely inspired pages of your *Handbook*, I have added twelve. This *Supplement* contains additional instructions for managing the unique challenges you will encounter in this country. Think of the *Handbook* and *Supplement* as one, just as the *Holy Bible* and *The Book of Mormon* are one. Elders, place it in the back cover of your *Handbook, now.*"

My mind left the room for a moment. In all the years I attended the Mormon Church, I had never encountered a character like this man. Images of the televangelist Jimmy Swaggart competed with those of Chairman Mao waving his "Little Red Book" before the masses at Tiananmen Square. By contrast, when I was growing up, our congregation was led by neighbors and friends. Bishop Murphy who, on weekdays, managed a frozen food company, ran worship services on Sundays. If he was not there, it was Doctor Oakes, our family physician. Both were kind and gentle figures.

The show in my head ended when I realized the President had stopped talking and was glaring at me. "*As I said,*" his eyes now boring into me, "place it in the back cover of your *Handbook, now.*"

The next two hours were spent in a page by page review of Thorsson's "new and improved" *White Bible*, much of it focused on the daily schedule. I was no stranger to hard work. I had studied hard and done well my first year at BYU, Brigham Young University. At the LTM, every waking moment had been spent learning and practicing the language. The *Göteborg* schedule, however, was on a whole new scale. We were required to be out proselytizing 10 hours a day, from 9:30 in the morning until 9:30 at night, with an hour break for both lunch and dinner.

Going door to door—known among Mormon missionaries as "tracting"—was how most of our time would be spent. Each week we were also expected to stop one hundred people on the street, asking for their name, address, and a commitment to visit with us in their home. The number of such "Golden Contacts," in addition to doors knocked, and lessons taught were to be written down on the official *Mission Progress Report* form and sent to office for collating and review by the AP's at the end of each week.

"You have to be bold," Elder Pierce counseled at one point, "When someone answers their door, ask immediately 'Får vi stiga in och berättar om vårt viktiga budskap?!'" (May we come in and tell you our important message).

Elder Payne followed, quoting directly from the *Handbook*, "Be affirmative in your thinking and your speech. Eliminate from your vocabulary the words and phrases 'if' and 'I'll do my best.' Say instead, 'I'll do it.'" Together, the two demonstrated the ideal way to approach people.

"Smile," Elder Pierce said, wearing the exact same expression that had been glued on his face since our encounter in the entry way, "Look people in the eye and offer your hand."

It was at this point I began laughing. Something about "looking people in *their* eye" and "offering *my* hand" struck me as wickedly funny. I tried unsuccessfully to suppress it, managing only to transform my giggling into an audible snort.

"I'm sorry," I said, covering my mouth but continuing to titter uncontrollably. I'd lost it. My capacity for rational thought was gone. I was giddy from exhaustion.

Judging by the response of my companions, the infection was spreading. Everyone, save the loyal O'Leary, soon joined. Elders Pierce and Payne stopped the role play, and with hands suspended in mid air, looked at me.

"I'm sorry," I repeated, slowly shaking my head from left to right, "I don't know why, but I had this vision of one-eyed Swedes and one-handed missionaries."

Obviously unmoved, they first turned to each other, and then back to me. With that, the room went silent and I somehow regained my composure. Heads nodded in agreement when I went on to explain, "It really wasn't that funny. I'm just tired. I've been up for 36 hours straight and I don't even know what time it is."

That is when the whole regrettable exchange took a turn to the surreal. Thorsson barked out what sounded to me like the Swedish word for herring, "Sill, sill, Äldste Miller!" (Herring, herring, Elder Miller).

"Sill?" (Herring?) I asked.

"Ja! *Sill*, Äldste Miller" (Yes! *Herring*, Elder Miller) he repeated, adding in English, "Speak *Your* Language."

"O, *SYL*," I replied, his meaning finally clear.

"Ja, SYL," he said, a note of disdain evident in his voice, "And so you know, the time is only 4 p.m., we have five and a half hours left in our work day. We'll end early today at 6 p.m., so that we can enjoy a welcome dinner at my home. Until then, we still have much to cover, if that's all right with you, Elder Miller."

I resolved to assume a low profile having already done enough to convince Thorsson that I was a complainer and troublemaker. I did feel relieved to know the correct time. We were going to be working long hours for sure, but at least not the whole night, as I worried when we first walked into the mission office. This close to the Arctic Circle, what we call night or day is stood on its head. Starting in November, it's rare for daylight to last more than a few hours. Whoever called Sweden the Land of the Midnight Sun obviously had never been here during the winter.

Finally, we got to the rules:

- *Missionaries should always be with their companions, except when using the toilet or bathing;*

Check, I thought. No surprise here. I had heard this before and was prepared. I knew there was a good chance of being paired up with an Elder at some point that I disliked, but thought of myself as a go-along-get-along kind of guy. Plus, even if it was really bad, most assignments were short term, lasting at most two or three months. I could manage that.

- *On the subject of personal hygiene, missionaries should avoid baths when possible, and restrict showers to five minutes or less;*

Avoid baths? What on earth for? Then it struck me: the big "M." I knew I didn't need a bathtub to do *that*, and five minutes was more than enough. Based on personal experience, I was certain I could even beat that time.

As much as we were instructed to banish the immoral act from our young lives, it was striking how much time was spent discussing the subject. We could never get away from it. In all interviews with church leaders, the question was asked "Are you worthy?" Starting around the age of 13, "moral purity"—meaning anything to do with sex— was a frequent topic of lessons at church. All boys were given THE PAMPHLET written by one of the Twelve Apostles, warning us not to tamper with the "little factory" between our legs lest it go into overdrive. The problem was considered so serious that another Apostle published a guidebook containing 30 specific steps for keeping our "release valves" closed. Diligence was required, he admonished, as "Satan never gives up." Among the tried and true methods, such as prayer and scripture reading, were others. For example, for those who had acquired the "habit of masturbating in a semi-sleep condition," he wrote, "it may be necessary to tie a hand to the bed frame with a tie." Should a tie be unavailable, the same result could be "accomplished by wearing several layers of clothing which would be difficult to remove while half-asleep." Masturbation aside, I knew that having only five minutes alone each day— no matter how well my companion and I got along—would be a difficult adjustment. I could already hear him knocking on the bathroom, interrupting my few precious moments alone, "You about done in there Elder Miller? It's been longer than five minutes. *Is the Spirit still with you?*"

• *Help protect your companion from temptation by reporting any and all concerns about his overall fitness as a missionary in your private weekly letter to the Mission President. If an immediate response is warranted, use the number provided to contact the President directly.*

I started feeling anxious. Mormons are a tight-knit community. That the Church is most famous for its choir is telling. Members work together, look out for each other, help and care for one another. When someone is in need, word travels along the "LDS Grapevine" at the speed of light—a party line open to everyone in the Church.

One Sunday morning, when Southern California was clobbered with a series of violent storms, our home began to flood. Mud and rock filled the backyard and flowed into the house. My father, younger brother Marc, and I had just sat down at a Church men's meeting when Bishop Murphy whispered in my Dad's ear informing him of the situation unfolding at home. We left immediately. Within a half hour, nearly every male member of the Church was in our back yard, digging drainage ditches, filling sandbags, and shoveling mud off the back porch. The ladies of the Church quickly followed and set to work consoling my mother, washing floors, and preparing food.

Growing up, I knew I could count on members in times of need, no matter the circumstances. Our family would be there for others as well. For many years, we prepared Thanksgiving dinners and secretly delivered them to needy families in our congregation. I loved doing this with my parents and brothers. It felt good to help. It felt right.

What Thorsson was proposing did not. This was not about "loving thy neighbor as thyself." This was about being a snitch. I felt sickened by the thought, especially when I considered that my companions were expected to rat me out, too.

• *Do not correspond with or contact any member, investigator, or missionary outside of your assigned area;*

Thorsson became visibly agitated as he broached this topic. His exact words, "Any missionary guilty of breaking this rule or gossiping and passing information via the 'grapevine' deprives himself and others of a full measure of the Lord's Spirit and aids Satan in his attempt to thwart the work of the Lord."

"We call this 'graping,'" Elder Payne added, "and it is OP, *off the program.*"

I thought of the one non-dress shirt in my possession, a colorful polo tee with a beach motif and the initials OP, for Ocean Pacific, boldly emblazoned across the front. Everything, it seemed, was taking on new meaning in the Sweden Göteborg Mission.

Looking across the room, I watched Cary Wells rub his hand back and forth over his curly brown hair. If he had a "tell," this was it. Cary was feeling annoyed. Me? Dismayed at first, then sad, really sad. If I obeyed this last rule, my friend and I would have no contact for the next two years.

"Maintaining relationships with members once you have been called to leave one area and transfer to another in the Lord's vineyard is forbidden. You are not to have any contact whatsoever with anyone outside of your assigned area. Not members, not your former companion and, lest you have any doubt, not with Swedish Sisters. Leave them alone. They are not for you. Female members of the Church living *here* are to remain *here*, to build the Kingdom of God *here*, to marry Swedish men and raise Swedish families *here.*"

I nodded affirmatively when Thorsson asked if we understood.

"While we are on the subject of women," he continued, "You are prohibited from ever being alone with a member of the opposite sex, member or not. No exceptions. Temptations of the flesh are widespread. Here, couples live in sin more often than within the bonds of matrimony. Fornication is rampant. Nothing would give Satan greater joy and satisfaction than having you sent home, back to your families, in disgrace, having broken the law of chastity on your mission. And mark my words, Elders, you *will* be sent home."

Thorsson paused, taking the time to point his finger at each of us. As he moved behind the desk and sat down, the two AP's took over the meeting, focusing on more mundane matters:

• *Missionaries are limited to two calls home per year, once at Christmas and the other on Mother's Day.*

"Calls should be brief, lasting no more than 15 minutes," Elder Pierce clarified, "and remember that permission must always be obtained from the Mission President prior to any call."

Of the 672 days, 16,128 hours, 967,680 some odd seconds left on my mission, I would have one hour of contact with my family. Time stretched out before me, like I was looking at my life through the wrong end of a telescope.

• *Avoid any activity that detracts from the work.*

Elder Payne read aloud from the *Handbook*, "Put out of your life all thoughts and discussions of home, school, girlfriends, and other worldly things."

"You *are* expected to write home each week," Elder Pierce followed, "Remember, keep it upbeat and spiritually uplifting and do not trouble your families with your difficulties and concerns. Do not exchange gossip about people and events back home. Always express your gratitude for their support and never miss an opportunity to bear your testimony, to be a missionary to your own family."

"I'm sure some of you have girlfriends back home," Thorsson interrupted, "if you feel you must correspond, think of what the Lord would want you to write in those letters. Do not introduce any content that invites impure thoughts."

Always on message, Pierce proceeded, "Displaying a picture of a girlfriend in your living quarters is OP. Carrying a picture of a girl in your wallet is OP. Do not distract you and your companion in this way. Your time here is to be spent doing the Lord's work."

Lucky for me, this was not a problem. No one was waiting stateside. The same could not be said for Elder Hedger. Turning in his direction, I could see he had a dead man's stare. He was panicked. During our two months at the LTM, he talked of nothing else except his girlfriend. Laurie, Laurie, Laurie, was all we heard. His wallet bulged with pictures. He was constantly writing her or listening to audio letters she recorded and sent to him. He even slept with their high school prom picture. Although he would not admit it, he lived in constant fear of her leaving him for someone else. None of us had the heart to tease him. He was such a sorry sack. On more than one occasion, after lights out, I heard stifled cries coming from his bunk.

Hedger's lifeless expression did not change when we were told letter writing was restricted to "Preparation Day"—the one day per week set aside for personal matters. According to the *White Bible*, acceptable activities included: getting a haircut, doing laundry, changing bed clothes, shining shoes, cleaning one's living quarters, grocery shopping, and planning the week's work activities. On this day, we were still required to keep our regular morning schedule; that is, rising at 6:30, conducting a Gospel study class at 7:00, eating breakfast at 8:00, and engaging in private scripture study from 8:30 to 9:30 a.m.

If any time was left over after completing all these chores and church related activities, we were free to engage in "uplifting recreational activities"—provided we had the President's approval. Going to a museum, art gallery, or cultural center was allowed. The *White Bible* expressly prohibited: playing musical instruments, listening to radio or TV, going to movies, engaging in contact sports, or congregating with other missionaries in groups. "P-day," as Elders referred to it, ended at 5:00 pm, at which time proselytizing promptly resumed.

"Suits are to be worn whenever you are in public," Pierce inserted, "and from November 1st thru April 15th that includes wearing the official mission hat. Out of doors, civilian clothes are OP."

Payne held up his, a tired, black felt fedora more befitting a prohibition era gangster than missionary. I was horrified. *How could I wear something like that?* No nineteen year-old would ever wear such a hat. I could see it. Together with my blue suit, white shirt and tie, thinly-lined trench coat and tortured Swedish, there was no doubt I would instantly be taken for the village idiot. The whole idea was preposterous. We were supposed to be emissaries for Christ's one and only true church on the planet. How was anyone going to take us seriously?

"The hat is for *your* protection," Thorsson remarked, "*Never* leave your apartment without it."

Yeah, I thought, *with that on our heads, no one would come near us. We'd definitely be safe.*

"The winters are severe here. Seventy percent of your body warmth escapes through the top of your head. Brethren," Thorsson carried on, a rare smile creeping across his face, "I see its 6:00 pm. Join me in song."

Following his lead, we stood. Elder Pierce conducted as we sang all four verses of LDS Hymn number 252, "Put your Shoulder to the Wheel."

> "The world has need of willing men,
> Who wear the worker's seal.
>
> Come, help the good work move along;
> Put your shoulder to the wheel.
>
> Put your shoulder to the wheel; push along,
> Do your duty with a heart full of song,
>
> We all have work; let no one shirk.
> Put your shoulder to the wheel."

Another prayer followed, this one distinguished by its brevity. No doubt the President was in hurry.

"Sister Thorsson is waiting for us at the Mission Home, having lovingly prepared a meal for your first night in Sweden. After dinner, we will drop you at the hotel. Lights out tonight Elders by 9:00 pm, meet in the lobby at 8:30 *prick* (sharp). Elders Pierce and Payne will take each of you individually to the train station, where you will be informed of your assignment, and dispatched to your designated area."

"Form a line," Elder Payne directed, marching us single file past a series of "stations" outside the oval office. At the first, we were given a box of

Books of Mormon. We would be giving out this "cornerstone of the LDS faith," to prospective converts. Moving to the next desk, stacks of missionary tracts bound together with rubber bands were placed on top of the box. Titles included, *Joseph Smith Tells His Own Story* and the *Plan of Salvation.* Conveniently stamped on the backside was the location and meeting times of the closest LDS Church.

The next to the last stop turned out to be a checkpoint. Elder Hedger had preceded me in the line and just finished. When I approached, the AP's placed my two bags on top of the desk. That's when I noticed a pile of pictures neatly stacked on the side table. Poor Hedger, Laurie was OP.

"Let us help you pack those books and pamphlets," they said, opening my two bags, "This is also a good opportunity to remove any items that are OP."

Doing a quick check and, miraculously, finding nothing, they stuffed the printed materials into my luggage and signaled the next in line to move forward. I started breathing again, grateful they had not found several pieces of contraband, including audio cassettes of Steve Martin's, *Wild and Crazy Guy,* and Cheech and Chong's, *Big Bambu.* They were OP to be sure but actually the least of my worries. I was more concerned about losing my dog-eared copy of *Catcher in the Rye* and another book Cary Wells had given to me at the LTM, a scholarly and controversial history of the Mormon Church.

"Your total, Elder Miller, comes to $100.00," said the missionary seated at the last desk.

"A hundred dollars?" I said in surprise, "What for?"

With all the warmth of a cash register, he replied, "For the books, and the pamphlets, your train ticket, your share of tonight's welcome dinner, and the hotel room."

"The welcome dinner? What?"

"Why yes," he interrupted, looking up from his ledger. Lifting his right hand, palm up, "The meal is ten dollars."

I didn't know what to say. What I did know is of the three hundred dollars we were permitted to have on hand per month, I now had two left. *How long would that last?* I wondered, knowing that this amount had to cover all my living expenses. Not only that, Sweden, we'd been told, was a high priced place.

We had been instructed to bring cash for our first month in the field.

After that, checks would be sent from home. In my case, part of that money would come from the meager amount I had been able to put aside working a summer job. The balance fell to Mom and Dad.

A big bowl of Spaghetti and meatballs (not a Swedish one among them), awaited us at the President's residence. It was obvious Sister Thorsson was accustomed to feeding large groups, having five children of her own and another on the way. As worn out as I was feeling, it was nice being around a family. The stern and uncompromising atmosphere of the last two hours lightened a little here. With the kids running about and playing, it was the first time since landing I was in a place that felt familiar.

Watching them reminded me of home, being around my family. I thought of my brother, Doug, and his wife, Liz. Two days after I entered the LTM, their first child, Tylor, had been born, my parents first grandchild, and my one and only nephew. He'd be two years old before I would have the chance to meet him.

I couldn't help but smile thinking of the day when I would have my own. Families are *everything* to Mormons. The message is everywhere and starts young: go to church, find a faithful partner, marry, have lots of kids, and by following the commandments, live together forever in the presence of God. The slogan "Families are Forever" is a trademarked logo popular among Mormons. You can find it on bumper stickers, cards, platters, clocks, decorative tiles, refrigerator magnets, needlepoint, and placards. Far from mass marketing of merchandise for the merely sentimental, it is an article of faith within the Church.

The Mormon emphasis on family explains their obsession with genealogical research. The Church of Jesus Christ of Latter Day Saints Family History Library is the largest in the world, with more than two billion names of deceased people gathered from over 100 countries. It is a duty of every living LDS Church member to identify those who died without having the opportunity to hear and accept the "Restored Gospel" in life. In an act of love and devotion, church members serve as proxies, performing the religious rites necessary (e.g., baptism, marriage) for the dead to enter Heaven.

Within an hour, we were back in the van headed for the hotel. The respite over, the warm feelings gave way to a sense of dread. My chest tightened and I broke out in a sweat. I'd heard the word many times before, but I now understood what it meant to be homesick.

The *Tre Kronor* hotel wasn't *The Ritz*, not even a *Motel 6*. A musty odor greeted Cary, Ken, and I when we opened the door. The room itself, the décor, and furnishings were straight out of a film noir—threadbare carpet, ill-hung, dark-green pleated drapes, an old-fashioned, tube-type, single dial radio, wobbly, brass floor lamp, two well used full-size beds and a rollaway. The bathroom was equally dated and dingy, plain white ceramic sink, toilet, tub, no shower. A dead body outlined in chalk was all that was missing to complete the scene.

We stood in the room, bags at our feet looking back and forth at one another. I don't recall who moved first, but we were soon in a huddle, arms around each other, and our heads pressed together. I could feel myself tearing up. I was really going to miss these guys.

"Ah, shit," Cary said, briefly pulling away to wipe his eyes.

"This sucks," Ken joined in, clapping each of us hard on the shoulders and then tightly gripping our necks.

"What are we going to do?" I blurted out, "I don't think I can do this. I *can't* do this."

"You can do it Dew," Ken replied, using the nickname they had given me at the LTM, "What else can we do? Can't back out now, my man."

"I dunno, Popeye."

"That Thorsson guy, what a prick," Cary spoke up, moving to the bed.

"Guy, Elder Wells, *guy*?" I asked, feigning disdain.

"Ya, tsk tsk, Elder Velz," Ken followed, using the worst imitation of a German accent I'd ever heard, "haz du already forgotten zie verds av vor commandant, Thorsson? Such verds ist verboten."

"Ya! First names, nicknames, and especially words like 'guy' and 'gal'," I clarified in the second worst imitation of a German accent uttered in the room, "zeez verds add a zense of vamiliarity zat detrax from zie Spirit, dummkopf, und az zuch, ist OP."

"*SYL, SYL*, Äldste Miller!" Wells cried out, pointing back at me, a horrified look on his face, "*Speak your Language*."

"Just det!" (Swedish for, that's right) Ken and I responded.

Spontaneously, we exchanged fascist salutes and broke into laughter.

"We have learned from sad experience", Ken broke in, affecting a serious tone of voice. He was quoting a passage penned in the late 1830's by the Prophet Joseph Smith while jailed in Missouri on charges of treason. We knew it well. Next to, "All for one and one for all," it was a favorite saying of our threesome. All Mormons know Smith's words. They are recorded in the *Doctrine and Covenants*, a book of scripture considered equal in authority to the *Bible* and *Book of Mormon*. The volume is in part a chronicle of the early Church and a compilation of revelations believed given to the Prophet by God.

Smith was at a low point in his young life. Members of his newly organized church, wherever they settled, were being treated brutally by their neighbors, forcing the group to flee from state to state. Church leadership, plagued by conflict and disaffection, left the Prophet battered and alone. Finally, in 1838, just a few months prior to his arrest and imprisonment, Governor Lilburn Boggs—notorious for his personal dislike of the Church—issued "Executive Order 44," authorizing the extermination of its members.

As Ken spoke the opening lines, we snapped back to attention and recited in unison using our best FM radio voices, "It is the nature and disposition of almost all men, as soon as they get a little authority, as they suppose, they will immediately begin to exercise unrighteous dominion!"

"You are exercising 'unrighteous dominion!'" was the charge Ken leveled at O'Leary when he reproached the three of us for choosing to sit together instead of by strangers on the flight over as we had been instructed.

Where these words had once given us comfort and a sense of solidarity, they now fell flat. Tomorrow, the *Three Musketeers* would be no more. In the morning, each of us would be among strangers.

"We may be OP," Cary remarked, "but Thorsson, he's E.U.D."

"Yeah, definitely: *Exercising Unrighteous Dominion*," I added.

Ken turned toward the rollaway bed standing upright against the wall and began unhooking the straps holding the frame together. With a tone of resignation, "It's late, guys."

In silence, we undressed down to our G's, the special underwear worn day and night and considered sacred by Mormons. Bearing a strong resemblance to long johns, the "garment" is worn by faithful members following their participation in a most holy temple ritual known as the "Endowment Ceremony." Members promise God to be obedient, chaste, and loyal to the Church. In return, the Lord is bound to provide joy, protection, and entry into the Kingdom of Heaven. The underwear serve to remind the wearer of the covenants made. Mission leaders also said our "G's" would shield us from physical and spiritual peril.

As I went to lie down, the bed creaked nosily. Gravity instantly pulled me to the crater in the center. Still sitting on the edge of his, Cary tore a piece of notebook paper into pieces and began scribbling.

"I'm giving you guys my home address. Send letters there and my parents will forward them to me. That way, we can stay in touch."

"Would they do that for you?" I asked, "Won't they know we're not supposed to talk to each other?"

"Who's going to tell them?" Cary answered, "They weren't there for Thorsson's rant."

Nodding, I took his address and asked to borrow his pen and a piece of paper, "You're right. Here's mine, I'll tell my folks to forward any letters I get."

Ken did the same. Then, reminding us of our nightly ritual, he suggested we pray. In the last two months, I'd spent more time on my knees praying than I'd spent in my entire life. As a family, we prayed before meals, prior to leaving on a trip, and in times of crisis. No more, I thought, than most. The prayers we offered at the LTM were an altogether different variety. Mere formalities, they were not. Morning, noon, and night, the three of us pleaded passionately for God's help, asking Him to fill us with His spirit, make His will known, and give us the strength to do His bidding.

I threw my legs over the edge of the bed and took to my knees. Cary did not, choosing instead to remain seated hunched over, elbows on knees and head in hands while Ken prayed. I turned toward Cary, briefly placing my left hand on his leg. I knew this guy, knew what he was feeling, what his refusal to kneel meant. His behavior was not some form of adolescent rebellion. Cary was angry. Not so much at Thorsson or the AP's, as with himself. All three of us had struggled with our beliefs at the LTM, only Cary more so. He'd been quick to tell me that he really had not wanted to serve a mission. Instead, he wanted to stay and finish school. Pressured by family and precedence, he relented. After all, how could one of the descendants of the "Eight Witnesses" not go?

"Amen," I said in response when Ken concluded the prayer. Standing, he pulled the chain on the old brass floor lamp. Cary was looking down, rubbing his fingers back and forth through his hair, shaking his head slowly from left to right as the light went out. In silence, we crawled into our beds.

≈

In bed, I laid facing the wall, tears in my eyes. I didn't know what Cary was doing. I could tell Ken had drifted off. Despite being bone-tired, sleep wouldn't come. I was torn, unsure what might gain the upper hand, feeling sad or feeling desperate.

"We have travelled 5,400 nautical miles from where we started," the pilot had announced over the loudspeakers when we landed. Before leaving home, I'd traced the distance on the world globe in my bedroom. Home felt so far away now—and two years, an eternity. When I was 17, my Mom was diagnosed and treated for breast cancer. *Would she still be there when I got home? What about Grandma Christina, my 91-year-old, Icelandic-Swedish relative and matriarch of our family?*

I exhaled, holding my breath once my lungs emptied, working hard not to cry. *Why was I doing this? Why would anyone want to do this? Come to a dark, cold, depressing place and find Thorsson waiting for you. Cary was right, he was a first-rate prick. And the AP's? Who'd want to end up like them? Stepford Wives of the Mormon Church. What about Swedish? My God, the language was impossible.* Mastery, like my family, seemed light years away. I couldn't speak or communicate with anyone, only catching a word here and there. *How was I going to connect with people, live? Use sign language, barter at the local market?*

I squinted hard, wiping my nose on the sheet. I did not want to risk waking the others with my sniffling. The thoughts continued.

What the hell? Maybe this is it; the way it's supposed to be. I've been called by the Prophet to serve, and not just anywhere—the home of my ancestors, Sweden. I could have been sent to Treefrog, Louisiana. I'd spent four years studying German in high school. Why hadn't I been sent there? Sending to me to Göteborg instead of Munich was surely evidence of divine intervention, right? And if God chose me to go to Sweden, then it was no mistake Thorsson was here. The Church authorities must know and approve of his methods.

Of course, there must be rules! You can't turn a bunch 19-year-olds loose in Sweden, a morally dangerous place, the Sodom and Gomorrah of the modern world. *Maybe Thorsson is trying to help us. That's what he said.* Over and over at the LTM, we'd been told, "When the leaders speak, the thinking has been done, the debate is over." *It is my duty to obey, to humble myself before authority and submit. Maybe the problem is me, my pride and arrogance?* That is the message of *The Book of Mormon*: don't think you know better than God. Be faithful and live the commandments and you will be blessed with success and happiness. Do otherwise and you will be, "beaten with many blows" (Luke 12:47).

Back and forth, round and round, my mind raced. I'd listened to returning missionaries praising their experiences as "the best two years of their lives." *Were they nuts? Liars?* I knew and was prepared to sacrifice, but something about Thorsson's outpost of Mormonism struck me as wrong. *If there ever were a case of "unrighteous dominion," isn't this it? Then again, here I am, called by God, I guess. Even if Thorsson is out to lunch, going along is the right choice in the eyes of the Lord and His Church. What else can I do? Who am I to question?* Before I criticized others, maybe I needed to consider the "beam in my own eye." *And my parents, what would they say?*

That's when my mind went blank.

I turned over, laying on my back, and stared at the ceiling. After several minutes of nothing, it came to me, *I've not thought this whole mission deal through AT ALL.* In fact, I'd never really had reason to think too deeply about much of anything. My life was simple, carefree, good. No dramas, no traumas. Growing up, it was much like a 1950's sitcom with a stay-at-home Mom, devoted, hard-working Dad, two fun, rough and tumble brothers, dog, cat, and three-bedroom ranch house.

It was obvious why Cary was on a mission. His family made him. From our lights-out, late night talks at the LTM, I also knew why Ken had chosen to go. He regaled us with his tales of frat house parties, boozing and screwing while a student at Utah State University. One day he decided he'd had enough. It was time to straighten up and fly right. As is required by the Church, he made a full confession of his sins to the local ecclesiastical authority, known in Mormonism as the bishop. Some of his transgressions were considered so grievous he had to demonstrate his contrition and worthiness for an entire year before being allowed to serve.

So why was I on a mission? I wasn't forced. Sure, I'd partied and fooled around a bit, but no more than most kids my age. I'd had no epiphany, seen no burning bush.

When I was 15, the Church's view of missions changed in a big way. Spencer W. Kimball, the twelfth Prophet, Seer, and Revelator of the

Church, ordered all young men to serve missions. Members refer to it as the "Eleventh Commandment." Along with the other boys in my Sunday school class, I watched a film of the Prophet talking about the importance of preparing for and serving missions. His short stature, elfin features, and soft voice belied his supreme authority. As he spoke, diagrams identical to WWII invasion maps were displayed, with arrows depicting the relentless advance of the Mormon faith across the planet—if we would only do our part. Still, I felt no call to arms. All it did was remind me of documentaries and war time news reel footage I watched with Dad on Sunday afternoons.

My year at BYU probably played a role. Everyone there was, without exception, Mormon. There, no one asked me *if* I'd be going. It was a question of *when*.

"No 'celestial smile' I see," Katie Barrett remarked the first time we met. I had no idea what she meant.

"You're not wearing garments, silly," she said, playfully tracing a line with her index finger from the top of my left shoulder, down to the middle of my chest, and then up to the right. She was referring to the deep, looping collar of the G's. The special underwear was often visible through clothing. The "smile" formed by the collar was a badge-of-honor among returned missionaries. Besides married couples, they were the only ones permitted to wear the garments. More important, G's were a serious chick magnet—the Mormon equivalent of a mating call. About the same time Spencer W. Kimball made going on a mission a commandment, church leaders began encouraging girls to do everything in their power to persuade boys to serve.

"So, you haven't gone on a mission, yet," she said, adding "You're not M.E."

"M.E.?" I replied, once again uncertain.

Flipping her straight, blond hair over her shoulders, "Yeah, you know, *marriage eligible*."

I laughed, "You want to get married or dance?"

"Why limit your choices?" she responded quickly, the innuendo strong and seriously alluring.

Oh my gosh, I fell in love instantly. Within a half hour, we'd left the dance and were making out in the back seat of my 1976 Toyota Celica.

I closed my eyes momentarily, a rare smile crossing my face as I thought about Katie; her lips, the feel of her skin, the perfume she wore, her body. She was the prettiest, most sexy girl I'd ever met.

When Ken stirred in his sleep, snorting loudly and changing positions, my eyes shot back open. Not wanting my hands tied to the bed, I pushed Katie out of my mind. Anyway, I knew she wasn't responsible for me going on a mission. Every once in a while the subject came up when we were together. Most of the time, we were like most freshman couples. We went to the movies, listened to music, studied, and ate meals together in the dorm cafeteria. Midway through the second semester, our relationship lost steam. We agreed to write each other over the summer break. We never did.

When I returned in California after my freshman year, life had changed. My non-Mormon buddies were either working or still in school. My Mormon friends were on missions—every single one. Wesley Murphy, the local Bishop's son, and kid with the hottest car, was in Peru. Peter Blake, the drummer for our on-again, off-again rock band, was in upstate New York, birthplace of the Church. And my very best friend, Bill Price, had left for Germany a few weeks before I got home from school. We'd been inseparable growing up, doing everything together; surfing, school, scouting, lusting over girls and dreaming of rock stardom. In the band, I sang. He played lead guitar.

The prospect of being one of the few sophomores at BYU who was not an "RM" (returned missionary) didn't exactly inspire hope for a successful year. I did not want to be the odd man out. Who would? I did have other choices. My ACT scores were solid enough to get into any University of California school. In the worst case, I could have attended Citrus, the community college down the street from our house. *Why didn't I do that?* When no answer came, I closed my eyes, crashing into a deep sleep.

I pulled down the neckline of my G's. I can't feel it but I can see the "Endless Summer" tattoo covering my entire chest. Bill Price and I had driven to the midway at Balboa Beach to get the work done. Surfers silhouetted in black against a hot pink and burnt orange background. I love this film. The soundtrack is outstanding. I'm riding the perfect wave.

"Dew," I heard a voice whisper quietly. It was Cary.

"Dew," he said again, this time shaking me, "Wake up man, its 6 am, we've got to get going."

I sat up with a start, instantly looking down at my chest. No tattoo. I'd been dreaming.

"I'm awake," I said, my voice trailing off, "I'm awake."

2

FIRST STEPS

∽

"If a missionary works, there will be no homesickness, no worrying about families, for all time and talents and interests are centered on the work. Work, work, work–there is no satisfactory substitute."

Ezra Taft Benson
13ᵀᴴ Prophet, Seer, and Revelator
Church of Jesus Christ of Latter Day Saints
(*The Teachings of Ezra Taft Benson* [1988], p. 200)

∽

"Prata inte, Äldste Miller!" (No talking), Elder Pierce barked. "Förlåt," (Sorry), I instantly replied. I knew I was breaking the rules. We had already been told once—on the ride from the hotel to Göteborg's Grand Central station—to button up less any idle chatter distract us from the work.

Truth is I was hungry. Starving, actually, having passed on what the Swedes call breakfast, fish swimming in a sundry of unsavory looking sauces. I would come to know these all too well: senapssill (herring in mustard sauce), löksill (herring with salt and onions), and skärgårdsill (herring with flecks of pepper and fish roe). The *piste de resistance* was *Kalles Kaviar*, a fish roe spread, brilliant orange in color, more suggestive of nuclear waste than cherished delicacy. Together with knäckebröd (keh-neck-ah-brood), a tasteless tooth cracking hard bread the size of a credit card, the fish were the featured foods of *Storfrukost* (literally, big breakfast) typical of the fare served in all Scandinavian hotels.

If the fish wasn't to your liking, then a variety of cheeses were always on hand, including *Brunost* (brown cheese). Velveeta this was not. Imported from Norway in bright red packages the size of bricks, it would be more accurate to call it, "a salty goat fudge." Placed along the country's borders, the smell alone of this substance would repel any invading army.

The hope of finding something to eat among the morning offerings came to an abrupt end when I tried to pour milk on the Swedish equivalent of corn flakes. The carton I grabbed had a picture of a happy little cow on the side. What else could it be, I thought? When I turned the container over, nothing happened. Finally, after vigorous shaking and a mighty squeeze, out it plopped, a thick white glob of goo. Not yoghurt. Not cream. *Filmjölk* (feel-m-yilk). A singularly Swedish dairy product made from soured cow's milk.

With that, I'd given up. Cary had skipped breakfast as well. Once out of the van and seated in the station, we had resumed our conversation. It was all above board, nothing OP. Pierce and Payne had left with Ken Arnold, escorting him to the train that would convey him to his first assignment. Cary and I were only discussing our empty stomachs.

"Äldste Wells, det är dags," (Elder Wells, it's time) Payne said, suddenly materializing in front of us as though he'd stepped out of a *Star Trek* transporter beam.

Without saying a word, Cary stood, ran his hand back and forth over his hair, looked me in the eyes, then turned and walked away. This was no fond farewell; more like my friend was being escorted to the gallows.

"Vänta här," (wait here) Elder Pierce directed, "Vi kommer straxt tillbacka. Du är nästa," (We'll be right back. You are next).

As Wells and the AP's walked into the crowd and disappeared, I sat motionless on the bench, wool gathering, watching the bustle, and wondering about the people passing by. *Who are they and where are they going?* They were all so skinny compared to Americans—and tall, and blond, and smoking, a cigarette dangling from the lips of nearly all.

Every once in a while, someone would look at me, catch my eye and just as quickly look away. With all that impersonality, I was surprised when a woman sat next to me on the bench. She was pretty. I gave her a wan smile. She remained expressionless. Rummaging through her purse, she retrieved a pack of cigarettes and lighter, then belched, snorted loudly, spit, and lit up. This picture of horror was complete when I caught a glimpse of her legs; thick black hair matted beneath her hose. The ways of Viking women were lost on me! If she were representative of hot catches, temptation would never be a problem.

The next thing I noticed was a pair of blue suit pants at eye level.

"Äldste Miller, det är dags," (Elder Miller, it's time). It was Pierce. With Payne's assistance, he lifted me to my feet. I wasn't sure why, but I felt light-headed, my legs weak, like they might give way.

As we walked the hundred yards to the platform, Pierce spoke, slowly and deliberately, giving me my parting instructions. In Swedish, he said, "What great fortune you have Elder Miller, God has called you to serve in Huskvarna (Whose-k-far-nah), a small village near Lake Vättern (Veh-turn) in the center of Sweden known as Småland" (Smoe-lahnd)

"Your senior companion," Payne continued, "will be Elder Church, a righteous missionary and great teacher. You're blessed to have him. He'll meet you at the station."

Looking at his watch, Pierce said, "The train ride takes 3 hours. Don't fall asleep because, about half way there, you'll have to change trains in the city of Borås (Bore-ōse)." Checking a pocket time table, he added, "You won't have much time, about 6 minutes."

After hefting my bags onto the train, the AP's once more, grabbed me under the arms, and pushed me aboard.

"Vi ses," (See you soon), they said in unison wearing their customary beatific smiles.

"Hej då," (Good bye) I said feebly.

As I turned to retrieve my bags, Payne admonished, "By the way, make sure you don't sit in first class. You'll wind up paying extra." Immediately, I could feel my anxiety start to boil. Before I could say a word, the door slammed shut. *First class? Where the heck is that?* This was my first time on a train, ever. I didn't know first class from the caboose. Not knowing which way to go, I mentally flipped a coin, and went to my left.

Unlike me, all of the passengers were seated, bags stowed, and attention directed to their copies of the *Göteborgs Posten*, the city's morning tabloid.

The train jerked into motion and me along with it. I stumbled down the aisle, bags banging into the seats and elbows of my fellow travelers. Few seemed to notice or care, as their eyes were glued to a full color, large-breasted nude woman on page three of their papers. Sure enough, she was wearing clogs. No wonder it was against mission rules to read the newspaper.

Finding no place to sit, I made my way through the connecting tunnel and into the next carriage. There, by the luggage rack, stood a man storing his bag for the trip. Not wanting to continue wandering up and down the aisles, I decided to ask him if I was in the first class car.

"Är detta första klass?" (Is this first class?)

Like a big herring, he pushed his lips together, and made a loud sucking noise.

I stood and stared at him waiting for a reply. When none came, I decided that my first attempt to speak the language with a native had failed. So I asked him again, more slowly.

"*Är detta första klass?*" (Is-this-first-class?)

With a puzzled expression, he looked at me directly, repeating his fish imitation.

Never mind, I thought. I smiled, and not wanting to be rude, thanked the man. Continuing my odyssey through the train, I now found myself in a cabin car. *Separate cabins? This has to be first class.* When a porter appeared, I asked him.

"*Är detta första klass?*" (Is this first class?)

He breathed in sharply, creating a gasping sound not unlike a patient with emphysema struggling to catch his breath.

Once again, I waited for a reply. *He must be a smoker like everyone else around here.* Curiously, it seemed as though he was waiting for *me* to respond. So I asked again, slowly emphasizing each word.

"*Är detta första klassen?*" (Is-this-first-class?)

Damned if he didn't do it one more time! Now annoyed, I reflexively thanked the man and walked away. I didn't know what to do. *Why won't anyone talk to me? And what is all this sucking about?* Later, I would learn that such sounds were, in fact, ways of saying yes specific to certain regions in the country.

I finished my tour of the train ending in a car jammed with baby carriages, a few bicycles, and the restroom. I could see a few fold-down seats, but so much "stuff" was piled before them, I gave up and resolved to stand.

And stand I did for ninety minutes, my attention divided between keeping my balance and listening for the name of the station where I was to change trains. *What was that name again? Borax? No that was my Swedish grandmother's favorite cleaning product.*

While I struggled to remember, the train passed through a number of small villages with difficult to pronounce names: Mölnycke, Landvetter, Bollebygd. It was sheer luck I recognized the name Borås when it was announced. Knowing I had only a few minutes, I moved toward the door, leaving the storage car behind and readying myself for the sprint to the connecting train.

The doors opened with a click, followed by a long hydraulic hiss. Stepping out, my right foot connected with open air, and down I went. The next I knew, my face was pressed to the asphalt and my bags were splayed about me. The crowd pressed on as though I wasn't there. Raising myself up, I looked down and saw I'd managed to tear my suit pants and bloody my knee.

Great, I thought, *here one day and I'm already down to a single pair of pants.*

"Are you all right?" a voice asked in perfect English.

"Well, I've cut my knee," I said, working to cover my embarrassment.

"I can see that, I'm sorry."

I stood, brushing myself off, and turned toward my Good Samaritan. She was drop dead gorgeous. I gawked.

Eighteen or nineteen years old, long blond hair, blues eyes, and an infectious smile. I could not help but think of Katie Barrett, my girlfriend at BYU. But this woman was more, much more.

"Let me help you," she said, moving closer to straighten my tie and adjust my suit coat. I shuddered when her breasts briefly brushed against me, my attention shifting immediately from the pain in my knee to the initials embroidered across her sweatshirt: U.C.L.A.

"Are you American? Your English is perfect."

"No, I'm Swedish, one hundred percent but I worked as a nanny for a year in California."

"California?" I said in surprise.

"Yes, why?"

"That's where I'm from!"

"Hmm, small world isn't it?" she replied, stepping back, eyeing me from head to toe.

"Yes ... it is," I stammered, my voice trailing off, "But wait, how did you know *I* spoke English?"

Tilting her head ever so slightly, she laughed, "Are you kidding? The suit, the tie, the shoes? You're a Mormon Missionary."

"I am?" My tone more a question than statement. Looking at my watch, I then said, "I AM, and I've got a train to catch in less than a minute, and I don't know where to go, what track it's on."

"Where are you off to?" she asked, helping collect my bags.

"Huskvarna, in Småland."

Pointing, she said, "its right over there, 'Track Two,' better hurry."

I turned and started a mad dash toward the train. I hadn't made it twenty feet when it hit me, *What am I doing?* My first friendly encounter and I hadn't even said thanks. It wasn't like me to be so restrained, rude even. I didn't like it.

Slamming on my brakes, I pivoted, and looked back. She was still standing there, watching me. I yelled out, "Tack så mycket!" (thank you).

She smiled.

"What's your name?" I shouted, "And where do you live?"

"Elin ... Elin Olin," she replied, "I'm a student in Lund, at Lund University."

"Hej då," (Good bye) I yelled back, waving.

"Vi ses" (See you later), she replied. With that, I waved smartly once more and was off.

Reaching the train, I could see the number "2" boldly painted, a meter tall, on the side of the car. The one adjacent was clearly marked with an equally large "1."

So, that's how you tell first from second class! Why hadn't Pierce and Payne just said so? What pricks.

Entering the cabin, I could immediately see that Huskvarna was not on everyone's A-list for a visit. All the seats were empty.

Straining a bit under the weight, I lifted my bags up onto the overhead rack and sat down with a sigh. My knee looked a mess. *Should I change my pants?* I decided against it. Better to save them. I only had one pair left.

The train whistle blasted and the wheels engaged. I could feel myself relax. I'd made it.

Reaching inside the breast pocket of my suit jacket, I pulled out my small, leather bound diary. Spencer W. Kimball, the same Prophet that had ordered all young men to serve missions, had also admonished all Church members—men, women, and children—to keep a journal. "Begin today," he said "for this is what the Lord has *commanded*."

I'd started journaling four days before I left California for Provo. Sunday, September 18th, was my first entry. There, I'd quoted a passage from a favorite book, *Catcher in the Rye*—the one thankfully the morality police overlooked the day before during their search for contraband at the mission office. For some reason, it had spoken to me:

"If you really want to hear about it, the first thing you'll probably want to know is where I was born, how my parents were occupied and all that David Copperfield kind of crap, but I don't feel like going into it...I'm not going to tell you my whole goddam autobiography or anything. I'll just tell you about this madman stuff that happened to me...".

I hadn't written anything in my journal since arriving in Sweden. Reading this, my first entry, I thought, *Man, did I hit the nail on the head.* This was some madman stuff for sure.

Turning to the first blank page, I wrote down the date, Elin's name, and where she lived. It seemed kind of pointless. The chances of my seeing her again had as much of a future as a snowball in hell. Plus, I had no intention of finding love in Sweden. I knew what was required of me and I'd made a commitment.

At the same time, meeting Elin and talking—even if only briefly—felt so normal. In my journal, I wrote, "Why did that have to be such a big deal? And how had talking with a girl become so twisted in the minds of the church elders, an everyday event suddenly a one-way ticket to *Dante's Inferno*?" I understood their logic, slippery slopes and all. They were always quoting Matthew 5:28, "As a man thinketh in his heart, so is he."

But what exactly was I thinking? Sure, I liked women. What guy didn't? Somehow, from the church leaders' perspective, we were all dogs in heat, any contact foreplay—a short step and hop from jumping in the sack and then, of course, being sent home in disgrace. I didn't get it. It didn't fit me. Then again, *they* were the leaders.

Gosh, Elin was pretty …

Hop, hop, hop.

~

I spent the time on the train to Huskvarna writing in my journal, catching up on what had happened since leaving the LTM and arriving in Sweden. Every so often, I'd look up and out the window. The sky was grey, the terrain mostly nondescript: dense pine forests broken up by flat, barren, snow covered tracts of land. It reminded me of the Pacific Northwest, but without the mountains.

By the time the conductor announced our arrival in Huskvarna, the measly daylight had faded to black, and gale force winds were blowing snow in every direction. Not wanting to tear out the other knee of my suit pants, I looked twice before stepping off the train. The station was deserted except for a lone, rail-thin figure holding what appeared to be a bicycle, barely visible through the storm. The person remained motionless as I trudged toward him, snow crunching underfoot.

"Äldste Church?" I yelled, hoping to be heard over the din. Actually, at this point, I was sure he was my companion. The bicycle and goofy looking black fedora—tightly pulled down over his head—left no room for doubt.

"Välkommen til Huskvarna, Äldste Miller." (Welcome to Huskvarna, Elder Miller) he said.

In Swedish, "I'm from California," I replied spritely. When he fixed me with a blank stare, I concluded I'd misunderstood. As it were, such confused exchanges would dog me my first few months in the country.

Ignoring my gaffe, he continued, this time louder, "Let's get going, we have a couple of appointments this afternoon. If we hurry, we'll be able to go by the apartment first to drop off your bags."

I struggled to keep up with the language. He spoke so quickly. *Would I ever be this fluent?* For now, I'd be stuck asking either, "Vad sa du?" (What did you say?) or "Hur säger man …" (How do you say …? Followed by the word or words in English).

My mind now raced. I guess we were going to get right to it. Church was certainly all business. Not so much as a, "How do you do?" I should be grateful, I supposed, that I wouldn't have to lug my bags around while we worked.

"We have appointments this afternoon?" I asked, being sure to S.Y.L., "What time is it?"

"Three o'clock," he answered, barely audible "reset your watch."

Three o'clock. I've only been in Sweden 24 hours. My, how life has changed.

I could feel the chill on my skin as I pulled back the sleeve of my overcoat and began fiddling with my blue-faced Seiko®. That's when I noticed that Elder Church had turned and was rapidly walking away from me.

"Äldste Church," I shouted, "Wait for me."

Sure enough he stopped. Then, without moving his body, he first turned his eyes in my direction, followed by his head. He looked like an owl. It was creepy. *What is with this guy?*

It wasn't until we had both exited the station and passed a short queue of taxis that I realized I was going to be stuck carrying my bags to the apartment. Eager to escape the weather, "Äldste Church, are we walking?"

"Yes," he replied, matter-of-factly.

I laughed, hoping he was kidding. When he kept walking, even quickening his pace, I implored in English, "Elder Church, my bags are heavy. Can't we take one of these cabs?"

"Äldste Miller," he said, reprising his owl impersonation, "we cannot waste our limited funds on such luxuries—and, Äldste Miller, S.Y.L."

"Just det. Förlåt," (Right . Forgive me). Then I shut up.

For the next 45 minutes, we marched, with me schlepping, sometimes dragging, my two grey bags. In no time, I was covered with snow. My shoes and socks were completely soaked, my toes numb. No matter how hard I tried, I couldn't keep up with Church. The distance between us grew by the second.

For the most part, the streets were empty, bereft of cars and people. Aside from the constantly blowing wind, the only sounds to be heard were occasional groans and a low, rumbling noise off in the distance. I knew where the groans were coming from: Me. The source of the other sound, I soon discovered, was a large, sprawling, smoke-belching factory, surrounded by twelve foot high brick walls, topped with barbwire.

Perhaps I'd watched too many World War II documentaries with my Dad.

I pictured myself on the Eastern Front, perhaps Stalingrad. *Yeah, Stalingrad.* I could see me. Walking single file, following my comrade, as we picked our way through a mine field, clutching my Russian made PPSh-41 burp gun, constantly on alert, lest we be taken out by a sniper. Strangely enough, the thought of being in Russia in thick of battle was preferable to the reality of walking the streets of Huskvarna, trailing my peculiar companion.

That's when guideline number 5 on page 22 of the *White Bible* kicked in, "Be positive about everything. Do not speak negatively of the weather, the people, the country, or the area. Be grateful to your companion. *Stay focused on the work.*"

Right. I was failing on all counts. What was I thinking? Church history was replete with stories of missionaries who had endured far worse. In the early days, men left their homes, families, and belongings behind, to preach the gospel—news of the "Restored Church"—to every "nation, kindred, tongue, and people." In fact, they were commanded to go without "purse or scrip," taking no money and only what they could carry. Anything less was a demonstration of one's lack of faith.

Once more, I remembered the example of my great-great-grandfather, David Bowen. He'd travelled a thousand miles in a wagon to get from Council Bluffs to Salt Lake City. Hundreds and hundreds died along the way. And I was complaining about being refused a taxi ride? *Buck up. Brace up. Have faith. Scott, remember why you are here.*

Before I could say Jack Robinson—or in my case, Joseph Smith—we were in and out of the apartment and on our way to the afternoon's appointments. The only glimpse I'd caught of my new home, Johannesvägen 5J, was a hallway leading into the flat. Back down the hill we went, past the factory, my companion leading the way, his bicycle in tow.

HIS BICYCLE IN TOW!

"Are we riding bikes?" I'd innocently asked as we were leaving.

"You have no bike."

"Yeah, ok, then why are you taking yours?"

"It's a rule," he stated affirmatively, his head trailing his eyes, "We do not have and are not allowed to ride in cars."

Ride in cars? What on Earth is he saying? I am talking about bicycles. Uncertain of whether he was nuts or I was on the brink of going nuts, I once again shut up.

On we went. Signs of our earlier passage on the still abandoned streets had vanished, covered by snow. Thirty minutes or so later, we arrived at the door of a non-descript apartment building. No matter where you were in the country—North, South, East, West or somewhere in between—all such dwellings looked identical. Bland. Utilitarian. The design reflected a historic period of rapid economic growth and political revolution. "Social Equality" was the slogan of the day, a time from the 1960's through the 1970's when no one was afforded special status or privilege.

As we entered the portico, my companion tapped the ever-present, glowing red button, filling the stairwell with light and triggering the timer. Tick-tock-tick-tock-tick-tock. It was the same kind of switch I'd seen the day before at the Mission office. Bypassing the elevator, we hustled up the winding, spiral staircase to the fourth floor. We had to get to the right apartment before the lights went out.

The name on the door above the mail slot read: D. Ander. Without hesitation, Church loudly knocked. When no one answered, he rapped again, this time harder and, simultaneously gave the hand cranked doorbell a sharp twist. The sounds echoed throughout the stairwell, answered by the piercing cry of a baby in the adjacent apartment.

I took a step back when that door flew open, and a young, bearded man stepped out, screeching infant in arms, and began yelling.

"Jag visste att det var ni, era Jävlar!" (I knew it was you, you fuckers!)

"Forgive me," I reflexively replied in Swedish, not understanding a single word of what he'd said. Falling back on my well-rehearsed set of phrases for newbies, I continued, "Can you please speak more s l o w l y?"

For reasons lost on me at the time, my response only further incited his rage. As my thick-headed companion continued to pound away, the neighbor sat his still-screaming baby on the threshold of his flat and turned back toward me. His face crimson and veins bulging, in my mind's eye he was transforming into a Viking berserker. All that was missing was his horned helmet and battle-axe.

Tapping my companion lightly on the shoulder, I squeaked, "Äldste Church, I think we should go."

"Jävla rätt Ni borde gå (Damn right, you should go)!" the man shouted at the top of his lungs, "It's always one of you bastards or the other, Mormons or Jehovah's Witnesses. You're a plague." Then, as though accommodating my request, he added, slow enough for even me to understand, "None of us are interested in your stupid religions. Leave us alone! Stick åt Helvete (Go to Hell)!"

Fearful of what might happen next, I reached over and shook Church, "It's *really* time to go." My companion's only reply was, "I guess Dean Ander isn't home."

I was stupefied. How could he miss what was happening? Church was Mr. Magoo. In my best Swedish, and with all the politeness I could muster, I said to the man, "Thank you. It was a pleasure meeting" and turned to head down the stairs. *Screw Church*, I thought, *let him deal with Eric the Red.*

By the time I made it to the entry way, I was having second thoughts. We were companions after all. My duty was to stay with him, to provide support and protection. As I wrestled with the horns of the dilemma, I could hear Church casually clunking down the stairs. That's when the lights went out. I tapped the switch again and immediately, the man resumed his raving.

"You assholes better be leaving. Don't you *dare* come back up these stairs!"

No argument there. We were on the same page. *Yes, yep, yes-sir-ee, Bob.* Yanking open the door, I could feel the blast of the winter air super chilling the sweat on my forehead and neck. When I removed my scarf to wipe my face, I could see my hands shaking.

"The Devil has gotten to Dean Anders," were the first words Church uttered when he joined me outside.

Getting in his face, I blurted out in English, "The devil? What the hell are you talking about? We could have died in there! Anders Schmanders. Did you see that man? How pissed off he was?"

"Of course," he said, taking a step back. "It's all part of it." Clearing his throat, he began reciting the oft repeated words of the Prophet Joseph Smith, "The Standard of Truth has been erected. No unhallowed hand can stop the work from progressing."

I shook my head in disbelief. My companion was giving a speech! Clearly, there was no stopping him. I could have jogged around the block, smoked a pack of cigarettes, and on top of it, read the Sunday paper—all before he finished.

"Persecutions may rage, mobs may combine, armies may assemble, calumny may defame. *But the truth of God will go forth boldly.*"

Pausing momentarily, he looked off in the distance, his face beaming with inspiration. Excitedly rubbing his hands together, his next words were, "Let's go tracting!" And off he marched.

"Wait," I shouted, standing my ground, wishing I had my own battle-axe.

Elder Owl (my new name for him as of this moment) stopped, turned and stared at me.

"Tracting?" I asked, incredulous, "Are you kidding? After that?"

"It's time to be thankful, Elder Miller. God has given us an opportunity. This missed appointment means there must be someone else out there ready and waiting to hear our message."

For the third time that day, I shut up. Church led the way and I followed, keeping my distance. I didn't want to hear another word come out of that man's mouth. I had to think—a commodity that, so far, had been in very short supply today.

We knocked on doors for the next two hours. Judging by the results, I concluded God must have changed his mind. This was not the opportunity Church had prophesied. No one let us in. A pattern soon emerged. If someone did answer—which was rare—they either screamed or quickly slammed the door once they caught a glimpse of us. Others never opened the door, retreating once they'd spied us through the peep hole.

"Watch the peephole," Church advised, his hushed tone suggesting I was on the receiving end of a super-secret missionary intelligence briefing, "When it goes dark, you know someone's home."

On those doors he drummed away, knocking again and again, and cranking the bell for good measure. I just wanted it to end. I could only imagine what the people on the other side were thinking. I was mortified. Left with no recourse, I stood off to the side, head bowed and eyes closed.

I could hear Rod Serling's menacing voice, *You're moving into a land of both shadow and substance … there's a signpost up ahead. Your next stop? The Twilight Zone. Do-do-do-doo, doo-do-do-doo. Is this how I will be spending the next two years?* This whole way of working can't be right, provoking people in this way, being so pushy, so obnoxious. *What happened to being nice? Thoughtful? Respectful?* God and the Devil had nothing to do with it. We were like blind bulls in a china shop, bringing all this on ourselves.

Checking my watch, I could see we were coming up on 6 p.m. Desperate to find the Owl's off-switch, I fell back on protocol.

"Elder Church, the *Handbook* says we are supposed to eat promptly at five."

"True," he replied, "but, we lost time picking you up at the train station. We have an appointment with Fru Nilsson at seven. She always feeds us. Her apartment is not so far from here. Until then, we can work."

More shrieks, slammed doors, and peepholes followed. We took turns being rejected, Elder Owl thrusting me onto the front lines, insisting that I take every other door.

"Hejsan" (Hello), I'd start, as we'd been taught to say, "My companion and I are two representatives of the Church of Jesus Christ of Latter Day Saints. We have an important message to deliver to you. May we come in?"

"I am not interest*ing*!" the few who opened the door would declare, mangling the English language with the same abandon as I did Swedish.

When Church announced that the ordeal was over, I was so relieved I could have wept.

"You'll like Fru (Mrs) Nilsson," he yammered on to no one in particular, "Her heart is open to the Gospel. Tonight, we give her 'the bud'" (pronounced, boo-ed).

"The bud?" I asked.

"Yeah, 'the bud,' discussion H."

Once again, I began trailing him, preferring my own company to his. My mind went to "The Discussions." The LDS Church's official *Uniform System for Teaching the Gospel.* I knew it well. Eight lessons. Color-coded scripts, labeled C through J, to use word-for-word when meeting with potential converts. Each lesson was linked with pictures and simple text, printed on 8 X 10" glossy paper, bound in a large three-ring binder known officially as, "the flip chart." One missionary delivered the lines; the other, like the *Price is Right* models, turned the pages and pointed at the illustrations and bullet points. Nothing was left to chance.

I'd been studying the stuff from the moment I'd entered the LTM. Committing the canned dialogue to memory was the principle way missionaries learned the language of their assigned country. We spent hours and hours seated in a room, hunched over the discussion book, reciting the lines over and over. Within a week, we'd all purchased the blue Peltor® noise silencing headphones available in the LTM commissary to avoid being distracted by the constant mumbling of our fellow memorizing missionaries.

Once weekly we were tested. Prior to departing for Sweden, most of us—myself, Cary Wells, and Ken Arnold—had managed to pass the first, tan-colored, discussion C. Only that sniveling, suck up O'Leary had managed to learn more. At the mission office in Göteborg, President Thorsson announced we had eight weeks to learn the remaining seven.

Back to "The Bud." The fact that we were about to deliver the baby-blue colored discussion H meant Fru Nilsson was close to taking the baptismal plunge. For most, "H" was *the* make or break lesson, the defining line in the sand, what separated the Mormons from the rest of the Christian world. If you made it through this one, and still wanted to hear more, you were joining the Church for sure. All one had to do was swear off cigarettes, coffee, cussing, tea, booze, and sex—unless, of course, you were married (preferably to a Mormon). You also had to tithe, turning over 10% of your income before taxes to the Church every month. In a country where most, as Thorsson had pointed out, "lived in sin," and citizens already dished out 50% or more of their income in "skatt" (taxes), converting to Mormonism was a mighty hard sell.

When Fru Nilsson opened the door, I was instantly transported back to Payson, Utah and the home of my 91-year old grandmother, Christina. I loved that woman. She was a saint. In her eyes, I could do no wrong.

"Stig på grabbar!" (Come in boys) the elderly woman said, shaking Church's hand as he entered the apartment, "I've been looking forward to your visit all day."

"And you," she continued, reaching up and patting my cheeks gently, "you're new. I heard you were coming. You must be *very* tired after your long journey, and hungry ... both of you, I imagine."

I was struck by her warmth and friendliness. She was actually glad to see us. More than glad, happy even. What a contrast with the last three hours, starting with the indifferent reception I'd received from my companion at the train station. I could have hugged the woman.

"Ta' av Er (Take off your coat and shoes)," her voice soft and reassuring, "Don't stand there by the door. Come in. Come in. Sit. I'll call you when it's time to eat." She turned and shuffled down the hallway.

I melted into the couch and began taking in the room. I noticed it was surprisingly dark, lit only by a couple of candles placed in brightly colored holders called *ljusstake* (youse-stock), common in Swedish homes. The furniture was straight out of an IKEA catalog, plain and simple. Pictures adorned the walls, including several primitive landscapes. I wondered whether she had painted them herself. There were also many old photographs, presumably of her family. One person appeared again and again. A man captured at various ages: graduation, in military uniform, in front of a factory wearing a suit. The last one, in color, was of an old man leaning on a cane. *Could this be her husband?*

From the kitchen, I could hear the occasional clatter of dishes and Fru Nilsson happily humming. I didn't know the tune. Whatever she was cooking smelled delicious. Yet, as much as it made my mouth water, it could not compete with the overpowering aroma of coffee.

If Sweden had a national smell—as countries do flowers, birds, and trees—it would have to be of coffee. They are obsessed with it. The brew ranks right up there with King and country. To Swedes, it is part of the Holy Trinity. In fact, they have a favorite saying about it, "Fader, Sonen, och det Heliga Kaffet" (Father, Son, and the Holy Coffee).

Kokt Kaffe, boiled coffee, as it is known, has all the consistency and flavor of motor oil. I knew it well. Despite the Church's longstanding prohibition, my Grandmother kept a pot cooking on the stove all day, every day. Whenever anyone came to visit, out it came. It was one of my strongest memories from childhood; Grandma Christina and her old Nordic friends, Mormons all, seated around the kitchen table drinking the substance with the same zeal as Arabs passing a hookah.

My mother was equally fond of coffee. Right up to the day I left for the LTM, she kept a Mr. Coffee Maker in the back bathroom of the house lest any prying nose from our tight-knit Mormon community discover her transgression. They were always dropping in unannounced. She was never caught.

The Mormon's tortured relationship with coffee—as well as tea, alcohol, and tobacco—occurred around the same time the Temperance Movement was gaining popularity in the United States. Circumstances in Joseph Smith's home also contributed. Fed up with the smell of stale smoke and tobacco stained floors, the Prophet's wife loudly complained. A revelation soon followed.

When first received and disseminated, the *Word of Wisdom* was treated as a set of general guidelines which most, including the Prophet, and my relatives, ignored. Nearly a century would pass before church leaders transformed the recommendations into divine law—a decision which closely followed the ratification of the 18th amendment, prohibiting the "manufacturing, sale, and transportation of intoxicating beverages." While prohibition was repealed, the *Word of Wisdom* remained in force. Violators no longer face excommunication but are banned from the Mormon temple and, of course, baptism.

O boy! Fru Nilsson is in for a big surprise tonight. Goodbye coffee, hello Holy Ghost.

My historical musings over, I looked to see what Church was doing. There the Owl sat, perched on the edge of the couch, back erect, hands on knees, looking straight forward, anything but relaxed. He reminded me of a statue of an Old Kingdom Pharaoh—cold, stern, unfeeling. Elder Robert Church, my companion for who knows how much longer. *Robert the Redeemer.*

"Hoo hoo," Fru Nilsson called, "the food is ready."

Hemlagad ärt soppa (homemade split pea soup), hushållsost (Swedish cheese), and Skogaholms limpa (seedless rye bread) awaited us.

"Tack så mycket" (Thank you very much) I said as I took my seat, "it looks and smells so good."

"Det är så lite," (It's so very little) she replied, the characteristic Scandinavian shunning of compliments once more recalling my Grandmother.

Contrary to habit, I picked up the fork with my left hand and the knife in my right. We'd been taught the Continental style of eating at the LTM. I was pleased with myself until I remembered we were eating soup! I quickly placed the knife back down on the table and exchanged the fork for a spoon. This is when Church announced it was time for a prayer.

Mormons always say grace before a meal. Usually it is short, to the point. Not this time. I thought I might lose consciousness before he finished. On and on he went, making little mention of the meal, neither thanking God nor blessing the food. He switched into speech mode, with Fru Nilsson in the crosshairs of his oration. "Fru Nilsson, open your heart." "Fru Nilsson, be accepting." "Fru Nilsson, humble yourself before God." The feverish delivery made me think the smell of coffee had gone to his head. He was having a major contact high.

Just when I thought he might reach across the table and shake the stuffing out of the old lady, he stopped. When I opened my eyes and looked up, birdman was already eating. Surprisingly, Fru Nilsson seemed utterly unfazed. I guessed she had been through this before. Such aplomb. I envied her coolness under fire.

No one said a word. It was hard to know what to say after that. Picking up the spoon with my left hand, I dipped into the soup bowl.

"This is really delicious," I said.

"Homemade. From scratch," she answered.

"Is it difficult to make?" I asked, pleased to be following the conversation.

Before she could answer, Church interrupted, "It's a very common dish," then switching to English added, "The recipe is in the missionary cookbook, right next to 'pigs in a blanket.'"

Out of the corner of my eye, I could see Fru Nilsson look down. Clearly, he'd hurt her feelings. Pigs in a blanket, I wanted to kick him. The only pig around here was him—and an ungrateful prick of a pig at that.

If Church could have his way, there would be no chit chat, no friendly banter. Changing back to Swedish, Church brought the focus back to the mission.

"So, have you been praying, asking the Lord for guidance?"

Fru Nilsson set down her spoon, and in a polite, grandmotherly voice, said, "We can talk about that later, after dinner."

For the next half hour, we talked. Actually, Fru Nilsson and I talked. Thankfully, she spoke slowly as I was translating every word from Swedish to English and back again.

I learned she had graduated from college and worked as a nurse her entire life. She had two grown children and three grandchildren, all living in the far northern part of Sweden.

"I don't get to see them as often as I'd like," she told me, "We talk on the phone, but it's not the same." After pausing briefly, she added, "I hope they'll be coming for Christmas this year."

The man in the photos was her husband. He'd died 10 years earlier after 42 years of marriage.

"Oh, I miss him," she said. I heard in her voice the same kind of stoicism I'd come to know so well from my Grandmother, "Life moves on though … more soup, Elder Miller?"

"Ja, tack!" (Yes, thank you).

Without asking, Fru Nilsson also ladled soup into my companion's bowl. The look on his face was a study in dread, much as one would imagine an inmate sitting in the electric chair waiting for the switch to be thrown. I knew what he was thinking: the proselytizing would have to wait through yet another bowl of soup!

As we finished the meal, and stood up from the table, Fru Nilsson pointed to my knee and remarked, "Your pants are torn."

"Oh gosh, yes," I said, taking time to think how to say what I wanted to say next. Fru Nilsson waited patiently. "I fell down the steps of the car when I was changing trains in Borås this morning."

"Stackars …" (You poor thing), let me fix those for you, right now."

A babbling noise came from the Owl, unrecognizable as human speech. Looking over, I could see his face twitching, eyes blinking rapidly but not in unison, first the right, then the left. *Could this be? Was I actually seeing this?* There was more, his mouth was opening and closing, his arms were fixed by his sides, fingers stiffly extended, his feet marching in place. Robbie the Redeemer's circuits were frying.

"No, no, no," he finally blurted out, "we have a very important message to deliver to you tonight."

"This won't take long," she quickly countered, her friendly tone unchanged, "Take off your pants, Äldste Miller."

"What?" the alarm apparent in Church's voice, "Pants? No. Off? No. Must leave pants on at all times."

"Fy. Sånt struntprat skall vi inte ha!" (Oh, Poppycock) "Come, come," she continued, gesturing, "The bathroom is over here. I'll bring you something to wear."

Through the crack in the door, Fru Nilsson passed a well worn robe, "It may be a tad small for such a healthy young man as you. It was my husband's, Sven."

Small it was, the two ends barely meeting in the middle. I had to cinch the belt really tight to keep me from hanging out.

"Hmm," she remarked as I emerged from behind the door, "It's been many years since I've seen that robe on anybody."

Looking down, I thought, if I wasn't careful, there would be a good chance she'd see a lot more of me.

When I walked into the living room, Fru Nilsson behind me, her sewing basket and my pants in hand, we found Church sitting on the couch. He looked at me and his eyes widened to what seemed an impossible dimension. Apparently, the vision of me in such an ill-fitting robe, my G's visible from chest to crotch was too terrible to contemplate. Without a word spoken, he handed over the flip-chart.

While Fru Nilsson busied herself with my pants, my companion commenced "The Bud." He talked. I followed along showing the accompanying pictures at the appropriate moments. I marveled at his performance. It was flawless, his cadence was constant, and he delivered each word as prescribed the manual.

In response to each query, Fru Nilsson gave the answer I knew the Church would want to hear. Yes, she would follow the Ten Commandments. Yes, she would obey the law of tithing. And, despite her clear love of coffee, yes, she would give up that too, as well as tea, cigarettes, alcohol, and sex.

For my part, I felt nothing. I was in the room, but could just as easily have been standing outside watching the entire scene through a plate glass window. This meeting was supposed to be a religious experience, a major step in conversion. We were talking about saving her soul; the rules that, if faithfully followed, would keep her from eternal damnation. *Where is God in all of this? The promptings of the Holy Spirit?* For all Owl's piety and dedication to the mission, his words were empty, devoid of passion. He may as well have been reciting the periodic table: H, hydrogen; He, helium; Li, lithium; Be, Beryllium; B, Boron.

What in Heaven's name are we doing here?

That is when Fru Nilsson spoke, instantly providing an answer, "It's so nice to have you boys here in my home." Pow! Fru Nilsson was not interested in our message. She liked *us*—our company, eating a meal together, and talking. That was the real deal.

As Church neared the end of Discussion H, she interrupted, "Elder Miller, I've finished mending your pants." Smiling, she held them up. I could see she was pleased with her work. So was I. The repair was barely visible. In fact, it was so good I might be able to wear the pants for the duration of my mission so long as I didn't pray out the knees.

"Put them on, so I can check that they look right."

"Before you do that, Elder Miller" Church firmly inserted himself, his voice growing louder with each word, "Fru Nilsson, I *must* ask you a question. "

"OK," she replied, first looking at him, then me, then back at him. I had no idea what was coming.

"Fru Nilsson, do you truly want to follow the Savior?"

"Ja visst" (Of course).

"Fru Nilsson," he continued, "Will you follow the Savior by committing today to obey all of His commandments and become a member of His Church by being baptized by those in whom He has invested His authority?"

Holy moly. Now I felt something. Shock. The birdman was giving Fru Nilsson the "baptismal challenge." I certainly didn't expect to witness this on my second day, let alone without my pants on.

"Visst. När?" (Sure, when?)

"Soon. Real soon", he responded, at once retrieving the flip chart and placing it in his black, hard-sided briefcase, "I've got some work to do now, making arrangements."

"I have a few ques—"

"I'll sort everything," he interrupted her, "I have the authority. *I'll* be the one to baptize you. We'll drop by later with the details."

Turning to me, "Elder Miller. Get your pants on. There's a lot to do. It's time to go."

Before I knew it, out the door we went, back into the freezer. The Owl, Mr. Mission-Accomplished, was on the march, charging ahead, leaving me behind. I stopped to look back. Fru Nilsson was at her door, waving good-bye. I returned her wave and did my best to catch up.

Still ten paces back, I could hear him talking excitedly over the wind, "This is great!"

Had he not been pushing his bike, I could imagine him clapping his hands and dancing a jig. He was definitely stoked.

"I did it. I did it. I got my first one. Now, I just have to get her in the water while she's still hot."

Hearing him, I knew what I should have done, what was expected. I should have made an effort to catch up, clap him on the back, and shake his hand. I couldn't bring myself to do it. Let's just say, I was not having Christian thoughts. Charity be damned. All I wanted to do was get away from him.

The second we made it back to the apartment, Church made a beeline for the phone. His soggy shoes and overcoat created a puddle on the floor as he dialed the Zone Leaders apartment in the nearby city of Jönköping (Yeun-shoop-ing) to relay the news.

"Thank you, thank you," he cooed.

Not knowing what to do, I stood, taking in the place. Burnt orange paisley paper adorned the walls. Known in Swedish as an "Ett-an," the flat was made up of a single room, with adjoining kitchen and toilet. Although hopelessly dated, I couldn't complain as my new home was bigger than my dorm room had been at B.Y.U.

A plain wood table was pushed up against one wall. Above it hung a bookshelf crammed with the very missionary tracts I'd been forced to buy at the President's office the prior day. There were enough pamphlets there to blanket the entire southern half of the country. *Why did I have to buy more? Wait a minute, why did I have to buy any at all?* Next to the shelves was a huge, professionally printed, dry-erase board, *The Missionary Planning and Goal Chart*. Every day of the week was broken down hour-by-hour with space set aside for recording specific performance targets and results. From the copyright, I could see the Church had produced it. *I wonder if there's one of these in every apartment?*

Two twin beds made up the rest of the furniture. Above one hung a patchwork of pictures, Mormon temples and leaders, cut from the pages of the Church's monthly magazine, *The Ensign*. The other bed was empty, save a bare pillow and duvet rolled up at the foot. The walls were also bare, unless you call rips and tears in the wallpaper decoration.

The Owl continued to talk into the phone, his back toward me. From the sound of it, I guessed the call would not be ending anytime soon. *What the heck, guess I'll unpack.*

Opening my bag, what I saw first were my parents and brothers looking up at me from a framed 3" X 5" photograph. I smiled and set the picture on a cardboard box that would serve as my nightstand.

Next, I took out my clothes and laid them on the bed. Looking around, I could see no closet or wardrobe. Near the bathroom I found a dilapidated coat rack on wheels. Listing and rusted, it looked like someone had fished it out of a dumpster. My companion's few articles of clothing hung to the left, I took the rest. Cardboard boxes, a general utility item among missionaries, would serve as my chest of drawers. I placed my two bags upright in the nearby corner, taking extra care to insure the contraband books and cassette tapes missed by the mission censors were well hidden inside.

When I turned around, Church was standing there, staring at me, his face a smiling rictus. Without thinking, I jumped back two steps.

"Uhhh," I croaked.

"Let's make 'gaggies,'" he chirped, his tone positively chipper. Before I could reply, to the kitchen he went. Along the way, he kicked off his shoes and let his wet coat fall to the floor.

Pots and pans banged. Water, oats, sugar, and copious amounts of Hershey's unsweetened cocoa were combined and whisked together. All the while, Church crooned the popular Mormon hymn, "We Thank Thee O God for a Prophet." Congregations around the world are coached in the LDS Hymnal to sing the words, "brightly"—and my companion's rendition did not disappoint:

> We thank thee, O God, for a prophet,
> To guide us in these latter days.
>
> We thank Thee for sending the gospel,
> To lighten our minds with its rays.
>
> We thank thee for every blessing,
> Bestowed by Thy bounteous hand.
>
> We feel it a pleasure to serve thee,
> And love to obey thy command.

Like most Mormons, he only knew the words of the first verse, which he repeated over and over for the six or so minutes it took him to finish.

"The date for the baptism is set: this coming Saturday," he sang, keeping the musical moment going. Simultaneously, he plopped a generous blob of his creation on a plate and handed it to me.

We both sat at the small kitchen table. His rendition over, he stuffed a spoonful of the brown, gooey mixture into his mouth. Pointing at me with his utensil he said, "I'll do the baptizing, you'll do the confirmation."

Similar to Baptists, Seventh Day Adventists, and Jehovah's Witnesses, Latter Day Saints believe in full immersion baptism. Immediately following the ritual bath, Mormons administer the ordinance of confirmation. Elders place their hands on the head of the new member and pray, bestowing the "gift of the Holy Ghost." The convert is now eligible to receive divine inspiration, spiritual gifts, and blessings from the Holy Spirit—or that's the story at least.

"We'll get our names in *The Harvester*," he gushed, referring to the monthly mission newsletter, "President Thorsson will be so pleased." Pointing to my plate, "Don't you like the gaggies, Elder Miller?"

I looked at the substance, poking it repeatedly with my spoon. The steamy, congealed and misshapen mass turned my stomach, looking more like a bathroom accident than celebratory offering. Tentatively, I placed a small bit on my tongue. I wasn't surprised to find that the taste lived up to its appearance. It was crap.

"Did you smell the coffee brewing in Fru Nilsson's apartment?" I asked, changing the subject.

"Yeah, so? He said, munching away.

"I'm not sure she'll stop drinking it." I couldn't help but think of my own mother and grandmother. "I doubt she'll do it."

Church stopped chewing, the elation immediately draining from his face. He stiffened, and his eyes resumed the owl-like movement.

Uh-oh, I thought.

A long pause followed as he finished his last bite. "Don't get in the way of Fru Nilsson's salvation, Elder Miller," his voice a monotone.

"I'm not sure I understand what you are saying."

He paused again.

"Why are ye fearful, O ye of little faith?" in even more of a monotone, if that were possible. "Your doubt, Elder Miller, is placing Fru Nilsson's salvation at risk."

I sat there, unable to speak. *Really? What? I am in the way?*

"Just like when we were tracting earlier, God gave us an opportunity when Dean Ander didn't keep his appointment, the chance to find that one person who was waiting to hear about the Church tonight. And your negative attitude gave Satan the opening he needed to prevent our success."

"What? I, my, er—" I stumbled, struggling to respond to his accusation.

Church abruptly stood, took our plates, and put them in the sink. "It's 10:15. Too late to set our proselytizing goals for tomorrow, enough time to write in our journals and pray before lights out at 10:30."

For the fourth and last time this day, I shut up. Silently, I stripped down to my G's and began making my bed. My companion was already on his knees, elbows leaning on the edge of the mattress, praying away. Mirroring his position on my cot, but only pretending to pray, I thought back over the day.

I could see where he might have a point. I'd not been the most enthusiastic companion. Within minutes of meeting, I'd wanted to take a cab. I'd told him we better leave when Dean Ander's neighbor got so pissed off at us. I'd griped when he suggested we go tracting. I'd accepted a second helping of soup. I'd taken off my pants!

Most of all, I'd felt nothing remotely spiritual the entire evening. Not when Church delivered "The Bud." Not even when Fru Nilsson agreed to be baptized. At the LTM, I'd heard that most missionaries in Sweden *never* baptized, never even came close. I should be feeling fortunate, blessed. Instead, it was a big zero.

I stood up thinking I'd better brush my teeth. As I turned toward the bathroom, Church made his way to the light switch.

"Lights out, Elder Miller."

"I was just going to brush my teeth. It's only 10:25. We still have 5 minutes."

"Yes, the rule states that we are to be in bed by 10:30, but it's the spirit rather than the letter of the law that demonstrates our faith."

Click. The room went black.

Feeling my way to the bed, I pulled back the duvet cover, plopped down and slipped between the sheets.

Slowly, as my eyes adjusted to the dark, I could make out the frame of my family's photograph. I thought about my Mom and Dad, my brothers, wondering what they might be doing. I missed them. Wished I could be with them. The past two days had left a taste in my mouth worse than the Owl's gaggies. At least the LTM had felt familiar. It was like being in school. Not so Sweden.

I couldn't fall asleep. I kept going over the last two days. *Fucking rat bastard Church, who is he to question me? Stupid Norman-the-Mormon. And what does he really know about me anyway? My people sat on the right hand of the prophet Joseph Smith himself!*

At that moment, I thought how enjoyable it would be to get out of bed and smother the little turd with his own pillow. Just as I was working out the details of how I might get away with it, my rage gave way to recognition. He was right, of course. I knew he was right. *I don't have his faith—or Thorsson's, or Pierce's, or Payne's.* All I knew about Mormonism was what I grew up with at 421 North Marcile in Glendora, California. The faith of my childhood, my house, my home, my parents, my brothers, and the members of my local congregation.

I felt so exposed, reminding me of a dream I'd had on more than one occasion. I could be at school, the mall or a party, and in the next moment I realize I'm buck-naked. People are staring at me. They can see everything. I can't hide.

What in the hell am I going to do? Boy, did that question feel familiar. It was the same one I'd struggled with the previous night and for the past two months. The last 48 hours had only added fuel to that fire.

How could I stay? Isn't going home the right choice? I didn't like what I was being asked to do. I didn't believe in the methods. And, the message I was here to deliver—everything from golden plates to coffee being the "gateway drug" to hell—seemed as foreign to me as the Swedish language.

I turned back and looked at the picture frame.

3

NO WAY OUT

~

"Faith isn't tested so much when the cupboard is full as when it is bare.
In these defining moments, the crisis doesn't create one's character it
reveals it."

LYNN G. ROBBINS
GENERAL AUTHORITY
CHURCH OF JESUS CHRIST OF LATTER DAY SAINTS

~

Shit. I shouldn't, I really shouldn't. It'll pass. Damnit, it won't, I know it
won't. Do it and get it over with. Don't, and it'll be on my mind all day.
Cracking open the door, I peeked out. *Where is he?* I'd already been
in the bathroom longer than my allotted five minutes. Any second he could
start banging away. I couldn't see him but the clatter of pots and pans told
me that he was still in the kitchen. The Owl was cleaning up after breakfast.
I still had a few minutes.

I shut the door and turned back to the mirror. I was naked and my dick
was hard as a rock. Since I'd arrived in the country the same scene greeted
me almost every morning, I'd wake up and there it was, standing at attention, making a pup-tent out of the bed sheet.

Like most kids my age, I discovered masturbation quite by accident. It was the summer between sixth and seventh grade. I was lying down in my room, listening to the Beatles, thinking about nothing in particular. I began stroking myself as I'd done before. This time was different. Where I once would have stopped now I kept going. It felt good. I liked it. I didn't want to stop.

I closed my eyes. Soon, a pressure built up inside me. If I hadn't been laying flat on my back, I swear I would have fallen over. My whole body tensed, then jerked, then exploded. Bang.

Holy shit, what just happened? And what is this stuff that just shot all over the place?

Panic quickly replaced pleasure. *What have I done?* At the time, the extent of my sex education was some vague idea that penises went into vaginas. Beyond that, I was clueless. *Have I just hurt myself? If so, how will I know? Who can I ask? What will I say I'd been doing at the time the injury occurred?*

Hurriedly cleaning myself up, I decided the best course of action was to keep my mouth shut, just watch and wait. My resolve lasted to the next day. Deciding my plumbing was unharmed, hanging out in my room listening to the Beatles became one of my favorite pastimes.

I didn't know that what I was doing was called masturbation. I wouldn't hear that word until I started *Seminary*—religion classes held every morning at 6:00 am during the school week. Beginning in the 7th grade, all Mormon kids are expected to attend throughout their high school years.

Hard as it may be to believe, the teacher's name that first year was Dick Heurtz. His charge was to begin the Church's lessons on "moral purity." That meant no kissing. OK, I knew what that was. No petting. I wasn't sure but could imagine. No fornicating. Sex outside of marriage, I got it. And no masturbating.

"What's that?" I whispered to my best friend, Bill. He shrugged his shoulders. We always sat next to each other at Seminary.

At the end of the first class on proper conduct between young men and women, he and I briefly huddled and decided to approach Brother Dick. If our eternal salvation was on the line, we needed to know what it was that we weren't supposed to do.

We waited, lingering by our desks, until the classroom emptied. This didn't take long. A mad dash always accompanied the end of class as the young Latter Day Saints rushed to get from Church to school on time.

"I'll ask him," my friend said, uncharacteristically brimming with confidence. With a wave of his hand, "Come on."

By the time we made it to the front of the room, Bill lost his nerve. He stood stiffly, his eyes riveted on the black board behind Heurtz.

I cleared my throat hoping he would regain his courage and ask our question. Nope. It wasn't going to happen. He had turned to stone.

"Yes boys?" Heurtz asked, looking at his watch, "Don't you have a ride to catch?"

Not a sound.

I don't know how I looked, but Bill's face was bright red. I couldn't tell if he was breathing. He was not going to talk. He couldn't talk.

"Uhh," I stammered.

"Bretheren?" Heurtz invited.

Out it came, at a pitch perhaps only a dog could hear.

"WHAT IS MASTURBATION?" I squeaked.

"I gotta go," the near comatose Bill blurted out. Now reanimated, like a guided missile, he flew from the room, his book bag flapping behind him.

Standing alone, the spot on the blackboard that had so captivated my friend suddenly reached out to me. Out of the corner of my eye, I could see movement. Heurtz was rubbing his chin, thinking.

"Well, Brother Miller," he started, his tone learned, "Masturbation is … um, let me put it this way, it's doing bad things with your bodily fluids."

"Oh … thank you," I replied, "Goodbye." With that explanation, I pivoted on my heels and ran out of the room.

Doing bad things with my bodily fluids? Bill and I would debate the meaning of this enigmatic answer for days. To two 13 year old kids, the list was short: saliva, snot, sweat, and urine.

Having exhausted the possibilities, we turned our attention to the bad things one might conceivably do with each. Hawk a loogie? Seriously, could God be concerned about that? Blow one's nose? If so, a lot of the old people in Church were going to hell. B.O., sweat? Hmm, a new discovery for most boys my age. And urine? That's it, we decided. Pee was our prime suspect. After all, it came from a body part that we'd surmised was off limits.

But what exactly could one do with urine that was so bad it would jeopardize our immortal souls? Our secret deliberations continued. Pee in the swimming pool? I'd stopped doing that after our neighbor, Mr. Kindrick—the owner of the only pool in the neighborhood—told us he added a special chemical that turned red on contact with urine. "Piddle" on the rim of the toilet, to use one of my Dad's favorite terms? Nah, we decided. Leave it for mother to find though and there would be hell to pay. Save it in jars perhaps? Too kooky for words; yet, what else could it be?

Strangely, it never occurred to us that semen was a bodily fluid—not that I knew the meaning of that word either. Other kids laughed and laughed whenever the announcer at the High School football games called out the name of one cheerleader in particular, Veronica Seaman. To theirs, I added my knowing laugh, not really knowing what was so funny. Perhaps it was because I considered semen an accident, a bit like crapping your pants. Certainly God could not hold one accountable for that?

The meaning of masturbation eluded us for some time to come. Eventually, the dots were connected. The revelation came in the form of THE PAMPHLET, titled "Overcoming Masturbation: A Guide to Self Control," passed out by Dick Heurtz without comment at a later class. Therein, all was laid bare. Whoever had authored that tract had to be the person the world had in mind when the word, "killjoy" was coined. Although published anonymously, we later learned it had been written by one of the Church's Twelve Apostles, Mark E. Petersen. *Peter*-sen and *Dick Heurtz*! You couldn't make this stuff up.

Step 3 of Petersen's manifesto specifically stipulated, "You must break off … friendship … with other persons having this same problem." I didn't know if Bill was doing it. I was. Gosh, he and I were best buds. We were constantly together. We took the same classes at school, liked the same music, and were in the same Scout troop. We even were interested in the same girls. Not surprisingly, Bill and I never discussed the subject again. The stakes were too high.

We were further incentivized to avoid our explorations of the subject by passages read to us in Seminary from a then popular book by the Prophet-to-be, Spencer W. Kimball. In these, he wrote that masturbation, "too often leads to grievous sin, even to that sin against nature, homosexuality." How so? "For, done in private, it evolves often into mutual masturbation—practiced with another person of the same sex—and thence into total homosexuality." That was enough for me. I couldn't look Bill in the face for weeks.

$\sim$

Standing in front of the bathroom mirror, dick in hand, I found it difficult to look at myself. Man oh man. None other than Spencer W. Kimball had signed my mission letter, the one calling me to serve. His signature was inscribed at the bottom of my missionary credentials, my double-o "license to convert." And his words left little doubt: masturbation was a "sinful habit ... a self-gratifying activity [that] ... separates a person from God, and defeats the gospel plan." Those who did it, he continued, were "spiritually unclean," their "missionary work ... offering no joy and limited success."

No joy and limited success. These words certainly summed up our results over the last six weeks.

S-i-x w-e-e-k-s. Six weeks. It felt more like six years. On top of it, my brainstorm of crossing out each day on the calendar—in the hope it would make time go by faster—only made it worse. What a dumb idea.

Ever since Fru Nilsson's baptism, my companion and I had not been invited into a single home. I counted the hours we tracted. Five hundred and four spent outside in the freezing cold and snow. We knocked on hundreds of doors, stopped scores of people on the streets—all to no avail. We'd become kryptonite. When people saw us coming, they quickly crossed to the other side or darted into a shop, anything to get away from us.

A thought intruded. *Could my whacking off be "defeating the Gospel plan?"*

I thought about some of the *Book of Mormon* and *Old Testament* stories. God always seemed pissed at somebody and when He was, mercy, you didn't want to be in the neighborhood. Can you say, "Collateral damage?" Most of the people in Palestine could. If the Big Guy upstairs could sanction wiping out every living creature in the city of Jericho—"man and woman, young and old, and ox, sheep, and donkey"—He could certainly punish the citizens of Huskvarna for my indiscretions.

More thoughts followed. *Is God really like that? A sinister Santa Claus? Making a list and checking it twice? Gonna find out who is beat'n off and nice?*

I recoiled at the prospect. In this case, it wasn't just me risking a bag of coal and a sack of switches. The very salvation of mankind was in my hands or, at least, in my right hand.

Scott, get a grip. This is batshit crazy. Stop taking this stuff so literally. You haven't done that since you were eight years old and confronted your Sunday school teacher. Remember that ...

Sister Cox had told us the story of Jonah and the Whale: how Jonah was swallowed, lived inside the beast for three days and three nights, before being spat out unharmed. *Could this be true?* I wondered at the time. In the Disney film, Pinocchio was reunited with Gepetto inside the great whale, Monstro. I loved that movie, but that was a cartoon. *Could the real, flesh and blood Jonah live in a whale?* I resolved to find out.

As soon as I got home, I consulted our family oracle, the source of all knowledge: the gilded pages of the white, 22-volume *World Book Encyclopedia*. I carefully researched the anatomy of whales and other cetaceans. I discovered there was no special room where a person could live.

The following week, without asking my parents, I took volume *W* to church. What happened next, I don't recall. I only have what my parents later told me. Apparently I stood up in class, pointed to the diagram in the encyclopedia, and boldly announced it was impossible for anyone to live inside a whale for three days, much less pray one's way out. In response to my challenge, Sister Cox read the specific passage from the Bible, noting that it was actually a big fish, not a whale. "What kind of fish?" I quickly asked, and then confidently, "I'll look it up." That was too much. She sent me to the Bishop's office.

Driving home in Dad's 65 VW bug, he asked me what happened. I spoke, he listened. As much as I recall, he was neither angry nor critical. He was more interested in what I believed to be the moral of Jonah's story. That was my Dad, the school principal, the educator. *What's the lesson here? What is to be learned?* It was the same approach he took when discussing *Aesop's Fables*—an oft read book in the Miller house.

Dick still in hand, I looked at myself in the mirror once more. *If Dad were my age, how would he handle this? What would he have done? Would he have tried to find a moral lesson …?* I didn't know, and it didn't seem to make a difference. In *this* Mormon world, with *these* people, no in-between existed. Masturbation was forbidden. Church doctrine was right. The stories in the *Bible* and *Book of Mormon* were true. No other higher principle existed to which one could make an appeal. It's was God's way or no way.

I was on my own. I had to decide. What side was I on? And yet, no matter how hard I tried, or fervently I prayed, I just could not make myself believe what some never questioned. I did not believe Jonah was swallowed by a whale when I was eight and I certainly was not going to start now. Where did this leave me?

If I chose not to believe the tale of Jonah then what of the others? That the earth was destroyed in a great flood and all life, except the poor dinosaurs, was preserved by Noah and his ark? An angel leads the 17-year-old, Joseph Smith to a set of golden plates on which the history of God's relationship with the Indians was written? Jesus rose from the dead? That whacking off.

The phone rang. I could hear the Owl leave the kitchen and clunk his way down the short hallway.

"Hejsan," he answered using his best telephone voice, "this is Elder Church of the Church of Jesus Christ of Latter Day Saints. How may I help you?"

In his next breath, I could hear his tone change, going from chipper, to serious, to sniveling toady. "Visst, Äldste Pyle. Ja visst. Vi kommer direkt!" (Yes, Elder Pyle. Absolutely. We'll come straight away).

Crap, I gotta get out of the bathroom.

I was frantically pulling my G's over my now limp rod when the Owl burst into the bathroom. He was totally amped.

"We've got to go!" he exclaimed excitedly, "it's a … the Zone leaders called and … we're … we've …".

"A surprise inspection?" completing his thought.

"Yeah, yes," he said, "we're meeting them … take, take the bus … and Elder P, Pyle …"

"In Jönköping, at the bus station?"

"Yes, in an hour, we'll never … we can't be late, we'll be …"

Seeing that he was not going to move until I did, I pushed my way by him. "We'll make it," I said firmly.

Surprise inspections. This was to be our second. The first took place two weeks into my assignment to Huskvarna. The Zone Leaders (ZL's) called early in the morning. We dropped everything and raced to the bus station, meeting midway between our two areas to switch companions. I went with ZL Pyle back to his area, Rosenlund, a crowded public housing project. This was a ghetto in every sense of the word: poor Swedes and immigrants densely packed into high rise apartments and stuck on the outskirts of town. Elder Harris, the other ZL, went with the Owl back to Huskvarna.

Although it's hard to believe, within a few hours, I actually found myself missing Church. Pyle was one scary dude. Square jaw, butch haircut, cold blue-eyes, and steely demeanor—all in a 6'5" frame that towered over me and screamed, "Storm Trooper." All that was missing was the brown uniform and swastika.

Drilled and grilled is how I would describe the two days we spent together. We marched from one set of apartments to another to tract. Early in the morning and before bed, he ordered me to recite out loud the discussions I was memorizing. If not on the streets or being tested on the missionary lessons, he was interrogating me:

What time do you two get up in the morning?

What time do you leave the apartment to proselytize?

Do you speak Swedish with each other all the time?

What time do you go to bed?

On and on.

My answers never seemed to satisfy. The next day, he asked the same questions all over again, as though he was trying to trip me up, and catch me in a discrepancy.

"Do you want juice with dinner?" he called from the kitchen—it was our first night together.

"Sure," I replied, without daring to look up from page F-9 in the black, three-ring discussion binder. I was up to "F," the fifth and longest of the eight. It was titled "Truth versus Falsehood," laying out the Mormon version of Gospel history. Latter Day Saints believe that shortly following Christ's crucifixion and resurrection a great apostasy took place. The true church was taken from the Earth until being restored by God through his new Prophet, Joseph Smith, in 1830. All other churches were and are false. The only path to salvation was becoming a Mormon.

Anyway, I'd managed to learn A through E word-for-word my first two weeks in country. As soon as I was able to recite them all without mistakes, the ZL's would send a note to President Thorsson. My name would appear in the *Harvester* newsletter. "Passing" the discussions was a big deal, a major hoop, an expectation of every missionary, proof one was no longer a rank Greenie.

"Dinner is ready," Pyle called, "We didn't have much to work with."

Oh boy, breakfast for dinner, again. It was standard fare among missionaries. Cheap, easy to fix, and fast. No matter. After having run around all day, I was ready to eat. A LOT. What greeted me was a single piece of bacon and one scrambled egg. I swallowed my disappointment and picked up the glass of juice. *What a treat!* Citrus does not grow anywhere in Scandinavia. Missionaries rarely bought it as it was so expensive.

I took a big gulp and instantly gagged, spraying some of the juice out of my mouth and the rest up and through my nose. That's when the burning started. My nasal passages were on fire, my eyes watering. Reflexively, I grabbed at my throat, bolted upright from the table, knocking my chair to the floor. That's when the coughing started. I thought I'd puke.

Pyle just sat there eating his food, unmoved.

When I finally stopped sputtering, I rasped, "What is this?"

"Juice."

"What kind?"

"Pickle," he replied flatly.

Close to screaming, "Pickle juice?"

"Yes," he said, rising from the table. Opening the fridge, he retrieved an empty bottle of pickles. Pointing to it, "Pickle juice."

"That's not *juice!*"

"It's all we had."

"You can't drink that stuff. It's full of salt and vinegar."

Pyle merely shrugged, opened the jar, and drank the rest. As he turned to leave the kitchen, he tossed the empty jar into the trash, and said, "You're on dishes."

I was speechless. What could I say? I couldn't believe this just happened. My grandmother used pickle juice to lift stubborn stains off copper pots! Now we were drinking it. *Dumbkaupf!*

∾

I was seated on the bus on the way to meet the ZL's for our second inspection. This time around I was going to be with Elder Harris. *Thank God.* I looked over at the Owl, mentally rubbing my hands together. *I hope he gets the pickle juice this time.* Church and Pyle. Pyle and Church—cut from the same cloth. They deserved each other.

Harris was different. I knew him. We'd spent several days together following the first surprise inspection, the one with Elder Pyle. After being juiced by that jerk-off, I'd left the ZL's area and returned to Huskvarna and the Owl. I thought it would be a relief to be back with my companion at Johannesvägen 5J. Instead, I became so homesick I couldn't sleep. Time slowed to a crawl. Whenever I was awake, I found myself thinking about the people I was with: Thorsson, Pierce, Payne, Church, and the Picklemeister. I couldn't stand them and was pretty sure they didn't care for me. *Good Lord, two years with this crowd.* They weren't like me, or my friends, or family. The short time I'd been in Sweden was already an eternity.

Each night became a vigil. Church would announce "lights out." I'd wait till he fell asleep, and then creep into the bathroom to cry. On Christmas Day, I rang my folks, homesick and lonely, asking, at times begging, to come home. They listened, at first supportive. When their loving reassurance didn't turn the tide of tears, my Dad intervened. In a kind yet firm voice, he simply said, "Scott, you can't come home. Just think about it, you can't come home." After a long silence, he reminded me of the cost of the call, and suggested we hang up. We said goodbye. I put down the phone and wept.

The next morning, I refused to get up. The Owl first pleaded. Next, he prayed. When none of that worked, he threatened to call President Thorsson.

"Be my guest," turning my back to him.

That's when he called the ZL's. Within an hour Pyle and Harris arrived. I could hear them whispering in the entry way.

"He's in there, in bed. I tried. I offered to pray for him. He won't listen to me. I *really* tried."

"We're missing out on tracting," Pyle responded brusquely, "the whole Zone's numbers are going to be off."

More was said. I couldn't make it out.

"Why don't you two go out and work," Harris suggested in a calm voice, adding "that way the numbers will only be off by half. I'll talk to him."

Elder Chris Harris was from Spanish Fork, Utah, the oldest of six kids. His father managed a grocery store. His Mom, like mine, stayed at home, looking after the family. Although he couldn't have been more than a couple years older than me, he gave the appearance of someone entering middle age; a bit on the pudgy side, slightly balding, his hair already showing grey.

"Feeling pretty low, eh?" he said once the Owl and the poster child for the Hitler Youth had gone.

I grunted in response, continuing to stare at the burnt orange, paisley wall paper.

He pulled a chair up beside my bed. For a long time, he just sat there, silent. Eventually, I started sobbing.

"I just want to go home. I can't stand this."

He listened. I turned to face him. Handing me a tissue, "I could write a book about being homesick".

I sat up in the bed, wiping my nose, and looked at him. He smiled, looked down, and said, "Yeah, homesick". A few more moments passed. Then, he told me his story.

"Gosh, where to start? I didn't think I was going to make it."

"What do you mean?" sniffing.

"Well, I'd been out a year. I was stationed in Krisitianstad, my first assignment as a senior companion. We came home at the end of the day. An envelope from my girlfriend Karen was waiting for me, you know, those large manila colored ones. Man, was I excited. Getting a letter from her was the highlight of the week. Sometimes, I got two or three, long ones, with pictures, and clippings from the *Spanish Fork Press*. And even though she wasn't supposed to, once a month, she recorded Casey Kasem's *American Top 40*. I'd hole up in the bathroom, listening to it on my tape player. Heaven. It was pure heaven."

I thought about the two contraband tapes hidden in my bags. Since arriving, I hadn't taken them out, much less listened to them, and I wouldn't dare tell anyone I had them. Not even Harris at this point.

"Leaving her to go on a mission was the hardest thing I ever did," he continued. "We'd gone together since eighth grade, went to every school dance together, attended the same college. Before I left, I gave her a promise ring. We'd already planned our marriage, where the reception would be, who we'd invite.

Anyway, I'm pumped. So, I rip open the envelope, shake it, and out fall some papers. One is a letter, the other a newspaper clipping. It landed face up on the floor. When I bent over to pick it up, there she was, her picture, a head shot, staring up at me. Some guy is next to her. I think, 'What the hell?' It's an engagement announcement!"

"No way," I said. Looking at him, I could see he was getting upset. "What did the letter say?"

"Tell you what," taking the time to collect himself, "let's get out of here. Grab a fresh set of G's, your toothbrush … whatever you need for a couple of days. We'll go back to my area and hang out".

And hang out we did. We spent the entire first day together in his apartment. It was a relief. No Owl. No Pyle. No tramping around in snow. No slammed doors. No bullshit.

The more time I spent with him, the more I came to see Harris as a good guy, cool. He reminded me of my older brother, Doug. How can I put it? We talked, a lot—and in English. Surfing, girls, school, you name it. Not once did I get the feeling that he was going to lay a guilt trip on me or narc me out to the Mission president. It was like I'd been furloughed from prison.

When I eventually expressed concern about the numbers, he waved me off saying, "All in good time. God's got this one covered."

That night, for dinner, he taught me how to make the classic Swedish dish, "*Pytt i Panna*," a kind of hash usually made with leftover meat, root vegetables, and fried egg on top. It looked great and smelled even better.

He cut onions and potatoes while I fried up *köttfärs* (hamburger) in a skillet. That was when I noticed his right index finger stuck straight out, all the time. Not once did he bend it. Curious, I asked, "Dude, what's up with your finger?"

"Oh that," he chuckled, "it happened while I was cleaning an outhouse."

"An outhouse?!"

"Yeah, you know, a portable shitter."

"Get outta here," joking, "Your family didn't have indoor plumbing?"

He laughed, "Nah, it was my job. I needed to earn money, you know, for college and my mission. This was the only one I could do after school and on the weekends. Basically, I was a grunt, the guy who did the dirty work on a honey wagon."

"A what?"

"The pump truck, they're called honey wagons. Anyway, we'd go to construction sites, parks—wherever there was a port-a-potty owned by the company—and use a big hose to suck out the crap."

"Whoa."

"Well, mostly I was on hose duty," he continued, "My partner, the senior guy, sat in the truck, smoking cigarettes. He was a first class jerk, always making fun of me, calling me 'the hoser,' or 'college boy,' constantly telling me I didn't know my ass from a hole in the ground, on and on. I tried getting along with him, shooting the breeze. When I made the mistake of telling him about Karen and me getting married and all, that's when the Mormon stuff started. 'What?' He'd say, 'Just one wife?' Ha ha ha. Real funny."

As he spoke, I couldn't help thinking of the job I'd had the summer before going to B.Y.U. I was driving a truck in East L.A., delivering 100-pound sacks of flour to tortillerias. "I know the type," I piped in, "I think I worked for his twin brother, Joe."

"It gets better. The guy was always pulling pranks. His favorite was telling me that the vacuum pump was on when it wasn't. I was supposed to hook the hose to the tank. 'Take the cap off,' he'd yell from the cab. I fell for this one twice. You know what happened. Without the pump on, once you took the cap off, shit sprayed everywhere, mostly on me."

"What a dick."

"One day, he pulled a new stunt. The pump was on. I'd made sure. I'm unscrewing the cap when he steps on the gas. The truck lurched forward. Somehow, my finger got caught in the chain that held the cap to the tank. Damn near twisted it off."

"Oh my!" wincing and shaking my head.

"They tried to fix it. The surgery didn't work. Guess my finger is going to be stuck like this for the rest of my life."

"Whatever happened to him?"

"You're gonna love this, he blamed it on me, and they believed him. I got fired."

"Fired?"

"Yeah, *for not following procedures.*"

My face burned. "Son of a ...," I shouted, throwing the spatula down on the skillet with the hamburger. Balling up my fists, I turned to face Harris, "That unfair lying ... why are people like that?"

Out it came. Rage. Two weeks' worth erupting.

"Thorsson, Pierce, Payne, Pyle? Who do they think they are? What gives them the right? Treating us like criminals ... going through our luggage ... charging us for *Books of Mormon* and those dumb tracting brochures when that crap is laying all over the place … making us pay for our own 'welcome here' dinner … telling us we can't talk to each other … playing B.S. cat and mouse games … their whole 'holier than thou' attitude.

"And Church, why am I stuck with him, that robotic, ass-kissing creep? Do you know what that little weasel has been doing? I thought I was losing it. Every morning, when I wake up, my family picture, the one on my nightstand, has been turned down. Face down. The fifth or sixth time this happened, I told him about it. I had no idea what was going on. 'Hey,' I tell him, 'I must be knocking this over in my sleep.' You know what he said? He said *he'd* been doing it. 'Why?' I asked him. He tells me my family is a distraction from the work. A distraction! Screw that, the only reason I'm here is *because* of my family.

"Oh, and the work, the work, *t h e 'h o l y w o r k.*' Riding around on bikes in the snow, wearing these stupid hats, stalking people on the streets, knocking on doors breakfast, lunch, and dinner, baptizing old ladies. It's ludicrous. What are we doing here? They hate us. We are making them hate us."

"Scott," Harris stopped me, pointing at the stove, "I hate to interrupt you when you're on a roll, but the meat is burning."

"What the … oh, the meat, the meat!" quickly removing the hamburger from the stove.

"Ett steg i taget," (one step at a time), he said, punching me lightly on the arm. I hadn't heard that expression in a while. It was a favorite of my Scandinavian Grandmother, Christina. I could feel myself relax, a bit.

"Let's mix this stuff together and eat."

We combined the vegetables and hamburger, and placed a couple of fried eggs on top. I dished out generous portions. Although calmer and surprisingly hungry, given how upset I'd just been, I wasn't ready to let this go. Handing him his plate, "Chris, I don't know how you do this? I'm ready to pull my hair out. The thought of going back to Huskvarna and Church, I don't even want to go there."

Without a word, Harris set down his plate, and motioned for me to join him at the table. Seated, he held up his index finger, the damaged one.

"What?" staring at his finger.

"You ask, 'how do I do this?' How have I made it through the last 22 months?"

I nodded.

"By staying focused on one thing."

"I don't get it. What do you mean?"

"Keeping my eye on the prize," he clarified. Continuing to hold his finger up, Harris matter-of-factly said, "This too shall pass. Right now, it's bad. So was sucking crap out of port-a-potties, having my finger almost torn off, getting fired when it wasn't my fault, being 'Dear Johnned' by my fiancé, living with maniacs like Pyle for the last 22 months."

"Yeah, but you're short; two months and you're outta here. I got two years left on this shit wagon. I want to go home now—"

"No you don't," he said, his tone dead serious, "you want to go back to the life you *had*. Surfing, hanging out, school, chicks. Well, that life is gone, man. It's not there. Poof, gone forever."

I sat there, saying nothing. Harris reached over, tapping me on the forehead with his unbending finger, "Start thinking about what you *do* want after this is all over, 'cause trust me, it's gonna end. Until then, you need to keep your head down and your eye on that prize."

"What's your prize?" I asked with obvious sarcasm.

"Besides going home, bro?"

"Yeah, your girlfriend is gone ... poof ... married to another guy." I instantly regretted my words and tone. Harris had been nothing but decent to me. "Sorry man, I shouldn't have said that."

"Don't worry about it. I get it. You don't like this. It sucks. But, just remember 'This too shall pass'," he slowly repeated.

For some reason, his words, *this too shall pass*, struck me this time round.

"Something else Scott, don't pile one bad decision on another." Seeing my puzzled expression, "You mean to tell me you really thought this whole thing through? Going on a mission? Coming here? And now, you're telling me you've *decided* to bolt?"

I sat there, listening. I didn't like what he was saying. At the same time, I knew it was true.

"Come on, stay or leave, whatever, but for heaven's sake, think it through this time."

I could feel my face flush. It was embarrassing. Harris was right of course. I had to get a grip, use my brain instead of just bopping along, going in whatever direction the wind was blowing the hardest.

"And while you're doing this, while you're making up your mind, deciding what *you* want, where *you're* going, what *you're* gonna do, you've got to keep a low profile, stay off their radar—"

"Radar?"

"Yeah, radar. This isn't *Father Knows Best*. Thorsson isn't Robert Young and the other Elders aren't your family. When you let these guys know you're upset, that you're unhappy with 'the program,' you think you're gonna get hugs and kisses and a mug of hot cocoa? Forget that. They are going to ask, 'what's wrong with you?' Then, *tell* you what's wrong with you. And after that, they are going to be all over you like ugly on an ape."

"So what, I just go along with them then?"

"For now, yeah. Look-it, being here, doing this is hard enough. Don't give them any reason, any ammunition to make it more of a hell than it is already. It's what's inside you that matters anyway … stuff they can't see unless you let them … what you think … what you feel … who you are …".

I sat there, taking it all in. My former life was gone, over—about that there was no doubt. It'd never be the same. What would I do if I went home anyway? I couldn't go back to B.Y.U. I'd never heard of a missionary going home early unless, of course, he'd committed a major sin like screwing a native. That's what people would think I'd done regardless of what I told them. I think Grandma would be alright if I came home, but my parents, forget it. They would be so ashamed. They wouldn't be able to show their face in church. And what did I want? Damn, I don't know. What did I even believe? Yeah. What did I believe? One thing was certain: I didn't want to end up like Church or Pyle. And I sure as shit didn't want them knowing my business or pushing me around.

I looked up at Chris who, at this point, had almost cleaned his plate, "I think I'm ready to pass Discussion F. I've got it down."

He smiled, "That's the ticket."

~

Just two minutes to go before Church and I arrived at Jönköping bus station for the second surprise inspection.

"Hat on, Elder Miller," Church ordered as we stood to exit the bus.

I gritted my teeth, stifling the temptation to roll my silly looking hat into a cone and stick it where the "sun don't shine." After first purchasing the hat my second or third day in Huskvarna, I'd taken to carrying rather than wearing the goofy thing. It was embarrassing. We might as well have been wearing cow bells around our necks. *Here we come, ding, ding, ding. Look at us, dorks, dorks, dorks.* Having taken Harris's advice from the emergency visit four weeks earlier, I plopped the hat on my head and said nothing.

We stepped off the bus into the Swedish equivalent of rush hour. I immediately thought of muskox—a massive herd of fur clad creatures gathered under a cloud of condensed breath and cigarette smoke. For all the hustle and bustle, the actual progress of the group in getting anywhere was close to glacial.

The Zone Leaders were nowhere in sight. In seconds, we were caught in the human undertow, sweeping us toward the edge of the station, the "utgång" (exit). There, the crowd thinned out, individuals running to catch another bus or get to work. We were alone. Almost.

Off to our right, in a section normally reserved for bicycles, stood a group of twenty or so teenagers with their mopeds. They were milling about smoking and, despite the hour, drinking Lättöl, a cheap, widely available, near non-alcoholic beer. Decked out in Levi® jeans, work boots, and leather jackets, they looked like extras from the set of Marlon Brando's *The Wild One.* To me, for all their tough getup, they were just children, little Swedish boys and girls.

I was ready to ignore them, when one of them yelled out, "Helan och Halvan" (Laurel and Hardy). The entire group turned to face us.

"Raggare," Church leaned over, whispering in my ear.

"What?" It was the first time I'd heard the word.

"A gang," he said in English.

"A gang? They're just kids," I responded.

When they started moving toward us, laughing, taunting us, chanting, "Give us your hats. We want your hats," I changed my mind. "Let's get out of here," I said, "How about the kiosk, the convenience store, we can go in there and get away from them."

Church reacted immediately, "Oh no, we can't go in there. It's against the rules. Too many newspapers and dirty magazines."

Idiot, I thought. Within seconds, we were surrounded. The jeering continued. As the group closed in, my hat was snatched away. I turned. One of the boys was jumping up and down, yelling in Swedish, "Look, I'm a Mormon."

He had our introductory script down pat, reciting it perfectly in English, "I am a representative of the Church of Jesus Christ of Latter Day Saints."

By now Church was also bare headed. A girl pranced about, "No, I am *the* representative, your extra wife, you wanna fuck me?"

"Yeah," the crowd chimed in, "Fuck her, fuck her, fuck her".

Just before I got shoved, I took a quick glance at Church. One of the other "raggare," a girl, was rubbing up against him, putting her arms around his waist, starting to dry hump his left leg. I thought he would dematerialize right there on the spot. Before that could happen, the crowd suddenly parted. Into the breach walked Harris, smiling.

Pointing with his special finger at my companion, he said "Elder Church you go with Elder Pyle back to Huskvarna and get to work." Pyle, the Aryan giant, was hanging back. *What a chicken shit*, I thought. He was the biggest one there.

"What about my hat?" Church squealed.

Narrowing his eyes, Harris calmly answered, "Go." Without waiting for a response, he turned back to the group, approaching one of the male members. Gently resting his hand on the young man's shoulder, he pulled him close, and spoke directly in his ear. The kids went completely silent watching the exchange. The conversation was brief. The apparent leader stepped back, first nodding to Harris, and spoke with authority to the gang, "Det här är tråkigt. Låt oss sticka grabbarna (This is boring, let's get out of here, guys) … och, ni två … ge hattarna tillbaka (and you two, give those hats back)."

As the kids made their way to the mopeds, my hat thief went over to Harris. The girl with Church's hat approached me, placing the Fedora on my head, while tenderly cupping my jaw with her hand, "Vad söt du är" (You're cute). And that was that. The rumble was over.

As the last of the gang headed for their mopeds, Harris walked over, handed me my hat, "I think this is yours. That one sure doesn't fit."

It is small, I thought, *it would barely cover the head of a pin.* I took Church's hat from my head, rolled it into a ball and stuffed it in my coat pocket.

"I want to stop in the kiosk before we head back to Rosenlund," Harris said.

Once there, he bought a newspaper and a small box of something I took to be candy.

"Läkerol?" he asked, extending the box toward me and giving it a shake.

What dropped into my hand looked like a cross between a throat lozenge and big black booger. Worse than its appearance, was the taste; a kind of sickeningly sweet aftershave. *Blech.* Turns out, it's hugely popular, like Tic-Tacs® in America.

Seeing the look of disgust on my face, "Give it time, it'll grow on you. Plus, it's a great way to start a conversation. No Swede expects an American to pull out a box of these, much less eat one."

All I could do was nod my head in agreement, the taste was so arresting. When I finally could speak, with Brut-y fresh breath I asked, "You bought a newspaper?"

The one he held was *Expressen,* one of two nationwide evening tabloids, the other being *Aftonbladet.* Its big bold headlines, garish colors, and half clad women in wonderfully provocative poses reminded me of the *National Enquirer* or *News of the World.* It was clearly, "OP," off the program. That's why the Owl was willing to risk getting beat up lest he "accidently" do what any other 19 year old would in the situation. Check out the babes.

"You can't talk church all the time with people," Harris replied, "You've gotta be able to carry on a conversation, be with people, talk about stuff they're interested in." Holding out the newspaper, "Look at this." The headline read, "ABBA Hits Number One Worldwide."

'You know Agnetha Fältskog, the blond one, is from here?"

Surprised, "I thought the whole band was from Sweden?"

"No, no," he continued, "I mean, she's from here, Jönköping."

On the bus headed for Rosenlund, I thought back on the past half hour. More than ever I was convinced that Church was a complete and utter, irredeemable moron. *How did some end up like him while others like Harris?* Church wouldn't jump in a pool to save a drowning man if the sign said, "no swimming allowed." Hell, he wouldn't even save himself. Harris was different. He was smart. Plus, he'd saved our asses.

"Good thing you showed up when you did," I said.

Harris chuckled.

"What did you say to him, that guy?"

"Nothing special. I know his Mom. Couple months ago, my companion—not Pyle, but Elder Stevens—and I, we helped her move. We'd been teaching her the lessons. Her 'sambo' (live-in boyfriend) was a drunk, liked to beat her up. So, one morning, when he was at work, we came over, packed up her stuff, and took it to her new place. I still check in on her."

Geez, I thought, *how does Harris get away with what he does?* He was fearless. Buying a newspaper, no less. Walking into a crowd of raggare. Helping that kid's mom move, despite the rules about fraternization. *We weren't even permitted to teach a single woman let alone go through her drawers, packing up her stuff.*

"Lars, the kid's name is Lars," Harris added.

"Right, Lars."

"Yeah, he's all right," grinning, "I told him he was scaring you guys."

I smiled. *What is Harris's secret?*

∾

We spent the day in Rosenlund going from one appointment to the next. It was unbelievable given what I usually did with Church. In Huskvarna, we vainly knocked on one door after another. Here, we didn't tract at all. And whenever we did knock, people invited us in and were genuinely happy to see us. More than that, they fed us. Constantly. I ate so many "bullar" (traditional Swedish cinnamon rolls) and drank so much "saft" (a homemade fruit juice), I thought I'd either burst or wet myself.

The subject of the Mormon Church seldom came up in any conversation. In fact, I don't think we said three words about it the entire day. At one home, Harris read an installment from a popular series of children's books about a boy named Alfons Åberg (Al-fonz O-berry). In this story, Alfons moves to a new town and struggles with loneliness. I listened intently, feeling a curious connection. *Where could I get these books?*

In other homes, we hung out and talked, catching up about the family—details Chris knew a surprising amount about. Harris also put his newspaper to work, talking about Victoria, the six month old Crown Princess of Sweden, about the new ABBA album, *Arrival* and hit song, "Take a Chance on Me," and of course, "Bordellhärvan," the sex scandal involving the Minister of Justice. Sex even. I didn't know word one about any of this stuff.

That night we ate dinner at a church member's house. I'd met the family before, my very first Sunday in the country. The Owl and I were attending services at the local congregation. The father, a tall, bear-like Finnish man bore a striking resemblance to a "Winkie," one of the Wicked Witch's castle guards from the film, *Wizard of Oz*. He came right up to welcome me.

"Hejsan," (Hello) he said, extending his huge paw, "Seikkula, is my name" (Say-cool-lah). His accent was unforgettable. Another movie came to mind, this time *Dracula*. As I was to discover, whenever Finns spoke Swedish, the tone and tempo recalled Bela Lugosi saying, "I am Dracula, I bid you welcome."

"You must be very tired after your long trip," he said clapping me hard on the back, a friendly gesture which almost sent me to the floor.

In the hope of being equally friendly, but also funny, I tried to say, "Yeah, if you see me drift off during services this morning, please throw some water in my face." Unfortunately, my vast command of the Swedish language led me to say, "If you see me drift off during services this morning, please piss in my face."

He laughed uproariously at my invitation, slapping me so hard this time it sent me careening into the Owl.

"I'll be sure and do that," he said, gesturing to his kids, "Come children, meet the new Elder. He is funny."

I was instantly surrounded. Six adorable little vampires—each not more than a year apart—all chattering at once in the same Transylvanian dialect.

Before eating that night, Harris and I played several rounds of "Horsey," crawling around in our suits on the white Linoleum® floors of their cramped, three bedroom public-housing apartment. Culturally, Swedes are regarded as a reserved people. When it comes to stoicism, they are rank amateurs compared to their sauna-inventing neighbors to the east. Owing perhaps to its long domination by foreign powers—first by Sweden for 700 years, then by Russia for 100—the Finnish people have cultivated a very special attitude toward words and speech. In a phrase, "why talk when you can be quiet?"

Not the Seikkula's. They were boisterous, fun-loving, outgoing, wild even. Each kid bore a bruise or scrape of some kind or another—not surprisingly, as when we were there, they took turns swinging from the draperies and jumping off their top bunk beds.

"Tulevat ja syövät, päivällisen on valmis," (Dinner is ready!), Brother Seikkula let loose in Finnish, a voice that could easily have reached across a soccer stadium.

Joki, Jukka, Jarvi, Jaacko, Jaakkina, and Jakk dismounted instantly, hooted in unison, and raced to the kitchen. Not understanding word one of what he said, Harris and I looked at each other and wondered, "What's going on?" In the next breath, in walked Count Seikulla who literally lifted us from the floor, and switching to Swedish, "Det är dags att äta, grabbar (It's time to eat boys)". Inspired by the children's example, I let out a hoot, too. I was starving.

By the time we made it to the kitchen, the Seikkulla children were quietly seated around the table looking positively angelic. Hands clean and folded, eyes sparkling and turned toward their father's chair—all that were missing were halos and small white wings.

In no time at all, Countess Seikkula brought the feast. Bowl after heaping bowl was placed before us; an assortment of vegetables, mashed potatoes, gravy, and bread. Last came an enormous, steaming platter of roast beef. *Oh boy*, I thought to myself, *this is going to be great*. I hadn't had a dish like this since my first step on Swedish soil. It felt like home. When I was growing up, mother served a pot roast every Sunday. I also felt a bit guilty. We were being treated like royalty. It was no secret the Seikkulla's were poor. This dinner had to be a stretch.

After a quick blessing, the food was passed. Wow, what a contrast. Gone was the mayhem. The children were so serious and well-mannered. Beyond our being there, I could tell that family meals together were a big deal.

"Don't be bashful," Brother Seikkulla encouraged, "We know missionaries are always hungry. Take more."

No argument from me. If I wasn't feeling lonely, I was hungry. I loaded my plate, doubly so when the meat arrived.

I looked down. *Gosh, I've never seen a roast served like this before.* It wasn't sliced. It wasn't shredded. Instead, it was cut into nearly identical, two by two inch cubes. *Maybe it's a Finnish thing. Maybe it's not beef; perhaps it's reindeer. Ooh, exotic. Who knows? Maybe this is the way it's served.*

I stabbed one of the cubes with my fork and leaned forward to take in the aroma. I wanted to make the most of this moment, savor every second. God only knew when I'd get to have this kind of meal again.

I breathed in deeply. Nothing. It was hot all right. I got that. The heat penetrated my sinuses. But that was it, no mouthwatering scent. No smell whatsoever. *What the heck?* I cut a piece and placed it my mouth. *WHAT IS THIS?* I screamed to myself. If tongues could speak, mine would have said,

"Let me out of here!" How to describe it? Foam rubber captures the texture, simultaneously mushy and chewy. The taste? This I knew. Dry dog food. When I was six years old, I'd shared a brief meal with my dog, Fritz.

Staring at my plate, I panicked. *What am I going to do?* I looked to Harris for help. He winked at me. The bastard knew. He'd taken only two cubes. I had at least ten, maybe more. In my mind, it looked like a hundred. They seemed to be reproducing. *I can't eat this stuff.* I needed a plan, quick. It wasn't going to be easy to come up with one because while we were eating, the family peppered us with questions; in particular me, as I was the new guy. Where was I from? Did I have a girlfriend? What were my hobbies? What did I think of Sweden? And so on, and so on.

At some point, Brother Seikkulla interrupted, "Children, let Elder Miller eat!"

This was my chance. It was now or never. No longer the focus, the family turned their attention to Harris. I began spearing the puppy chow block by block, first dropping each piece to the napkin in my lap, then transferring them one by one to my suit pockets. Thankfully, Jarvi and Jaacko, seated on either side of me were totally captivated by Harris's Kalle Anke (Donald Duck) impersonation.

Just when I thought I was home-free, Sister Seikkulla exclaimed, "Father look, Elder Miller has finished all his meat. Pass him some more."

I threw my hands up in the air as though I was being held at gunpoint, "No, no, no ... thank you, I'm good." I should have quit right then and there. But when she insisted I take more, out of my mouth came "Jag är så ful" (Yahg air so fool). Everything stopped and all eyes turned to me, staring. Thinking they hadn't understood me, or that I'd mispronounced one of the words, I repeated what I said—or so I thought.

"Jag är så full" (Yahg air so full).

That was it. The table exploded in a paroxysm of laughter. Jaako, seated to my right, fell out of his chair. Not to be outdone, the other kids followed.

Tears streaming down his face, Brother Seikkulla slapped the table, "See, I told you he was funny."

Although I had no idea what they were laughing at, I joined in. When the howling finally subsided, and all had regained their composure, Harris explained.

"Jag är *mätt* (Yagh air met [I am satisfied]) is what you were trying to say."

"What did I say?"

"Well, first," he started laughing again, "you said, 'I am ugly,' then, after that, you said you were drunk."

When the family saw the look of understanding on my face, it started all over again.

The evening ended with dessert (in Swedish, efterrätt). Sister Seikkulla served the traditional Finnish dish, "pannu kakku," a cross between a pancake and soufflé. It was delicious. This time I did not refuse offers of seconds and thirds.

As we said our goodbyes, each of the children approached and gave us a warm hug. Mother kissed our cheeks. Brother Seikkulla shook Elder Harris's hand. Turning to me, he grabbed my coat collar, pulled me toward him and crushed me in a bear hug. Just when I thought all of the air had been squeezed out of me, he smacked me heartily on the back and, in his booming voice, said, "You are a funny man, Elder Miller. You should be on television."

On our way back to the apartment, Harris said, "You can empty your pockets now." As I dropped the cubes on the snow, their appearance changed from that of dog food to dog.

"Funny, huh?" he continued, "I did the same thing the first time I was invited to their home. Once burned, twice learned. God bless 'em, their hearts are bigger than their pocket book. With all those kids and his job, they can't afford real meat."

"What was it?"

"TVP," he replied.

So that's what it was. I knew the stuff well. My last year in high school, and the summer before college, I worked for a company in East Los Angeles that made and delivered the product. Hospitals, soup kitchens, fast food restaurants and other businesses used it as meat extender. It was never meant to be served as a main course.

Within minutes of having laid the TVP to rest, we were back at Harris's apartment.

"Hey Chris, do you think there's time for me to pass the last discussion?" Discussion J was the green one, twenty-five pages about what it meant to be a Mormon. I was stoked, happy at the possibility of being finished with this mind numbing task. Once done, I would no longer be a "greenie."

"Yeah, sure," adding, "Go ahead and get ready for bed. I've got some paperwork to do then we can do it."

I undressed down to my G's, grabbed my overnight bag, and made my way to the bathroom. Shutting the door, I retrieved my toothbrush and paste, and turned toward the sink and mirror. *Here I am again.* Mint flavor filled my mouth as I brushed, mindlessly reviewing events of the day.

I looked at myself in the mirror. *I've actually had fun today. That's weird. Fun. What a concept. I thought those days were behind me. Well, wait a minute, tomorrow, I'll be back with the Owl in Huskvarna—the place where fun goes to die.*

I leaned over the bowl and spit. *The Seikkullas. That's what it's all about. I miss my family. My older brother Doug, his son Tylor, my parents' first grandchild, what is he, six months old now?*

The phone rang. *That's strange. It's déjà vu all over again. This is how the day started. I wonder who it is this time? Maybe Pyle is sick of my companion and wants to come home. Screw him, I've got one more day with Harris.*

I opened the door and poked my head out of the bathroom.

"Got it," Harris said, "We'll be ready" and hung up the phone.

"Anything important?"

"You could say that. You done in there?"

"Yep," emerging from the bathroom.

"Well," he said raising the finger I'd come to know so well, "I told you, 'this too shall pass.'"

"What? What's passing?"

"Transfers are coming. Tomorrow. You're outta here."

4

CROSSROADS

∽

"The sooner you take a stand, the taller you will be."

Spencer W. Kimball
12ᵀᴴ Prophet, Seer, and Revelator
Church of Jesus Christ of Latter Day Saints

∽

Lund, Sweden. My next destination. I was as clueless about this place as I'd been about Huskvarna. Actually, I did know a little about the town. This was the ancestral home of my mother's family, or at least a part of it. Her father's family came from a little town in Denmark just across the channel from this southern Swedish town. That's a love story to be told at a later time.

I also knew that Elin, my good Samaritan—the student I'd met some two and a half months ago at the train station on my first day in Sweden—lived in Lund. *Gosh, I wonder if I'll see her. Not much chance of that. No use really, what would I do if I did?*

The bus came to a stop with a jerk. *Where am I?* "Värnamo," (Vair-nah-mo) the sign said. It looked like so many other Swedish towns I'd been in or passed through so far. Dark, overcast, and the usual snowy cobblestone streets flanked by 18ᵗʰ century brick, copper-topped buildings. A few passengers stepped off, more boarded, paid their fare and took a seat. The driver, I noticed, waited patiently for the last traveler. After a minute or two, he finally said, "It's time. All aboard."

My transfer letter had arrived just as Harris said. The Owl and I had been out tracting the entire morning. It was finally lunch. I was glad to be going back to Johannesvägen 5J, if for no other reason than to warm up. We'd received the usual Huskvarna reception: slammed doors, swearing Swedes, and mostly, nothing, no response at all. Taking our now familiar, hilly route around the factory, I felt no small satisfaction in knowing that as pointless as these last two months had been, it was over. As petty as it might seem, I was also happy to know something my companion didn't.

"Go fix lunch," the Owl said as we entered the apartment. Mail was splayed about the floor in the usual way, the result of being shoved through the slot in the door.

I busied myself and waited. Closing the refrigerator, there he was standing, glued to the floor. He moved his head slowly, first left and then right and then back again—his eyes fixed on the letter he was clutching with both hands. *He is so strange. Thankfully, "this too shall pass."*

"Here, it's from the mission office."

I took the letter, setting down the tube of tomato paste I was about to use to make pasta. Even though I knew what the envelope contained, on opening it, I was surprised by its appearance: impersonal, no handwritten note or signature—just a single sheet of paper. Across the top was typed in large block letters, "TRANSFER NOTICE." Below that, were listed in order, my new assignment, Lund, the name of my next companion, Elder Wiggins, my missionary rank, still junior, and a few words about travel arrangements.

Looking up, I said excitedly, "I'm going to Lund!"

"Don't tell me that," he replied, brooking no further discussion, "that's 'graping.'"

"What?"

"It's OP," turning away from me.

Following him into the main room, "Hey, are you staying or leaving?"

He stopped in his tracks, and with his back still to me, "You know the rules. Leave me alone."

Right then and there I concluded he was staying—so I said it, "You're staying, aren't you?"

He turned to face me. For the first time, his eyes, head, and body were all in alignment. "No thanks to you Miller" he sputtered. And then, out it came—all in English.

"Your attitude, your poor work habits, your lack of devotion, your unwillingness to sacrifice," he continued, his voice rising, "You are so selfish. You've jeopardized the salvation of the people here, and squandered two months of opportunity ... the Lord's time and mine".

I stood there, listening, stunned into silence by his uncharacteristic eruption. *Jesus, did I want to give back what I was getting. Me selfish? You vulture. You don't give a hair off a rat's ass about these people. They are nothing to you, just an opportunity to flaunt your righteousness. You baptize Fru Nilsson and what do you care about? That your name will be in the* Harvester *for all to see, points and numbers, that's what matters to you, to impress Thorsson, Pierce, Payne, and the rest of them. FUCK YOU.*

I didn't say anything.

The Owl soon returned to his perch. Speaking calmly, "Since you're so determined to break the rules, I'll tell you. I am now a District Leader."

I couldn't believe my ears. *No way. Church, a District Leader? How could this happen? How could God let this happen?*

"We need to pack," he said, a smug smile shaping the corners of his mouth. Nothing more was said. Later, at the bus station, he waited till I boarded then left without so much as a good-bye.

∿

The route to Lund was a lot like the emotions I was feeling, twisted, convoluted. As with everything else in my mission life, I had no say in how I got from one place to the next in Sweden. The President's Office dictated the arrangements. Instead of traveling directly, they turned the trip into Homer's *Odyssey,* shuttling me up, down, and around the country, switching between buses and trains, trains and buses.

When done right, the trip should only take three to four hours. My handlers managed to add five to the journey. And the purpose of all this craziness? Ensure no missionaries' paths crossed on "Transfer Day." After all, if we happened to meet, we might talk. Who knows what devil's work would come of that?

I'd just pulled out my journal and was about to catch up on the past couple of days when a voice spoke, "Är den här platsen ledig?" (Is that seat
taken?). Looking up, it was the kid I'd been watching moments earlier. He
was pointing at the window seat. *Wait a minute, he's not a kid. Wait another
minute, why does he want to sit by me? There are plenty of vacant seats.*

More than surprised, "Ja, ja visst" (yes, yes, certainly), I said, standing so
he could get by me.

Once we got moving, the older, or was it younger man introduced himself, "Stefan Petersson heter jag" (My name is Stefan Petersson).

We shook hands, me using my best Swedish accent in response, "Skot
Meal-ehr, heter jag. Trevlig att träffa dig, Stefan" (My name is Scott Miller.
Nice to meet you, Stefan).

As was customary of Swedes hearing their language butchered, he
remarked, "Your Swedish is very good."

I just had to chuckle, although I didn't believe a word of it, "Tusen tack"
(Many thanks).

"So," he continued, "you're a Mormon missionary?"

"What, did my suit give me away?" struggling a bit with the language
now. I wasn't used to having conversations about everyday matters. Get me
on the subject of baptism or the plan of salvation and I could talk Swedish
circles around people.

It was his turn to chuckle, then switching to English, "How do you find
it here?"

I could feel my mood change. *How to respond?* I was stuck between putting on my Mormon happy face and wanting to tell him the truth. *I hate
this.* "Well ... I've only been here a couple of months ... I haven't really seen
too much of the country ... the language is ... hard ... the people have been
nice."

"Really?" he said, incredulous, "Swede's aren't particularly fond of religion, Mormons in particular. The whole 'mångifte' (polygamy) thing and
prejudice toward blacks."

I nodded. It was not the first time these two issues had come up. On
more than one occasion while tracting, people needled us, "Are you here to
find another wife, boys?" Others, with open contempt, questioned, "What's
wrong with the blacks? Good enough to clean your Church, but not join?"

The latter was a common misunderstanding. People of African descent had been *members* of the Church from the earliest days. In fact, Joseph Smith was an abolitionist. An 1833 prophecy declared, in no uncertain terms, "it is not right that any man should be in bondage one to another" (Doctrine and Covenants 101: 79). Later, in his 1844, failed bid for the Presidency of the United States, Smith forcefully called for an end to slavery. His platform went so far as to propose using money from the sale of public lands to purchase the freedom of the enslaved.

Unfortunately, Smith's enlightened position on the rights and freedoms of black Americans did not survive his death. When the Saints migrated westward and Brigham Young became the prophet, the policy turned decidedly discriminatory. Young, dubbed the "Lion of the Lord," boldly asserted "any man having one drop of the seed of [Cain] … cannot hold the priesthood and if no other Prophet ever spake it before I will say it now in the name of Jesus Christ I know it is true and others know it."

Similar to Southern Baptists and other denominations of the time, Young equated the black skin of Africans with the "Mark of Cain," a sign of God's condemnation. From his proclamation forward, although membership was permitted, both the priesthood and access to the temple were denied to anyone of black ancestry. The practice was equivalent to the Montgomery, Alabama segregationist seating policy for public transportation, only writ on an eternal scale. In effect, a black man or woman could enter LDS heaven, but never take a seat at the front.

Like most LDS Church doctrines, I'd not thought much about the exclusion of blacks prior to becoming a missionary. Mom and Dad were both Kennedy Democrats. They were hugely supportive of civil rights, appalled by white violence against blacks around the country. I never heard a prejudicial remark escape their lips. Come to think of it, I never heard an overtly racist remark from any Mormon I knew.

At the same time, one could say, my family and I were isolated. Despite growing up in Los Angeles, the suburb in which we lived was essentially all white. Hell, the pioneering black actor Woodie Strode—famous for his role as the Ethiopian gladiator, Draba, in Stanley Kubrick's *Spartacus*—was a member of our local congregation. Mormons, bigots? And yet, there it was plain as day: a racist policy all Latter Day Saints accepted without reservation. Or apparently so. No one talked about it.

And polygamy? When I was growing up, sure we knew about it. To us though, the practice was ancient history. The subject never came up. Whenever it did, most often, it was described as an act of benevolence, charity even. The many women widowed during the Mormon trek westward needed husbands! The need was there and the Lord provided.

"So, you are having success?" Stefan asked, breaking the silence.

Looking down at my feet, then back up at him, "Uh, well, er ... not really," adding, "And the people haven't been that friendly either."

"I'm not surprised. I've watched you boys, seen you work. How can I express it? Your way, knocking on doors without invitation ... stopping people on the streets ... Among Swedes, it is not usual. What is the word? It is pushy ... so American ... ah, rude."

What a great combination: rude, racist, moral degenerates. No wonder people love us.

With a sigh of resignation, "I don't know what to say ... you're right ... it's stupid ... I hate doing it, but we're not allowed to do anything else."

A look of concern crossed Stefan's face, "I'm sorry. I did not mean to cause any discomfort. It is rude of me to say."

"No, no," I replied, "it's all right. What you're saying is true. I guess everyone here knows it."

"I may be a little different than most Swedes."

"How's that?"

"We share the same line of work. I'm a Lutheran minister. I was once a missionary."

"Wow, really? Lutherans have missionaries? You guys knock on doors, too?"

He smiled broadly, "Som vi säger på Svenska, det är en lång historia! (As we say in Swedish, 'that's a long story!'). No knocking on doors. I worked in Africa, mostly with refugees—"

"Gosh—"

"Just det (That's right), ... mostly helping bring food and medical supplies ... the need was great ... much war, disease ... starvation ..."

He paused and looked out the window.

"Hmm, many memories. I've been back in Sweden for several years now. I work in a youth ministry in Lund."

"Lund? That's where I'm going."

"You should come see us," he said, taking a card from a pocket inside his parka and handing it to me."

"Thank you."

"We work with street kids. Maybe you know of them, they are called, 'Raggare.'"

"I know them all right. One of them took my hat once. I got it back …".

"May I ask, why do Mormons wear those hats? Does it have some special meaning?"

I was about to answer when the bus driver stepped on the brakes bringing us to an abrupt halt. Overhead, speakers crackled, "Tyvärr ser det ut som om vi har en bilolycka framför oss" (I'm sorry, it looks like there's been an accident ahead). Everyone strained to see what was going on. All that was visible was a line of vehicles leading up a small hill.

We started moving again.

"I can't see any emergency vehicles," Stefan spoke softly, "No wait, I see one, its coming, a police car."

"Mina Damer och Herrar," (Ladies and Gentlemen), the bus driver broke in, "from what I can see, it looks like this accident has just happened … please be patient, we will proceed as quickly as we can."

The bus inched along, all of the passengers sitting in silence.

As we came up on the scene, the driver, apparently unaware his microphone was still on, gasped, "Herre Gud" (Oh my God).

That's when Stefan stood up, "I must find out what's happened." He squeezed by me and quickly made his way to the front. Taking one look, he commanded the driver to stop, "Please let me off."

In no time at all, he was standing beside me, retrieving his bag from the overhead rack.

"I'm going to help," he said, then paused, looking at me expectantly.

I responded, stammering, "Uh, uhhh …" .

Seeing my reluctance, he reached over and, with his free hand, patted me lightly on the shoulder. "I must go, goodbye Scott." Up the aisle he ran and was gone.

I just sat there. *What to do? I should help. But I have to get to Lund. I'm already going to be late. I'm going to be in trouble. My new companion will be waiting for me. I have no way of getting in touch with him. I should do something. I am an Eagle Scout for Christ's sake. I know first aid. I got a merit badge in it. What if I do get off? How will I ever get to Lund? What can I really do anyway?*

I watched out the window as the bus crawled toward what turned out to be a crossroads. On my side of the bus, people peered out the windows. Those on the other stood in the aisle, forced to stoop to catch a glimpse. In sharp contrast to what would happen in America, the Swedes, true to form, except an occasional whisper, were quiet.

There were three vehicles—"en lastbil," or large truck, and two small sedans. *Someone must have blown the stop sign at this intersection.* One sedan was wedged under the truck, the top peeled back like a sardine can. The other was smashed into the back of the first car. Clouds of smoke and steam billowed up from its engine.

Where is everyone? I kept scanning the scene. *There's one guy, dressed in grey overalls. Must be the truck driver.* He looked dazed. A woman was sitting by the side of the road, holding a baby, crying, her face and hands streaked with blood. Next to her was Stefan. He was coatless, his dark, down parka now wrapped around her shoulders. He was leaning in close, speaking to her. The sole police officer on the scene, crowbar in hand, was doing his best to pry open the driver's door.

Once more the speakers came to life, "Would everyone please take their seats? We'll be getting underway again." Pausing briefly, he added, "Let us hope everyone will be all right."

As we cleared the accident, I turned away from the window and looked ahead. Ashamed, I struck down hard on both legs with my fists. *I should have gone with Stefan. I should have helped. He did; didn't give it a moment's thought. Me? I sat here, worrying about getting in trouble. Why? Why didn't I help?*

It's not like being a Good Samaritan was a foreign concept. As early as I can remember, our family, along with other members of the Church, fasted once a month. The money we would have spent on feeding ourselves was donated to feeding the poor. Four times a year or more, all of us worked picking fruit or canning vegetables on Church-owned farms. The products were later distributed to food pantries. Also, Dad and I were "Home Teachers," a program sponsored by the Church. We were responsible for visiting families—active members and those that seldom came to services, the elderly and the sick. We offered assistance, everything from mowing lawns, seeing to it that utility bills were paid, to shuttling people to important appointments. We strove to live up to Christ's teaching, "Inasmuch as ye have done it unto one of the least of these my brethren, ye have done it unto me" (Matthew 25:40). I never did "Home Teaching" with anyone else, only Dad. *For all I know, others were out there proselytizing, harassing more than helping. And when you get right down to it, that's what I'm doing here in Sweden.*

Unless I was trying to coax someone into joining the Church, I wasn't supposed to talk with any Swedes, much less offer assistance. When Harris helped that woman—the ragara leader's mother—move out from under the fist of her abusive husband, he broke about ten rules. For one, he'd struck up a relationship with a woman in need, in the midst of a divorce, involving himself and, by default, the Church in her personal affairs. More, he didn't ask permission. Like Stefan, he just acted.

Harris would have helped, I'm sure. And Christ? If he came upon an accident, he'd have been out there healing, right? Heck, I'm an Elder of the Church of Jesus Christ of Latter Saints. On a key chain, in my pocket, I have a vial of consecrated oil for blessing the sick—and I did nothing. I could have just gone out there and offered comfort, or something, any damn thing. Isn't that what this whole mission is about, making the world a better place?

Mormons! We're here on a mission. But what is the mission? Emulate the example of Jesus? Do unto others as he would have us do, on Earth, now? Apparently not. Our job is to be obedient, wear a funny hat, ride a bike, knock on doors, and follow the script. We're just clowns for Christ.

I don't like this … and I don't like me.

I reached inside my coat pocket, retrieving my journal. On a fresh sheet I wrote the date and, then in big block letters, the words, "Epistle to Self":

> If I'm going to stay here, and that seems pretty damn likely at this point, my parents and all, then I've got to find a way to make this work. For me. I've got to do what I've got to do and be prepared to take whatever comes. I'm not a bad person. I'm not thinking about doing bad things. I have to make up my own mind, decide for myself what is right, stand by that, and do it.

I looked up momentarily, then back at the page, re-reading my epistle. Before closing the cover, I underlined the word "right" three times.

~

Diesel fuel. The smell filled the cabin when the bus door hissed open. I didn't want to get off. I let everyone else exit before I stood to retrieve my briefcase from the overhead rack. *What would this companion be like? Another Owl? A Harris? A Pyle? Or some altogether new species?*

Holding the hand rail, I made sure my feet would make a solid connection with the ground before stepping off. I'd learned my lesson. No more falls, scraped knees, or torn pants for me. It was time to take up the reins of my life.

Easier said than done.

Not too far off, there he stood. True of all Mormon missionaries, he stuck out like a sore thumb. I could see people gawking. One man pointed at him. A couple covered their mouths, whispering back and forth. I'm sure they were gawking at me, too. *Gosh, just once, why can't we wear something different. Yes sir, clowns for Jesus, that's us all right.*

When my blue-suited twin saw me, he raised his hand in greeting, waved and smiled. My blood ran cold. *What does this mean? Is this what the fly feels like when the spider comes calling?* What I next noticed is the absence of two standard-issue, regulation items: a fedora and bicycle. In his case, a fedora would have been a definite improvement. His hair, how to describe it? Clumps, irregularly cut, and arranged in unnatural waves. One strand, like a radio antennae, stood straight up. *Maybe it's a toupee? If so, he's got it on sideways.* Whatever it was, I felt a strange impulse to run over, rearrange it or run a comb through it.

In English, "Hellooooo, Elder Miller," extending his hand, "Welcome to Lund!"

Uncertain of whether I was being tested, I took his hand, but replied in Swedish, "Hejsan Äldste Wiggins, trevligt att träffa dig" (Hello Elder Wiggins, a pleasure to meet you).

"Oh, speak English," his broad smile returning, "there'll be plenty of time to speak Swedish."

"Uh, ah, OK," I said, still leery. *Is this guy for real?*

"You gotta bike?" he asked.

"Oh, yeah, it's on the rack, at the back of the bus."

Grabbing my suitcases from the bags lined up on the curb, we made our way to the back of the bus.

"Wow, that's a nice bike," Wiggins complimented, "looks new ... I have a bike, but I don't ride it."

"Oh?"

"Been locked to the light post in front of our apartment for months," he chuckled, "I'll tell you later. Anywhooo ... we got about a five minute walk, you OK with that, or do you want to take a cab?"

"A cab? Are you serious?"

"What? You don't think we can get that bike in a cab? I'll betcha we can, we'll figure it out ...".

"Na, no, we can walk," I said, still trying to figure my new companion out.

"Cool, our place is near the University."

Instantly, I thought of Elin, "How many students go there?"

"I dunno, lots. Actually, we live in student housing."

"Really?" I responded, floored that the mission office would permit us to live among so many temptations.

"Yeah ... pretty small, this place, originally for one student, but it's all right, a bed and a cot ...".

"A cot?" alarm now creeping into my voice.

"Yeah, but you can have the bed if you want, whatever ...".

Despite his appearance and my initial suspicion, I found myself liking the guy. Grabbing my bike, he gestured with his chin, signaling the way forward. "Follow me boys!" he exclaimed.

Follow me boys? I had to laugh, "I'm right behind you."

The city, unlike Huskvarna, was bustling with activity. People everywhere—in the stores, on the streets, moving in every direction, young, old, and in between. It was a lot warmer here, only a light dusting of snow on the ground. *Maybe that's why so many are out and about.*

We passed by a giant church, its imposing grey granite towers jutting into the air, the façade darkened with what looked like soot. "Lund Cathedral," Wiggins remarked, noting my interest, "Been here for centuries, built in 1085. It's burned down several times. We'll go visit on P-day. It's got five organs and the coolest astronomical clock you've ever seen ... it tracks phases of the Moon."

We continued walking, first veering away from the main street, and then making a couple of turns onto smaller cobblestone lanes. As he pushed, my bike rattled as the wheels rolled over the neatly cut stones. The buildings on either side were old, some Medieval in appearance, their rooflines steep and uneven. Barren trees contrasted sharply against the brightly painted houses. One building at the end of the block was conspicuously modern, a prefab concrete and glass monster, having all the charm of a military bunker. Out in front, bikes littered the walkway.

I guessed that was where we were heading, pointing, "Is that our building?" No sooner had the words left my mouth when Wiggins set the kickstand and began running. Our pace had been steadily increasing over the last couple of blocks.

"Yup … and I've gotta go," yelling over his shoulder, "lock your bike up out front. We're in 4D." Then he streaked away like the Flash. Well, not exactly. His movement was a cross between a run and a waddle. *What the hell is going on?*

Finding an empty spot next to a garbage bin in front of the building, I locked up my bike. Once secured, I headed back for my suitcases. *This is weird. And I was just getting to like him, too.*

In the time I'd been in Sweden, the weight of my luggage had not changed. It still felt like I was schlepping cannon balls. Fortunately, 4D was on the ground floor. I knocked and the door gave way.

"Elder Wiggins?" I hesitantly called. Hearing nothing, I stepped in and was immediately greeted by the unmistakable smell of shit. *Gawd, what's that? There must be a problem with the plumbing or something. Man, this reeks.*

To my left, behind a closed door, I could hear water running. *Maybe the toilet has backed up. He's in there fixing it.*

"Hey, Elder Wiggins, can I help?"

When he didn't answer, I set my bags down, and deliberately shut the apartment door with a bang.

"I'll be out in a minute," he yelled.

Wiggins' description of our flat was spot on. It was small, half the size of the place in Huskvarna. The sick green paint and acoustical ceiling tiles spoke, "Early Institution." Off to one side was a tiny room—a kitchenette—barely big enough for one person. It was strictly gourmet: hot plate, toaster oven, pint-sized refrigerator, and Barbie and Ken sink.

The sleeping arrangements were just as upscale, the cot looking like a clearance item from an Army-Navy surplus store. A desk sat at the head of the two beds. On top was stacked the usual Mormon books and pamphlets I'd come to know so well. They were all neatly arranged, yet far from accessible. If you ever got the gumption to get one, you would have to turn and shuffle sideways up the eight inch gap between the bed and cot.

Above the desk was the apartment's only window. It was covered by an old Venetian blind; the slats were yellowed and several badly bent. The blind hardly seemed necessary as it looked as though the glass had not been cleaned since the last time Lund Cathedral burned to the ground.

I guess I'm sleeping on the cot. The bed is already made up with Wiggin's stuff. Oh well.

The bundle of sticks and canvas posing as a bed creaked under the weight of my luggage. *So, where do I put all this stuff?* As had been the case in Huskvarna, no closet, no chest of drawers. Stuck to the walls, above his bed, were the usual cut-outs from Mormon magazines: the Prophet, Twelve Apostles, a temple or two. *Wait a minute, who are these guys?* I moved to take a closer look at some of the pictures. One, I immediately recognized. It was Einstein. The others, I wasn't sure. *Well, maybe one. DaVinci.* Several had tiny captions. I read them. *Archimedes. Galileo. Copernicus. Edwin Hubble. Edwin Hubble? This stuff is OP for sure.*

So intently was I looking at the pictures that I didn't hear Wiggins come out of the john. I jumped about a foot when he spoke, "And if a person gains more knowledge and intelligence in this life through his diligence, he will have so much more advantage in the world to come." Wiggins was quoting word for word from the Prophet Joseph Smith's *Doctrine and Covenants.*

"Oh," I managed. Actually, I didn't know what else to say. *How many of Joseph Smith's revelations did this guy have memorized?*

"Great thinkers all," he continued, hanging his pants from a makeshift clothes line spanning the entrance of the kitchenette, "Besides, 'The Glory of God is intelligence,' *D & C* 93:36."

Although impressed by his powers of recall, I was no longer looking at the pantheon of intelligence arranged on his wall. I was looking at his pants. The seat was soaked. More than that, Wiggins himself had a towel wrapped around his waist, no G's to be seen.

"Got one more thing to hang up," heading back to the bathroom. I could hear water draining from the sink and above that, him humming *Ode to*

Joy—the last movement of Beethoven's Ninth. Soon, out he came, his tightly twisted G's in hand.

After placing them on the line next to his pants, he faced me, "Elder Miller," he paused, "um, uh, would it be OK to call you Scott instead?"

Wiggins was full of surprises, "Are you kidding? Of course. You OK with that?"

"Yeah, call me Wiggins, or Mike ... whatever ... um, I got something to tell you."

"Uh, OK," my voice rising.

"I've got colitis. You know what that is?

I shook my head.

"Inflammation of the large intestine," he said authoritatively.

Once again, I found myself without words. I had no idea what that was or what it meant.

"Basically, it boils down to this, I don't have control over my bowels. I can be anywhere and all of the sudden, I've gotta go. Sorry man, you're seeing what happens. I've gotta drop everything and get to a toilet as fast as I can. If I don't make it, out it comes." He let out a long sigh, "Sorry about the smell."

"Don't worry about it," I replied, feeling sympathetic, "What a bummer. Can't they do anything, can't they help you with that?"

"Not a heck of a lot. I gotta watch what I eat. Some foods set me off. You know, drink lots of water, 'cause it's easy to get dehydrated."

"Oh my," I said, taking a seat on the edge of my cot.

"The cramps are the worst, then there's the gas," retrieving a clean set of Garments from a cardboard box next to his bed, "it makes riding a bike impossible. Hope that won't be a problem."

Problem? Thank the Maker. Between the bike, the hat, the suit, and name tag, eliminating anything that would make us look more like residents of this planet, I was all for.

"Fine by me," I said, checking my delight lest he think I was happy about his illness.

Pointing to some empty cardboard boxes, "Why don't you unpack? I'm gonna lay down for a few minutes."

While he curled up on his bed, we talked back and forth. "How's your Swedish?" he asked, "I can help you with that. Tomorrow we'll get you a library card. You can check out these language tapes. It'll help with your accent."

Library card, I thought. *What's next? Sex with girls?*

Like most Americans, I struggled more with making my Swedish sound Swedish than choosing the right words to make a sentence. The language has a lilting, melodic quality, along with several letters not found in the English alphabet. Not only do you risk advertizing yourself as a foreigner, but depending on your intonation, you can seriously insult someone. The Swedish characters, ö, pronounced "uhw," and å, pronounced "ohh," are good examples. Mix them up and you are either opening a door (dörr) or calling somebody a fool (dåre).

"What about your knowledge of the scriptures?" he asked next, "I can help you with that, too. We've got a lot of J-dubs here in Lund. It's fun to bash with them."

"J-dubs?"

"Jehovah's Witnesses. They always let us in, whenever we knock. I got a whole tracting log full of their names."

I must have given him a blank look. He continued, now with excitement, "They *think* they know their scriptures. We barely get the first discussion started, and they want to bash."

"Bash?"

"You know, scripture chase, except you're not doing it with Mormons."

Now I got it. Scripture chases were a common activity in our early morning Seminary classes. Bibles before us, our teacher Brother Dick Huertz would cite a doctrine and challenge us to be the first to find the appropriate, supportive scriptural reference. If nothing else, the game worked to keep us awake.

"Grab my quad," Wiggins said, pointing to the desk near the window. He was referring to the four books of Mormon scripture bound in a single volume: *The Bible, Book of Mormon, Doctrine and Covenants, and Pearl of Great Price.*

Sliding my way up between the two beds, I grabbed the thick, leather-bound volume. Like so many other missionaries, his full name, "Michael Clark Wiggins," was embossed in gold on the front cover. That's where the similarity stopped. The gilded pages of the top edge and tail looked like a Roman mosaic. On closer inspection, the "tiles" turned out to be paper tabs, hundreds of them—blue, white, and red—arranged in columns.

Sitting down next to Wiggins, he tried to show me how his scripture finding system worked. In truth, it made about as much sense to me as a Rubik's Cube. He explained, "The columns line up with subjects on the blank page here at the beginning of the book. These subjects connect to the tabs on the side. Put your finger on any tab, and bam, you open right to the page with the scripture you need."

I nodded as though I understood.

"Lemme show you ... name a subject," he playfully demanded.

"Uhh."

"Come on!"

"Bah, um, well ... healing the sick," I blundered out. *Gosh Scott, I can't believe you said that. The man just told you he has an incurable illness.*

"Here it is," he said, either unfazed or oblivious to my indirect and unfortunate reference to his condition, "Doctrine and Covenants 42:48, 'he that hath faith in Me to be healed, and is not appointed unto death, shall be healed.'"

He looked at me with a broad smile. Obviously, he was proud of his system. And no doubt, I should have been impressed. It *was* impressive. He was impressive. For my part, I couldn't get past the irony. *Here he was serving a mission, literally working his ass off for the Lord, devoted as all get-out, and yet he's still sick. I'm sure Thorsson knows about this, maybe even anointed him with oil, laid his hands on his head, and gave him a blessing.*

I looked at Wiggins again. He was waiting expectantly for me to say something, do something. Suddenly, I felt an impulse to reach inside my pants pocket, get my vial of the special oil and go to town.

It didn't go any further than that. Instead, I returned his smile, saying, "Mike, wow, this is amazing. You've got to help me do this to my scriptures."

~

"Yes but who ... *who* I ask, did the sex with Mary?" a knowing smile crossing his face. Joakim (Yo-ah-keam) then leaned back in his chair, his expression suggesting he'd just scored the winning goal at last year's World Cup.

Tall with dusty blond hair and a freckle-face, Joakim was friendly enough but not especially warm. A third-year physics major, he had to be bright. In fact, I got the sense he thought he was smarter than everyone else.

We'd met earlier that week on the streets. He'd approached *us*, given *us* his address, asked *us* to come over. My first four weeks or so in Lund I was floored by the reception we received, by Joakim and others. In Huskvarna, it always seemed we were a few short steps away from being tarred and feathered and escorted to the city limits. Here, it was altogether different. The people, in particular university students, sought us out. Soon, I would come to understand, few were actually interested in Mormonism. Instead, we were a curiosity, less pariah and more oddity, subjects in a laboratory to be observed and studied.

Whatever the reason people let us in, and were friendly, I didn't particularly care. It was better than knocking on doors. Plus, with Wiggins being sick so often, our numbers were off. *Numbers. Yeah, numbers. The frigging numbers.* The Zone Leaders, Elders Lee and Larson, were constantly ragging on us for failing to meet our quotas. The absolute importance of these obligations had been drilled into our heads from "Day One." If our weekly tallies missed the mark, "the call" would come.

"How many people have you stopped on the street this week and asked the 'Golden Questions,'"—What do you know about the Mormon Church? Would you like to know more?—the ZL's would demand. "At the rate you're going, you'll never reach 100. You'll make the whole Zone look bad. You want that?"

On top, we had to teach 40 official missionary discussions. Forty! The pressure to produce was extreme. In Huskvarna, we were lucky to be invited into someone's home once or twice a week. Even the Owl, Mr. Righteous to the world, took creative license in defining what counted as a legitimate discussion. I remember the first time he turned to me after a near miss with a slamming door, saying, "That's a C1!"

We were out tracting. We knocked. A middle-aged man answered. "Hello," Church started, "My companion and I are two representatives of the Church of Jesus Christ of Latter-day Saints. We have an important message for you. May we please come in?" When the man refused, my companion started reciting Discussion C, section 1, the Joseph Smith story. Church's pace picked up dramatically as the man reached for the door handle, ending at a clip so fast I thought it might result in a sonic boom. "YES!" he said, clapping his hands once loudly, "I finished the section. That counts!"

By contrast, Wiggins was scrupulously honest. No slippery slopes for him. A discussion was, well, a *discussion*. People actually had to talk, share, you know, interact. Fortunately, in Lund, this wasn't a problem. On the other hand, tracting was out. Wiggins could barely make it up and down a flight of stairs much less spend four hours a day on his feet, the amount of time prescribed for the activity.

No sooner had Joakim delivered what he believed to be the *coup de grâce* when Wiggins pounced. I'd seen this before. Our host had no idea what was coming. He wouldn't until his arguments were fatally skewered. Wiggins knew his stuff. Where he stood alongside an international panel of debaters, I had no idea. The way he used his knowledge sure wowed the hell out of me though.

Wiggins retrieved his quad. Fingers flying along the tabs with the skill and alacrity of a master pianist, he quickly located a passage from the *Old Testament*.

"Point well taken," he started, "The birth of our Lord was the fulfillment of ancient prophecy. The Jews were awaiting their Messiah, a leader who would restore them, God's chosen people, to their rightful place as rulers of Jerusalem and eventually the world."

Joakim sat motionless, a wry smile the only indication he was listening.

Reading chapter and verse, Wiggins continued, "Isaiah prophesied, 'The Lord Himself will give you a sign. Behold, a *virgin* shall conceive and bear a son.'" On saying, he closed the book, fingered a new tab, opening to the *New Testament*. "That prophecy was fulfilled when Christ was born, and Luke tells us, 'the *virgin's* name was Mary.'"

Joakim chuckled, clearly amused, "My friend, *virgins* don't have children. *Sex. Sex* is required. So, I ask again, who did the sex with Mary?"

Wiggins calmly turned to a new page, this time laying the entire volume on its spine. A type-written sheet, cut to match the others, was revealed. I could see the title in capital letters at the top, "BIRTH OF THE SAVIOR." As was soon apparent, this was Wiggin's *Cliff Note* regarding the meaning of the word "virgin," in the original Hebrew and Aramaic languages. Clearing his throat, he proceeded to give a detailed summary, the upshot of which was, guess what, we really didn't know if Mary was a virgin in the contemporary sense. The specific word used in the scriptures may be interpreted simply as a young woman of marriageable age, not necessarily someone who has never had sex.

I was puzzled by the tack Wiggins was taking, and also feeling impatient. *Why doesn't he just tell him what Mormons really believe? What we've been taught since we were kids? I knew full well 'who had the sex with Mary'? God did. God got Mary pregnant.*

The birth of Christ was not an impenetrable mystery, at least to Mormons. It was a fundamental part of LDS cosmology—the literal belief in eternal progression. The story, as I understood it, from my earliest introduction to Mormon theology was that the God we worship was once a human being! Having lived a righteous life, he died, was resurrected, and ascended to Heaven. Then, together with his wife or wives, they sired spirit children. These children, as did their Heavenly Father and Mother, had to be born to earthly parents, and choose to lead a virtuous life. If they did, in turn, they would on death be resurrected, go to Heaven and become gods themselves. For Mormons, the cycle is never ending, resulting in a chain of humanity stretching back through the millennia and across endless universes. The often quoted couplet of Lorenzo Snow, the Church's fifth prophet, seer, and revelator said it succinctly, "As man is, God once was; as God is, man may become."

There is more. Each generation requires a redeemer—a messiah, one who will come, anointed by God, born without sin, and sacrifice his life to set the cosmic scales of justice right. Why? Because no matter how moral a life one leads, people can't help themselves. They sin.

The only question left is how the savior arrives? Once more, for our church, the answer was easy. Mormons are a practical people. Our God can no more escape the laws of nature than we can. The Gospel of John tell us, "For God so loved the world he gave his only begotten Son"—the operative word being "begotten," meaning, "generated by procreation!" Somebody had to put the beef in the taco. Frankly, I found this idea easier to accept than a virgin birth—a savior with only half the required number of chromosomes.

Now, Joakim sat up and gleefully retorted, "So, someone *did* have sex with Mary?!"

Yes, of course, I wanted to scream. *Making babies requires sex. Why is this so hard to understand or accept?*

Wiggins had a different idea. Obviously, we weren't on the same page.

"Joakim," he asked, "Do you know the origin of your name?"

"What?" Joakim responded, "What does this have to do with anything?"

"Your first name. Joakim. Do you know its origin? You share it with a very important person."

A look of confusion quickly replaced Joakim's smug certainty.

"Interesting that we're having this particular discussion," Wiggins continued, "Did you know that you share your first name with the father of Mary, the mother of Jesus?"

Where does he find this stuff? I thought.

Joakim merely sputtered, knocked off balance by my companion's question.

"Neither here nor there", Wiggins said, his voice suddenly soft, "The birth of our Lord is … a matter of faith. Whether Mary was a virgin or not—at least in the way we use the word now—we have to accept many things that we don't yet understand. God's promise is that all things will be revealed in time if we have faith."

Regaining his footing, "I don't accept things on faith. I'm a scientist."

Wiggins retrieved his scriptures from the table, opening to yet another type-written page, this one titled, "FAITH." In a knowing voice, he read, "The dictionary defines, 'faith' as belief, confidence, or trust in a person or thing. Scientists, like everyone else, take a great many matters on faith."

"Oh?"

"Of course. They have to. There are so many unknowns. The origin of the universe. The existence of quantum particles. The nature of light. Gravity, for Heaven's sakes. Gravity. You *believe* in it, have confidence in it, even though science has no explanation for it."

Joakim jumped in, "We may not know now, but with further research, we will. Our understanding of the universe will increase."

"My point exactly," Wiggins laughed, "In the meantime, it's not only reasonable, it's a good thing to believe. In gravity. *In God and his word.*"

"There *is* no God."

"Little wonder you think that, now is it?" setting his quad back down on the table, "science is only as good as the questions asked, and the scientists asking the questions."

"What do you mean?" showing interest for the first time.

"Werner Heisenberg. Remember him? He was a scientist, a contemporary of Einstein, Schroedinger, and Bohr. 'What we observe,' he asserted, 'is not nature itself, but nature exposed to our method of questioning."

Here comes another beef in the taco, I thought. *I gotta remember this.*

"Of course, God doesn't exist *for you*. Your questions do not allow it."

~

"You ever eaten a *Semla?*" Wiggins asked, stopping to look through the window of a typical Swedish bakery, known as a konditori (cun-deet-erh-e).

We were making our way home along Klostergatan, a main drag through town, following our meeting with Joakim. My companion was bordering on buoyant. Most days, by this time, we'd be back at the apartment with Mike exhausted, holed up in the john, turning his insides out.

"No, what is it?"

"Heaven on earth," he said, pointing at a bun filled to the brim with whipped cream, and topped with powdered sugar.

"Mmm," my mouth watering.

"Want one?"

"Was Christ born of a virgin?" I replied, "I'll take five!"

We both laughed. "Come on, my treat," he said.

The smell of coffee, rich, fresh-ground coffee, permeated the shop. I loved it, instantly thinking of my grandmother Christina. She wouldn't hesitate to get a cup. I could see her now, elbowing up to the bar, knocking people down, with her favorite mug in hand.

At the counter, what Swedes call a "gammal tant," a kind, elderly woman (literally, "old aunt") took our order: one semla, and two cups of hot chocolate. Poor guy, Mike had to pass on the pastry.

"I'd love to have one," he said, "but just looking at them … you know …".

As soon as we took a seat at one of the small bistro tables, Mike gave me the scoop. The Swedish delicacy is made once a year—during the Easter holidays—and consists of a cardamom-spiced wheat bun that has been cut in half, hollowed out and filled with a mix of bread crumbs, milk, almond paste and whipped cream. I'd never tasted anything like it. I could eat them every day, and then some.

Munching away, I listened as Wiggins chattered about the encounter with Joakim. If he were disappointed about forgoing the semla, it sure didn't show. His face was flush, movements animated. At these moments, the illness that so often compromised his life receded into the background.

"Science students," he complained, "They can be so sloppy and … unscientific."

We had had these discussions, debriefings, many times before—whenever we met with a student, Jehovah's Witness, anyone who would debate with us, or rather debate with *him*. I was more Little John to his Robin Hood, Alan Hale to his Errol Flynn. My companion had an encyclopedic mind. Never once did I see him fail to "split the arrow," lose an argument. Invariably, his opponent was either forced to surrender or shut up. Even though concession never led to conversion, I truly admired his ability. No one could touch him.

Wiggins stopped briefly to take another sip of hot chocolate, already having knocked back half the drink. He was about to say something when he abruptly set down the mug. His shoulders dropped and body went rigid as the color drained from his face. All the previous excitement was gone. I'd seen this look before. *Oh boy, here it comes.*

"I gotta go," he said, and took off. I watched him do the "Wiggins-waddle," heading for the bathroom at the back of the bakery. *Hope he makes it. Jesus, poor guy.*

The next week, Mike was in hell. The worst I'd ever seen him. He spent hours curled up on the bed. We didn't make it out of the apartment a single day. He couldn't. Lee and Larson, the ZL's, harassed us each morning when I called to let them know Wiggins was sick. Too sick to work. I wanted to tell them to piss off, especially Lee, who was a shorter, squat, square version of Pyle, the purveyor of pickle juice from Jönköping. Lee was forever using wrestling terminology, repeating lame analogies and metaphors. He'd once been the State champion of his high school team—a fact he never forgot and would not let us forget either.

When we spoke on the phone, I could picture him, the way he looked. Perhaps butts were on my mind a bit, but I imagined his face as an oversized sphincter, his every word having to squeak out between tightly pursed lips. If he told me one more time that we needed to "go to the mat for the Lord," I thought I'd lose it, tell him to fuck off, him and the rest of the boys-in-tights from Bumfuck, Wyoming.

"Oh, my B-team," he lamented, his tone sarcastic, "I'm gonna have to write this up on the 'dirt sheet' and send it to President Thorsson at the

Mission Office."

Wednesday of that week, a knock came at the door. It was early, around 10 in the morning. Wiggins and I were still in our G's, sitting on our beds. Mike was having a brief respite from his illness. We were using the time to prepare a presentation we'd been assigned to give at the upcoming zone conference. The topic was conjugating Swedish verbs common in daily conversation. It was hardly a crowd pleaser, even so it was right up Mike's alley. For the first time in days, he was smiling.

The two day conference would be held at the LDS Chapel in Malmö, a town about 20 kilometers south of Lund, and the third largest in Sweden. Among missionaries it was Mecca, being home to the only Burger King in the Sweden-Göteborg Mission. Along with everyone else, I planned to eat burgers and fries for breakfast, lunch, and dinner.

I'd been to one zone conference before, in Jönköping, and really enjoyed it. I was so homesick. It was a relief to take time off and hang out. I'm sure the Swedes living in our zone were also relieved; two whole days, we were out of their hair and hallways. Delivered from their oppressors, they could walk the streets freely, raise their faces to the sun, and breathe deeply without having to play duck and dodge with the boys in blue.

It wasn't all fun and games. Aside from the customary pep talks and presentations, plenty of time was spent going over the rules, and going over them again. "Tales of the Fallen" were also a main event; Elders who succumbed to the temptations of the "Great Deceiver"—or better said *the* temptation because, while the details varied, the offense was always the same. Some dumb schmuck snuck out, got laid, and was sent home. How were they found out? Without exception, they confessed during their P.P.I., or "Personal Priesthood Interview," a private meeting between each missionary and the Mission President. These little chit-chats, a central feature of every zone conference, were lengthy and unpleasant. Think of a moral colonoscopy performed by Spanish Inquisition.

Anyway, I opened the door not knowing what to expect. No one ever knocked, morning, noon, or night. There, were the last people on Earth I wanted to see—especially as I was in my underwear. It was them, the ZL's, Lee and Larson. *Oh shit.*

"God morgon," (good morning) Elder Lee barked in his best coach-like voice, "how's my team?" Before I could say, "Good morning," "Come on in," or "Go away," the pair pushed by me.

Mike stood as they entered. In fact, that's what we all did, stood there; Lee and Larson in their suits, hats, and brief cases, me and Mike in our baggy-assed G's. The only one showing any expression at all was Larson. He was smiling broadly, revealing a bounty of sharply pointed teeth that would have put a vampire to shame. It was quite a sight, riveting actually. Even though I'd seen them before, I couldn't help but stare.

Fortunately for all of us, Larsson was not one of the undead. If I hadn't known better, I would have concluded he was from that tribe in Sumatra I'd once read about in National Geographic—the one where the women file their teeth into spikes in the hope of making themselves beautiful to their husbands.

If you could get past that—admittedly hard to do—Larson bore a striking resemblance to Abraham Lincoln: gaunt and gangly. Like our 16th president, he was also a good guy, in marked contrast to his companion. He'd told me the story about his teeth my first Sunday in Lund. We were at church and he caught me staring at his mouth much like I was doing now.

"Pretty ugly, huh?" he asked, his question taking me by surprise.

Embarrassed, all I came up with was a long, "Ahhhhh."

Before I could think of anything to say, he continued, "I call 'em my gnashers. You know, 'weeping, wailing, *gnashing* of teeth.'" He laughed loudly, "It all happened at a church softball game. Our ward was in the championship. Bottom of the ninth, two outs, and I'm on deck. The Stake president is at bat. We're down by one. He's terrible, can't hit worth a darn so I'm just hoping he doesn't strike out. That way, I can have one last turn before I leave for my mission. Instead he fouls and I manage to catch the ball with my mouth. BAM!"

"Couldn't they fix them?" I asked.

"Yeah, they *could,* but it would have cost a fortune, and I didn't have enough money to get them fixed *and* go on my mission ... so ...", he growled like a lion, barring his teeth, "here I am."

Once again, I looked at his mouth, all busted up. Whatever embarrassment I felt gave way to shame. Compared to his, my devotion wouldn't fill a thimble.

Lee brought me back to the present. "How are my boys?" he asked.

"Boys?" I started, still marveling at how the man managed to speak with his jaws seemingly wired shut.

Wiggins shot me a quick shut-up-I'll-handle-this-glance. "We're fine," he said, "I feel bad we haven't been able to get out."

"Yeah, you guys have been pinned. Gotta do a 'reversal.'"

I hated this guy. My eyes rolled so far back in my head I thought they'd get stuck there.

"Elder Miller, I know you're probably dying to get back into the game, escape the 'full nelson' you're in ... I know I would ...".

He had no idea. Actually, what I wanted to do was kick him in the balls. Wiggins, and my better judgment, prevailed. I was sure Lee would take me, easily.

Still speaking through his teeth, "You go back to our area with Elder Larsson and work. I'll stay here Elder Wiggins."

"That's great," Mike said enthusiastically, "That way you can help me with the language lesson I've been preparing for the zone conference. It'll help me *and you.*" He turned slightly in my direction, quickly giving me a wink only I could see.

I instantly knew what Mike was up to. Lee's command of Swedish—despite having been in the country longer than any of us—was notoriously bad. He was the Mormon Norm Crosby, the master of malaprop, famous for dressing up English words and idioms with a Swedish accent, and then inserting his linguistic inventions into conversation. My first Sunday in Lund—the same day Larson told me about his teeth—Lee pulled the biggest language boner I'd ever heard. He was speaking in front of the entire congregation. After stopping mid sentence to take a sip of water, he began choking. Instead of saying, "it went down the wrong pipe" he proudly and, at the top of his lungs, proclaimed "it went in my vagina." Actually, the word he mangled was much more vulgar. I didn't even know the word, had never heard it used—especially in Sunday School. Suffice it to say, it started with a "c" and ended with a "t." Wiggins translated for me as Church members sat in stunned silence.

I looked at Lee. For the first time ever, his mouth was wide open and jaw hanging loosely. He'd been had. Mike found this guy's weak spot and pushed his shoulders to the mat. Match to Wiggins!

5

REVELATIONS

∾

"But, behold, I say unto you, that you must study it out in your mind;
then you must ask me if it be right, and if it is right I will cause that
your bosom shall burn ... But if it be not right you shall have no such
feelings, but you shall have a stupor of thought ..."

JOSEPH SMITH (1829)
FIRST PROPHET SEER, AND REVELATOR
CHURCH OF JESUS CHRIST OF LATTER DAY SAINTS

∾

I couldn't believe my eyes. *It's Cary Wells, my best friend at the L.T.M.,
one of the three musketeers boarding my bus at Malmö Central Station!*
The last time I'd seen him, after that first gloomy night at the *Tre Kroner*
hotel in Göteborg, was when Thorsson's henchmen, the A.P.'s Pierce and
Payne, led him away to his train the next morning.

We did our best to stay in touch with each other. Though it was a huge
pain, we sent letters through our parents. To reach me, he would send a
note to my folks who, in turn, forwarded it on to me. I would do the same
through his.

After the first exchange, we tried the direct route. He got caught. His
companion, Elder Burr, found my letter and went ape-shit wondering who

within the mission was contacting Cary. With no return address to go on, Burr demanded to read the letter. The little prick-turned-detective wanted to track down the other moral misfit. As Cary later related in a letter safely circuited through our parents, even the President got involved. He wrote, "I told Thorsson 'You don't like it? Send me home.'" Cary's ability to cut through the crap, quickly and with confidence, hadn't changed.

No sooner had he got on the bus and was paying his fare, up I stood, waving, yelling, "Elder Wells! Back here, back here."

A big smile crossed his face when he recognized me. I half trampled Mike getting from my window seat to the aisle to met Cary midway. We embraced.

"So good to see you man," I said, thumping him on the back.

"Sit by me," he replied, leaving our two companions to make their own introductions.

The doors were hissing closed as the two of us made our way to an empty row at the back of the bus. Within moments of taking our seats, Cary whispered, "I'm going home."

"What?" I asked in a hushed voice, stunned by his words, "You're going home?! What'd'ya do?"

That big smile returned, "Dude, I'm not being *sent* home, I'm *going* home." With that, he rubbed his curly brown hair in that signature way. *Man, I'd missed that. I missed him.*

Cary continued, "I'm telling Thorsson today, during my P.P.I. He's been dicking around with me for a month now, stringing me along, telling me to have faith and all, pray, give it another week. If he doesn't help me get home today, I'm taking the ferry to Denmark and catching the next flight out of Kastrup. I've got a credit card. The airport is only an hour from here."

"Jesus, Cary, what's happened?"

"What happened? Nothing *happened*. What are we doing here? This whole thing, … it's bullshit. It's been bullshit from the start."

Good heavens. Has he thought this through? Could he really go home? Won't this wreck his life? Gosh, will he be excommunicated? Won't his family be ashamed?

I wasn't sure what to say. Before I could say anything, he pulled a large, brown manila envelope from his briefcase and passed it to me. *Oh shit. What is this?* Suspecting I was being handed contraband, I instinctively looked up the aisle. Wells' companion, Elder Burr, was sitting next to Wiggins, the two of them talking excitedly. *OK, they're not watching. We're good.*

"You know this is crap. If what we're doing here isn't stupid enough, take a look at this stuff. I was gonna mail it to you when I got home."

"What is it?"

"More stuff about Joseph Smith and the Church. Read it. It'll blow your mind."

I thought back to our time at the L.T.M. and the book on Church history Cary had given me—one of the items that had miraculously escaped discovery that first day at the mission office when our luggage was searched. I still had it hidden in one of my bags.

I looked at the envelope in my hands, "What's in it?"

"More of the same," he replied, "Stuff about the 'First Vision.' Did you know that early church members didn't even know about it? Never talked about it. He didn't start telling the story until years later. Come on!"

The "First Vision" is a pillar of Mormon theology, an occurrence that establishes the faith's exceptional claim to being the one and only true Church on Earth. The story goes that the then 15 year old Smith went into the woods near his home in Manchester, New York, to pray for guidance about which Church to join. His prayers were answered with a personal visit from no less than God and his son, Jesus Christ. They told him, in no uncertain terms, that he was to join none of them. All were false, "abominations" in Their divine sight. Only a new Church would suffice.

Cary continued with a laugh, "Joseph Smith sees God and Jesus Christ and doesn't tell a soul—not his parents, his brothers, no one." He was rapidly building up a head of steam, his volume increasing. I looked up the aisle to make sure our companions weren't listening.

"You already know about all the different versions of his vision. What are there now? Three? Four? Smith couldn't even make up his mind about who he saw. In one, it's an angel, in others it's Jesus, in the canonized version, it's God and Jesus. You'd think you'd remember that!"

The bus hissed to a stop. More passengers boarded. Once again, I checked on Wiggins and Burr. They were still carrying on, oblivious to us.

I looked back at Cary. I knew what he was saying. It was true. Joseph Smith never got this story straight. We'd talked about it before. I just couldn't get as worked up about the varying accounts as he did. It reminded me of the children's game called, "telephone." You sit in a circle. One kid makes up a story. He whispers it to the next and it's passed to everyone in turn. By the time you get to the last kid, what's been shared bears little or no resemblance to the original. On top of that, I knew that everyone embellishes—"polishes the apple" as my Grandma Christina used to say. I know I did. Each time I told someone about the band my friend Bill and I had in High School, we got bigger and better, eventually rivaling the Rolling Stones.

"Mostly it's journal articles and newspaper clippings," Cary said, plowing ahead, "There are some copies of historical documents too ... stuff about the *Book of Abraham* and Joseph Smith as a translator."

Here was a subject I knew much less about. It was another basic tenet of faith though. Latter Day Saints believe that Joseph Smith translated the *Book of Mormon* into English from "reformed Egyptian" characters inscribed on gold plates. Church leaders are unequivocal on this point. "Either the Book of Mormon is what the Prophet Joseph said it is," the Apostle Jeffrey R. Holland wrote, "or this Church and its founder are false, fraudulent, a deception from the first instance onward." Strong words leaving little wiggle-room. Holland continued, it's a "do-or-die, bold assertion."

Although a handful of prominent early members claimed to have seen and even handled the gold plates—among them Cary's relative, who was one of the "Eight Witnesses"—it was not possible to check the accuracy of Smith's translation as he gave them back to the Angel Moroni upon completion. Turns out though, other evidence exists related to his abilities as a translator of ancient writings. In May 1843, a set of six small, bell-shaped brass plates with strange hieroglyphics were found near Kinderhook, Illinois, and brought to the Prophet. On examination, he noted the engravings were similar to those on the gold plates and told the story of "a descendent of Ham, through the loins of Pharaoh, King of Egypt." The only problem is the plates were bogus, fabricated by three of Smith's contemporaries.

The story of Smith's prowess in translating of ancient texts does not stop there. Five years after publishing the *Book of Mormon,* Smith translated a collection of Egyptian papyri. Word was he had acquired them, together with a set of Egyptian mummies, from a traveling side-show. He claimed the writings were none other than those of the biblical Abraham and Joseph, even containing the autograph of Moses and handwriting of his brother Aaron. The resulting *Book of Abraham* is part of the *Pearl of Great Price,* a volume canonized by Church authorities in 1880.

Although facsimiles rendered by the Prophet have always appeared alongside his translation, the original papyri were lost—that is, until 1967, when they were found in the New York Metropolitan Museum of Art. Translated by modern scholars, the papyri were nothing more than ordinary Egyptian funerary texts, dating from about 100 BC, or 2000 years after Moses, Abraham, and Aaron lived. Despite these facts, even today, the introduction to the volume unequivocally states it is, "A translation of some ancient records ... written by [Abraham's] own hand, upon papyrus."

I began peeling back the lip of the envelope. Cary immediately interrupted, "Don't read it now. And let me give you some advice when you do." He took a deep breath, thought for a moment, then began, "Pretend you're not a Mormon, that you're learning all this for the first time. I know that'll be hard but try it."

"Huh, ok," nodding.

"If you read it with your Mormon eyes, you'll just end up trying to make excuses, rationalizing it, explaining away all the problems and contradictions, the goofiness. You've got to approach it the same way you would if you were hearing about say, erh ... ffff ... the blue-faced deities of Hinduism or gods with elephant heads riding on tigers." He laughed. "That stuff sounds fantastic to us because we weren't raised with it. Hearing it for the first time as an adult, you wouldn't believe any of it for a second ... you'd know it's a bunch of crap."

"Yeah ..." I said slowly.

A bell rang overhead signaling the driver to pull over at the next bus stop. "Här skall vi stiga av, Äldste" (We're getting off here, Elders) Wiggins declared. Our eyes met as I hurriedly worked to secret the package in my valise.

"Vi kommer," (We're coming) I replied and exited the bus together with Cary.

Despite the early hour, the sun was shining. Each day, in fact, I'd noticed it was getting lighter and lighter. Within a month, the whole topsy-turvy night-all-day nature of Swedish winter would reverse. By midsummer, the sun would never set and it would be day-all-night.

"Kyrkan ligger cirka tre hundra meter härifrån," (The church is about 300 meters from here) Wiggins remarked, and took off leading the way. Burr walked alongside him, the two continuing to talk.

Turning to Cary, I said, "Thorsson's going to get a lot of bad news today."

"Who cares? Pious phony!"

"No, I mean, I was planning on talking with him too."

"WHAT?" Cary responded with surprise.

"I mean, it's not as important as what you'll be telling him … but … I, I'm not, it's not about me going home or anything like that …"

"What? What is it?" his interest piqued.

Leaning over and talking quietly, "I'm going to talk with him about Elder Wiggins … he's sick, he's really sick …."

With that, I related what had happened since my companion and I had been paired up: how he'd messed his pants on our meeting, spent days laid up in the apartment, couldn't eat without it giving him cramps or terrible diarrhea.

A few nights before the zone conference, I was reading my journal. Thumbing through it, I came across the entry from the day I'd been transferred to Lund, the one when I met Stefan, the former Lutheran missionary, and witnessed the accident. Reminded of how I just sat there, watching Stefan rush to help, I decided I was going to tell Thorsson about Mike. This time, I was not going to sit idly by. I was going to take action. Thorsson had to know. It was the right thing to do.

"Do what is right let the consequence follow …" the words of LDS Hymn number 237 rolling off my lips. Cary rubbed his hand back and forth over his head and completed the verse, "Battle for freedom in spirit and might."

We were still singing the song when we entered the Church.

"Elder Miller, Elder Wells, such great spirit!" It was Pierce, the Assistant to the President, his expression unchanged since our encounter at the Mission Office my first day in country. Next to him stood another missionary wearing the same saintly smile. I'd never seen him before.

"This is Äldste Smith," Pierce pointed, "He's the new A.P."

I was about to ask if the other half of the dynamic duo, Elder Payne, had gone home when I remembered the rules: as in Aboriginal culture, we weren't allowed to mention the "departed."

"No relation to our beloved Prophet," Smith said softly, reaching out to shake my hand, "Smith's a common name I suppose."

"Trevligt att träffas," (Nice to meet you) I responded, being careful to use Swedish.

The smell of brownies permeated the air. A herd of blue suits moving toward the Chapel stopped in place and massed together. In unison, noses tilted upward, taking in the rich aroma. Decorum surrendered to desire. I myself inhaled deeply. *How long has it been? I wonder if they're frosted? Let me at 'em!*

Sweden made some of the best chocolate candy bars on the planet. My favorite was "Ducat," a milk chocolate confection with a soft nougat center manufactured by Maribou AB in a little town just outside of the capital, Stockholm. I swear, given the chance, I would have eaten one every hour on the hour. Cake, on the other hand, never made it on any Swedish menu. And ever since "gaggies" had been officially banned—the letter from the mission office claiming the classic missionary dessert raised the risk of appendicitis—I'd been "jonesing" for a piece.

I breathed in once more. My mouth watered. The smell intensified, coming in waves, as we entered the chapel. Concentration was all but impossible. Through the opening prayer and much of the President's speech, visions of brownies, soon joined by cakes, pies, and donuts paraded through my head.

Meanwhile, Thorsson carried on, pounding the podium while delivering an impassioned speech about—no surprise—virtue, a Mormon euphemism for sexual abstinence:

"Satan is in our midst."

"He is cunning, working slowly and deliberately to bring us down."

Citing recent remarks of Elder George P. Lee, the first Native American member of the Church hierarchy, he admonished us, "Stay unspotted from the world, study the scriptures, pray unceasingly, and be obedient."

Native Americans occupy a special place in Mormon theology. They are the 'Lamanites,' one of several peoples whose history is believed to have been kept on the gold plates. While science confirms that the first Americans are of Asian origin, their ancestors crossing onto the American continent via a land bridge, ten to fifteen thousand years ago, the *Book of Mormon* says something completely different. The Indians are Semites! They took a boat from Israel, landing somewhere in South America, eventually populating the Western Hemisphere.

Silence filled the Malmö Chapel. Thorsson had stopped talking and was taking in the audience. I, for one, was hoping he was finished so we could go eat. No such luck. Wiping his brow, his tone softened. "Let me tell you a story about two missionaries," he started, "I am happy to say, this did not happen here. It was in the UK. Their day began innocently enough. Like you in Sweden, they were allowed to play tennis on P-day. Two women approached, and they agreed to play doubles. Nothing happened. The next week, the foursome met again, and the week after that."

I listened, even though I already knew how the story would end.

"Elders, Satan is cunning," the President continued, extending his finger and sweeping the room as though pointing at every one of us, "so unlike our Lord, who appears in righteous glory with trumpets and the song of angels. The Great Deceiver, the Evil One, comes unannounced, leading us astray one small step at a time."

Then Thorsson laid it out. As expected, two minutes of feverish humping followed by a tearful confession, excommunication from the Church, and an eternity of shame for the Elder and his family.

While he paused to take a sip of water, I scribbled a note and passed it to Cary. "He's going tell us we can't play tennis!" it said. Cary smirked.

Thorsson continued, his bulging blue eyes burning into the souls of all present, "Now ... *I* know what some of you are thinking ..."

Did he? Could he?

"... those of you with impure thoughts and hardened hearts ... you are thinking I'm going to forbid playing tennis."

Holy Moses. I could swear he was looking right at me. Instinctively, I bowed my head.

"But I'm not!" he proclaimed triumphantly, his hand raised, index finger pointing toward the heavens. Grabbing the podium with both hands, he leaned forward, smiled, and in a reassuring voice said, "You are of course free to play tennis ..." and paused again.

Where is he going with this?

"... to keep the proper spirit, however, from this day forward, you are expected to be properly attired when you play. You are representatives of the Church of Jesus Christ of Latter Day Saints. God's servants. All that stands between the Swedish people and perdition."

I sat there not altogether sure what I'd just heard. *What is he saying? Have I lost my mind?* Looking around, no one else seemed to be reacting. It was then that some part of me decided to act. I raised my hand and, without waiting to be called upon, blurted out, "Are you saying that we have to wear our suits when we play tennis?"

Thorsson froze. Slowly turning his head, he fixed his gaze on me. His eyes narrowed, unblinking, holding me in their grip, "Have I not been clear?"

Without warning, Mr. Big Mouth, my brave alter-ego, the one demanding clarification, decided to run out of the chapel, leaving me to hold the bag. The rest of me sat there, momentarily unable to speak. I was not trying to be impertinent. I wasn't sure what the President was saying. I just could not believe what I thought I heard and, with everyone else taking it so well, assumed I'd misunderstood.

Looking up from my seat, "I, I ... don't ... understand."

"Ask your question!" he demanded.

"Er, well ... um ... we *can* play tennis ... but have to wear our suits when we do?" my tone rising.

"As I said, to keep the proper spirit you are expected to be properly attired when you play ..."

That's when Mr. Big Mouth reappeared, "But President Thorsson it costs 200 crowns to have a suit dry-cleaned ... no one, who can afford ...?" Why I was acting like the LDS poster child for tennis—Elder Björn Borg—was beyond me. I didn't even play. Something about the absurdity of it all bugged me. With only 1000 crowns to live on each month, the President was effectively putting the kibosh on tennis. *Why won't he just tell us that?*

"I'm not sitting here for this," Cary interrupted, as he stood and exited the pew. Thorsson nodded to the AP's who, together with Elder Burr, trailed Cary out the chapel doors.

Turning back to me, "Elder Miller, you and I can take this up in your P.P.I. In the meantime ..." his tone noticeably softening, "I'm sure the rest of you have been enjoying the delicious smells coming from the kitchen. Sister Thorsson and I have prepared a special treat for you. Join me in the cultural hall!"

Mormon churches are remarkably similar. Simple, plain, and functional are perhaps the best way to describe them. No crosses, paintings, stained glass windows, high vaulted ceilings or awe inspiring icons. There was always a chapel, filled with rows of wooden pews facing a podium from where Church leaders would speak and conduct meetings. To the right of the lectern, there was usually a piano or organ; to the left, a table on which the sacrament, or Eucharist as it is commonly referred to in other churches, was prepared and served. In foyers flanking both sides of the chapel, one could generally find classrooms, a library, kitchen, the junior Sunday school meeting space, and janitor's office. The cultural hall Thorsson referred to was almost always at the rear, immediately behind the chapel, separated by a moving partition. This multi-function room was a kind of combination overflow area, basketball court, performing stage, and cafeteria.

A half dozen or so long, folding tables had been set up and covered with white butcher paper. Each place setting featured a glass of milk and a huge brownie. Next to each plate was a copy of Elder Lee's speech, the one Thorsson had used as the inpsiration for his.

I was relieved to see Cary standing on the far side of the room. When I moved in his direction, Pierce stepped in between to wave me off.

"Take your seats Elders," Thorsson directed, "Let's pray." Heads bowed, he began;

> "Our dear Father in Heaven, we are grateful, dear Lord, for affording us this opportunity to meet together as Elders of Zion to learn from Thee and Thy chosen leaders. We thank Thee, oh Lord, for this opportunity to serve in Your vineyard, for our Prophet, Spencer W. Kimball, and the Twelve Apostles, for their unswerving dedication and sacrifice. We ask that you bless them and watch over them so that they may continue to lead us in righteousness ..."

I opened my eyes, turning my head ever so slightly, stealing a peak of Cary. He was looking right at me, head up, eyes wide open. I did my best to convey an expression of concern. "I'm OK," he mouthed silently. The prayer continued:

> "... Lord, we give special thanks for Elder Lee, the first Lamanite general authority of the Church, whose appearance at this time is so clearly a fulfillment of *Book of Mormon* prophecy, whose words have alerted us to the dangers and inspired us to remain morally clean in thought and deed. On this beautiful spring morning, we ask thee, oh Father, to bless the food before us, that it will serve to nourish our spirits and help us remember the important lessons learned here today in this, Your house of worship. For these things,

we ask humbly in name of our Lord and Savior, Jesus Christ, amen."

"Amen," the missionaries responded in unison and then looked up at Thorsson. I turned and looked at Wiggins. No matter how good the brownies smelled, or hungry he might be, I knew he wouldn't eat them. He'd be sick for a month. Burr was another story. He was sitting across from me, his eyes wide with anticipation.

"Go ahead Elders, dig in," the President invited.

Watching missionaries eat is an experience. With all the bike-riding and tracting, they are a forever hungry lot, always just this side of starvation. Seated to my right, the rail-thin Elder Simms pushed the entire brownie into his mouth at once. Cheeks bulging, he looked at me and smiled.

For some reason, I hesitated. Something—I didn't know what—wasn't right. I just felt it in my gut.

That's when the retching started, the sound first coming from a nearby table, then all around me. I looked to Elder Simms who was frantically clawing the brown clumps from his mouth. Across from me, Burr was spitting and coughing, his eyes squinting and tearing up at the corners. A few missionaries stood up abruptly, one knocking his chair to floor.

"What's wrong with these?" someone yelled, followed by a loud, collective groan.

"Salt," Elder Simms croaked, gulping down his cup of milk, "the brownies are laced with salt!"

I could hear Thorsson's voice begin to rise above the din, his tone kind and fatherly, "Things are not always what they appear ... are they Elders? And by the time you realize the error of your ways, it's too late—just like the Elders in England, too late." He pursed his lips, and nodded knowingly, seemingly weighed down by the certainty that, despite his best efforts, many would fall. Wiping away a tear, he implored, "Remember this lesson Elders, what at first may seem innocent and wholesome may contain the seeds of your destruction."

I looked round the table at my fellow Elders, most still struggling to free themselves of the foul taste in their mouths and knew that was not the lesson I'd be taking home.

～

Burger King. I didn't even like it, really. The last time I'd eaten at one, I ended up with a bowel impaction so bad I had to go to the hospital and get hosed out. It was my last semester at BYU. I'd tried everything: straining, sitting in a hot bath, even an over-the-counter remedy—all to no avail. In the middle of the night, I called and woke Katie, asking her to drive me to the hospital; awkward doesn't come close to describing the experience.

As far as I was concerned, the best burgers in the world came from *In-N-Out*, a family-owned business with a handful of drive-through outlets in the Orange County area. You could get a "Double-Double," with cheese, a side of fries, and a coke for around three bucks. The ingredients, including two all-beef patties, were always fresh and cooked to perfection. On Fridays, the line of cars waiting to order trailed down the street, sometimes for blocks.

With no *In-N-Out* available, and the only *McDonald's* located outside the boundaries of the Sweden-Göteborg Mission, *Burger Butt*—as Katie and I subsequently called it—would have to do.

"Why so glum?" Wiggins asked, putting a spoonful of oatmeal into his mouth from an old Tupperware container. Understandably, he'd passed on the burger and fries. "I thought this would be a treat," he continued, pausing to swallow, "that you'd be happy ..."

"I dunno," I answered, uncertain of whether I should say anything. I hadn't told him about my plan to express concern about his health to Thorsson. I didn't want him to stop me. I knew he'd object. It was not because he'd feel I was going behind his back, undermining his authority as "senior companion." It was more because he'd see arguing with the President as pointless, or worse. "Direct frontal assaults almost always fail," I could hear him quoting some sage, or scripture, "What good does it do to kick against the pricks?" (Acts 24:16) So, I didn't tell him.

And while we're on the subject of withholding information, I'd never told Wiggins about the accident I'd witnessed on the way to Lund, my brief encounter with Stefan, the shame I felt at doing nothing to help the victims, or my resolution to start "doing the right thing." That's what talking with Thorsson was about.

Chewing a bite of Whopper®, I looked over at Wiggins. That hair. Now I knew why it looked so bad. The night before coming to Malmö, I watched him cut it using a set of Fisher-Price® safety scissors and a hand-operated blade clipper. He was trying to save money. Not only were the usual clumps and cowlicks in evidence, but one side was cut higher and more thinly than the other. I'm not sure how, but the result gave me vertigo whenever I looked at him head on, tempting me to tilt my head in the opposite direction to keep my balance. His hairstyle, if you could call it that, is also what made me decide to talk to Thorsson. I liked Mike, a lot. And while I'd never wanted him near my head with a pair of clippers, I admired his "do-it-yourself spirit" and dogged determination. Heaven knows, he'd never say anything to the President.

"What 's up?" he asked, returning my stare.

"My PPI," I replied, taking time to consider my next words, "it didn't go so well ..."

"Thorsson give you crap about speaking back to him during his speech?"

"Yeah ... among other things ...," I said as I took a french fry from the bag on my tray.

Wiggins furrowed his brow, causing a pointy bit of hair to jut out from his forehead,

"What things?" he asked slowly.

"*You.* I talked to him about you ..." and began relating what happened.

By sheer coincidence, I'd met Cary in the hallway as he was coming out of his interview with the President; otherwise, I might never have seen him again. The moment he saw me, he flashed a big smile. Although I was being led by the AP's to where Thorsson was holding court, Cary ignored them, stopped the procession, reached out and hugged me as hard as he could.

"I'm going home tomorrow," he said, "I'll miss you, Dew."

I patted him hard on the back, "Me too." I could feel my eyes well up.

"Don't worry man, I'll write you as soon as I get home."

"OK," nodding.

"Hang tough," were his parting words.

I stepped back, stifling a wave of emotion, and began walking the last twenty or so feet to Thorsson's door. Stopping short, I tugged reflexively at the bottom of my suit jacket, took a deep breath then knocked.

"Come in, Elder Miller," the familiar voice called.

The office, borrowed from the Bishop, could have been in any Mormon Church: vanilla-colored cinderblock walls, faux-wood laminate office desk, and a four drawer filing cabinet—all standard issue. Behind the desk hung a twelve-by-eighteen inch Warner Sallman print of Jesus in profile.

Thorsson came out from behind the desk, standing at its side, and extended his hand. As we shook, he took hold of my arm with his left hand, holding tightly while staring right in my eyes. If feeling bothered by the meeting with Cary, it didn't show. He was totally focused—on me.

After a reasonable time for a handshake passed, I loosened my grip. The President tightened his. "Elder Miller," his words slow and deliberate, "how are you doing?"

"Fine," I said, making my face as expressionless as possible. I was resolved, this time my eyes would not serve as his window to my soul. *If he wants to hold hands, I'm good with that.* Returning his grip, "How are you President?"

"What?" he asked, a look of surprise momentarily crossing his face.

"How are you?"

"Let's get down to business," he replied, ignoring my question. Releasing my hand and arm, he moved back behind the desk.

"Elder Miller," he started, retrieving some papers from a black faux leather briefcase sitting open on the desk. I recognized the material immediately. It was a stack of my weekly reports, the form my companion and I completed and mailed to the mission office. A note with several lines of handwritten scribbles was clipped to the bunch. Printed letters at the top read, "From the Office of the President." While scanning the documents, he exhaled loudly through his nose.

"Please, sit down," pointing to the chair directly in front of his desk, "I've heard really good things about the language class you and Elder Wiggins taught today."

"Tack så mycket," (Thank you very much) I responded using the Swedish accent known as "Stockholmska." I'd been practicing. True to his word, Wiggins had taken me to the library our first week together. Along with several "ungdoms böcker" (books for adolescents), I checked out a set of language tapes. During the long hours we spent inside, I read and listened, writing down new words—especially teenage slang—and imitating the sound of the spoken language as best I could.

"Impressive," Throrsson enthused, "Your accent is impressive."

I smiled, the rare feeling of pride dissipating with the thought, *if he only knew why.* Libraries and anything one might find there were O.P., forbidden.

We talked a bit back and forth in Swedish before switching to English, "And how is your testimony, Elder Miller? Is it growing along with your language skills?"

I knew exactly where he was going. He had to know about my relationship with Cary. That, coupled with the doubts and difficulties I'd expressed in the weekly progress reports from my time in Huskvarna, would have troubled even the most accepting Church leader.

Testimony is a huge deal in Mormonism. One Sunday per month, members fast and donate the money they would have spent on food to the needy. It is on this day that the only official, unscripted service of the Church takes place. Following an opening prayer, members who feel moved by the Holy Spirit are invited to come to the podium and, in front of the entire congregation, "bear their testimony."

As a kid, I actually looked forward to "Fast and Testimony" meeting. Although I never witnessed any of the spiritual manifestations common during Joseph Smith's day, there were fireworks nonetheless. Watching tearful testimonies and sobbing confessions broke the usual monotony. At the Glendora Third Ward, Sister Morrow was the star. Once at the podium, her words would dissolve into incomprehensible and uncontrolled blubbering. The cabaret only ended when her dutiful husband rose from the assembly to retrieve her. "In the name of Jesus Christ, Amen," he would say into the microphone before leading her back to their pew.

"I know this Church is true." Those are the words. The ones everyone was supposed to say. The ones everybody did say at some point during their turn at the mike—except Sister Morrow who usually didn't get past, "My dear Brothers and Sisters ..." before the waterworks started. I remember her standing outside the chapel doors on one occasion, apologizing to the members as they exited. I don't recall what she said in front of all of us, but figured she must have been embarrassed by her behavior. I knew I would.

My parents never stood up and, growing up, I never felt moved to speak. Plus, while I enjoyed attending, truly enjoyed it, I wasn't really sure what the expression meant. *I know this Church is true.* No one spoke this way outside of services, even members. Every place else, knowing meant that you actually knew something—your home address or telephone number, 2 + 2 = 4, and no way a person can live inside a whale for three days.

"I know this Church is true."

Little kids, three and four years of age, would stand on a special stool and, in cute Bam-Bam and Pebbles Flintstone voices, repeat the words. The audience always ate it up. I hated it when they went up there.

Now was not the time, however, for any musings about testimony, personal doubts, or anything else. I was a man on a mission. I'd been rehearsing each morning while showering in anticipation of my meeting with the President, going over and over it in my mind so as not to get distracted from my main objective.

Is my testimony growing along with my language skills? Yeah, whatever. Can we move on now?

"Every day," I replied without hesitation.

"Good, good, very good," he responded, and in the same breath, "And are you morally clean, Elder Miller?"

Nodding, "No problems there."

Thorsson sat staring at the papers. After what had to be a minute, if not more, he set the reports aside and locked eyes with me, "In *every way*?" he asked, his tone dead serious.

Rehearsed this one, too! And while I had no plans to tell him, the time I'd spent in the shower preparing for this meeting had proven a positive distraction from other activities. Scripture study also helped, but not in the way one might expect. Over time, Wiggins and I had carefully indexed every reference to sex and sin. Curiously, masturbation was never mentioned, much less forbidden in the *Bible, Book of Mormon, Doctrine and Covenants, or Pearl of Great Price*. To be sure, I was still conflicted about it, especially knowing the official LDS position—but less so.

"President Thorsson, I'm proud to say I have nothing to report."

"Good, that's good," retrieving the papers and making a note. "Be vigilant, Elder Miller. Satan is. He's working hard, right now, to thwart our efforts here."

I nodded, adopting a serious expression.

"And, do we need to talk further about the new dress code on P-day?"

"No," I said slowly and with feeling, "I feel bad I misunderstood."

"Good, good, very good. That's the right spirit," he said, obviously pleased with my response, "Properly dressed is spiritually blessed ..."

I noticed I was doing a lot of nodding and stopped.

"So Elder Miller, what is keeping the Lund area from being successful?"

Yikes! We were off script. *What to say? Think, think.* Then it came to me. *Wiggins debating principle number one: don't accept the premise of the question.*

"Uh, actually, President Thorsson," I started, "at the moment, we have a fairly serious investigator."

"Lindemann. Isn't that the name?" he said, taking me by surprise.

"Er, that's Lindfeldt," correcting him, hoping my swift response would deflect any suspicion. We were on dangerous ground here. Lise-Marie Lindfeldt was a 20-year-old college student Wiggins and I had met a few weeks earlier.

It was P-day. We were walking home from the ICA Supermarket near our apartment when, out of the blue, a couple of voices called out in English, "Elders, up here!" On the second floor balcony stood two incredibly attractive women, a blonde and brunette. "Come on up!" they said, waving, "We won't bite."

"Oh sorry, we can't. We have all these groceries to put away," Wiggins shouted back, "and some ice cream that'll melt if we don't put it in the freezer soon."

"We love ice cream," the two giggled loudly then, turning toward the balcony door, yelled, "Stay right there. We're coming."

Before we could split—not that I really wanted to even though meeting with single women alone was OP—the two met us on the street with four bowls and spoons in hand. To our surprise, one of them, the brunette, was American, and a member of the Church! Her family had hosted Lise-Marie when she was an exchange student in the States.

"Call me Lu Lu," the American said, extending her hand.

That was it. We changed our minds. Up to the apartment we went, spending the rest of the evening fixing dinner with our groceries, eating ice cream, laughing, and telling stories about home and our missions. Later, once Lise-Marie learned, by hanging out with them, I'd missed getting my haircut, she insisted on styling it for me. Although completely innocent, I could feel myself melt each time her hands touched me—well, not completely innocent. With her strong, southern Swedish accent and voluptuous shape, she looked and sounded like a blond, Sophia Lauren. What can I say? It was the best haircut I ever had. Heck, it was one of the most enjoyable times I'd spent in Sweden so far.

After Lu Lu went back to the States, we continued to meet with Lise-Marie, teaching her the discussions—alone, in her apartment, without a chaperon, in breach of mission rules.

How to get off this subject with Thorsson?

"We're working our way through the discussions," I said.

"Good, good," the President responded, "So, Elder Miller, is there anything else we need to discuss."

Here was my chance to speak up.

"Well, actually, there is."

I could tell Thorsson was annoyed. Obviously, he was ready to turn me loose so he could bring in the next missionary to interrogate. After all, this fishing expedition landed nothing.

"What is it?" he asked, his tone suggesting that whatever I was about to say better be important.

"President Thorsson," I said, beginning the speech I'd carefully crafted and rehearsed, "it's about Elder Wiggins …"

"Yes, I'll be meeting him shortly. What is it?"

"I'm really concerned about him."

"Hmm," he nodded, leaning back in the chair, and resting his chin on the upturned palm of his left hand, "He's not been feeling well?"

"Yeah, yes, he's sick, really sick. He …"

"I know," he said, talking over me, "The ZL's have been keeping me informed."

Wiggins was doomed for certain if he had to depend on those two idiots to look out for him. Larson was nice enough, but oblivious. Lee, the midget wrestler, was a first rate prick in the mold of Elder Pyle, the pickle-juice pusher. Neither of them had shown a lick of interest in Wiggins' health.

Got to stay on track. This is no time to let my feelings about the ZL's distract me. Returning to what I'd planned to say, "The first day I met him, on the way home from the bus station …"

"Have faith Elder Miller," talking over me once more, "The Lord will not allow Elder Wiggins to suffer beyond what he can endure."

"President Thorsson," I responded, my tempo picking up, "He's getting worse. He's lost weight. The food he eats goes right through him. He's worn out all the time." At this point, I started feeling good. I wasn't letting him stop me. I was staying on message. No way can he ignore what I'm saying.

"Have you given your companion a blessing, Elder Miller?" he inquired, leaning forward and lifting his eyebrows.

A blessing? Anoint Mike's head with the oil? Lay my hands on him? Pray for his recovery? Hmm. Thorsson had me. I hadn't. It had crossed my mind, for sure. But that's it. Why? Because I thought he needed to see a frigging doctor!

"No, I haven't," I answered, not seeing any way around his question.

Thorsson stared long and hard at me. "What does this say about you Elder Miller?" his tone disapproving, "That you have the priesthood authority to heal the sick and haven't used it?"

Wait a minute! Somehow I'd not only lost control of the conversation, but also become responsible for Wiggins being sick!

Although taken aback, I stuck to my guns, "President Thorsson, Elder Wiggins cannot do the work. He's sick. He needs to see a doctor and maybe go home."

"You are out of line" he snapped, then stood and came around the desk, "You are not entitled to revelation for this mission or Church. If and when the Lord deems it appropriate for Elder Wiggins' assignment to change, I'll let you know."

I bit my lip, considering what to do next. Thorsson beat me to the punch. "You may go," he said, opening the door. And that was that, the whole crummy exchange lasting less than ten minutes.

Walking back up the hallway, I was soon joined by the AP's. I felt stupid and humiliated. Why had I expected anything different?

As soon as I finished telling the story to Wiggins, he reached over and slugged me on the shoulder. "Thanks Scott, I really appreciate that."

"You're not mad?"

"What?" he said with a laugh, "Heck no." His voice breaking up the tiniest bit, "Uhh, no one has ever done anything like that for me here. But, you're gonna pay for it, you know."

I smiled, "Let's split."

"All right," he responded and stood. I carried my tray to the trash bins, dumping the wrappers and few remaining fries.

As we pushed our way through the revolving door, Wiggins came to an abrupt stop. "Oh no," he moaned, then turned and hurried back inside.

6

A NEW SUIT

∽

"One of the grand fundamental principles of Mormonism is to receive truth,
let it come from whence it may."

JOSEPH SMITH
1ST PROPHET, SEER, AND REVELATOR
CHURCH OF JESUS CHRIST OF LATTER DAY SAINTS

∽

I hesitated before knocking on the door. It wasn't fear, so much as anticipation I was feeling. I'd only recently told Wiggins about what happened the day I transferred to Lund from Huskvarna—meeting Stefan, the accident, and me sitting on my butt when he rushed out to help.

I'd wanted to go and visit him ever since. I felt like I needed to apologize, explain myself, something. I was also interested in finding out more about him, his ministry, why he did what he did. Stefan was different. His was not the Mormon way. He didn't wait to consult the rules or get permission from the President's office. He acted as his heart and conscience told him to.

Geez, I wonder if he'll let us in? Will he even talk to me after the way I acted?

I'd glued the business card he'd given me that day into my journal. Not surprisingly, his address was on a main drag, near the train station—perfect for keeping in touch with street kids, the "raggare."

"No 'Discussions,' and no bible bashing," I'd told Mike, "I just want to meet him again, talk, hang out a bit."

Chuckling, "I'll behave Scott, don't worry."

I took a deep breath, slowly exhaled, then knocked. I could hear footsteps coming toward the door.

"Äldste Miller!" Stefan exclaimed the moment he recognized me, "What a pleasant surprise!" Looking over at Wiggins, he smiled, adding, "Is this a professional visit?"

I laughed. We all shook hands.

Standing aside and motioning with his hand, "Stig på, stig på!" (Come in, come in).

We entered the apartment and, as is the custom, removed our shoes leaving them on the mat near the door.

"Ta av er," (Take off your coats) Stefan instructed, pointing to our suit jackets. Mission rules were clear: we were forbidden to remove our suit jackets in public. Sensing our discomfort, he retreated, "It's OK."

I looked over at Mike and thought, "What the heck?" then took off my jacket. Mike followed my lead.

"Are you hungry?" he asked, "I've just finished making a pot of mushroom soup."

"That sounds great," I replied, "It smells great."

He smiled, "I picked them myself last fall."

This came as no surprise to me. The Swedish people are devoted mushroom hunters—it's in their genes. When the time is right, whole families venture into the woods to fill their baskets. What they cannot eat, they freeze to insure a steady supply throughout the year. So great is the quantity and variety of wild mushrooms harvested, the country has become a major worldwide exporter.

When they're not hunting, eating, or shipping them abroad, you can find Swedes glued to the TV, watching documentaries about the fecund fungi. These shows describe the various species, the best time for finding and picking them, which ones are deadly and to be strictly avoided, and the annual fatalities—obviously people who missed the show.

We followed Stefan as he made his way down the hallway. African tribal art adorned the walls, mementos from the time he'd spent in the country. Where there wasn't a mask, spear, or shield of some kind or another, there were bookshelves, all packed tightly, several bowing under the weight. The décor extended into the bedrooms and a large room at the end of the hall. In it, a collection of carved wood figures, drums and other primitive musical instruments were on display. A dozen or more oversized pillows were spread about on the floor. Clearly, this room served as a meeting place.

Stefan's flat had to be the most unusual I'd ever been in—packed full of "stuff." Most Swedes take a simple, utilitarian, even Spartan approach to home décor. Light colors and clean lines, but most of all, no stuff. Not Stefan, there were bits and pieces of his life and interests everywhere. Nevertheless, all was neat as a pin.

"The pillows are pretty cool, eh?", continuing, "The kids like them."

"They come here?" I asked, making conversation, "To your apartment?"

"Sure," he said, "all the time. I never know when they'll show up."

I was envious. If only we were allowed to do this. Why do we work the way we do? Who thought it up? Clearly, a bunch of old guys more familiar with the Fuller Brush Company® than the "Summer of Love."

Adjacent to the large room was the kitchen. We sat down at a small table, next to a window overlooking a typical Swedish "trädgård" (small garden with trees). Stephen dished up the soup while I cut slices of bread from a newly-opened Skogaholms limpa (loaf of seedless rye bread).

The Swedes have a ritual for eating soup. Having been in the country for seven months, I knew what to do. In order not to touch the loaf with my fingers, I used my napkin to hold the bread while cutting a slice. There's always a tub of butter on the table, a wooden knife stuck in the center. After passing the loaf to Mike, I used the wood knife to spread a generous amount of butter onto my piece. Setting the slice on my plate, I picked up the "osthyvel" (cheese slicer). I'd already bought one of these little gems to take home with me at the end of my mission. They are found on almost every Nordic kitchen table. The slicer—invented by Norwegian Thor Bjørklund in 1925—works in much the same way as a carpenter's plane. Instead of being pushed, the blade is pulled across a block of cheese, lifting a perfect slice almost every time.

"Hope it tastes good," Stefan said, using a common Swedish expression equivalent to *bon appetit.*

We started eating. I looked over at Mike. He dipped his bread into the soup and, as is the custom, took a bite. "It's great."

"Mmm," I added, nodding.

"So guys, what do you think about the big change in your church?" Stefan casually asked, setting his spoon on the table and taking a bite of bread.

"What are you talking about?" I replied.

"You know," he said, chewing, "the Black thing."

"What *black thing*?" I asked, confused.

Stefan stopped, looked back and forth between the two of us, and continued, "Oh, you don't know, do you?"

"Know what?" I asked, at a loss.

"That ... just a few days ago, your Church ... it announced that Blacks could be priests."

"What?" I sputtered, confusion giving way to embarrassment.

"Sure," he said matter-of-factly, "It was in the newspaper ... I think I still have a copy."

As he went to retrieve it, Mike and I just looked at each other, him mouthing, "What?"

"Here it is," Stefan said, setting the paper between us.

Silently, we read the story—two full pages in the center of the paper—complete with pictures of the Prophet Spencer W. Kimball, the Twelve Apostles, and a copy of the actual announcement released by the Church.

June 8, 1978

To all general and local priesthood officers of The Church of Jesus Christ of Latter-day Saints throughout the world:

Dear Brethren:

As we have witnessed the expansion of the work of the Lord over the earth, we have been grateful that people of many nations have responded to the message of the restored gospel, and have joined the Church in ever-increasing numbers. This, in turn, has inspired us with a desire to extend to every worthy member of the Church all of the privileges and blessings which the gospel affords.

Aware of the promises made by the prophets and presidents of the

Church who have preceded us that at some time, in God's eternal plan, all of our brethren who are worthy may receive the priesthood, and witnessing the faithfulness of those from whom the priesthood has been withheld, we have pleaded long and earnestly in behalf of these, our faithful brethren, spending many hours in the Upper Room of the Temple supplicating the Lord for divine guidance.

He has heard our prayers, and by revelation has confirmed that the long-promised day has come when every faithful, worthy man in the Church may receive the holy priesthood, with power to exercise its divine authority, and enjoy with his loved ones every blessing that flows there from, including the blessings of the temple. Accordingly, all worthy male members of the Church may be ordained to the priesthood without regard for race or color. Priesthood leaders are instructed to follow the policy of carefully interviewing all candidates for ordination to either the Aaronic or the Melchizedek Priesthood to ensure that they meet the established standards for worthiness.

We declare with soberness that the Lord has now made known his will for the blessing of all his children throughout the earth who will hearken to the voice of his authorized servants, and prepare themselves to receive every blessing of the gospel.

Sincerely yours,
SPENCER W. KIMBAL
N. ELDON TANNER
MARION G. ROMNEY
The First Presidency

Reading it, I could feel my mood darken. I should have felt happy. This is what Mormonism was all about, *supposed* to be all about, continuing revelation. The scriptural canon of the LDS Church was open to change, revision, and addition. Prophecy did not stop with the Bible. God was still in contact with His people, making His will known through His chosen prophets. The Articles of Faith—a collection of thirteen fundamental doctrines composed by Joseph Smith—categorically assert, "We believe all that God has revealed, all that He does now reveal, and … that He will yet reveal many great and important things pertaining to the Kingdom of God." For all that, I wasn't happy. Not at all.

We read the article to the end. It was less than flattering. Left with no explanation for the Church's longstanding exclusion of Blacks in the first place, nor reason for God's abrupt change of heart, the "skvallertidning" (Tabloid newspaper) used the occasion to trot out every peculiarity of Mormonism they could find. Along with polygamy, gold plates, the exclusion of woman from the priesthood, our large families, magic underwear, and historical controversies of record, was a picture of two expressionless Mormon missionaries in their Al Capone hats—the caption reading, "Elders ecstatic over Church announcement."

A knock came at the door. Stefan motioned for us to stay seated. "Eat. Eat, while it's hot. I'll see who it is," as he trailed off down the hall.

"This is big," Mike said in a whisper, emphasizing *big*.

I groaned, thinking of the reactions we were in for when out and about. "Why," I asked, in a hushed tone, "are we reading about this in the newspaper? Why didn't somebody get a hold of us? Why didn't Thorsson let us know? He's gotta know."

At the door, I could hear Stefan. "Gunnar, tjenare! (Gunnar, how are you?). I couldn't hear the response, only Stefan.

"Come in."

"Are you hungry? I just made some soup."

"That's OK, come in anyway."

"Really, it's OK. It's just me and a couple of friends."

Mike and I rose from our seats when the two entered the kitchen. Although he tried to cover it, a look of surprise crossed the young man's face as soon as he saw us. I'm sure he wasn't expecting two Mormon missionaries.

"Hejsan," (hello; pronounced, hay-sawn) I said, extending my hand, "Miller heter jag" (My name is Miller).

"Hej," he grunted, his grip as limp as piece of boiled spaghetti. Although it would be tempting to conclude his weak handshake had something to do with meeting a couple of blue suits, I'd grown used to this. Unlike us Mormons, who used the strength of our handshake as a statement of faith, the Swedes were far less enthusiastic about this form of greeting. Most—especially teenagers—were content simply to wave and say, Hi."

The awkward process was repeated with Wiggins.

"Join us," Stefan invited in Swedish.

Looking at us, Gunnar responded, "Nah, I should go. I'll come back later. It won't take long."

"Vänta lite, Gunnar" (Wait a minute, Gunnar), Stefan said, then turning to us, "Ursäkta mig ett ögonblick, Jag kommer strax tillbacka" (Excuse me for a second, I'll be right back).

As Wiggins and I sat back down at the table, the two walked toward the large window in the main room, the one with all the pillows on the floor.

I could hear Gunnar's voice. "Why are you with those two cockroaches?" (Varför är dom där två kackerlackorna här?), his words full of contempt.

"How quickly you forget," Stefan replied warmly, but firmly.

"What are you talking about?"

"Gunnar … how often have I heard you and your friends say that people don't give you a chance …"

The young man said nothing.

"So quick to judge," Stefan added calmly, "Treat others as you want to be treated. We're all God's children …"

"Them? Bullshit! They're not like you Stefan. They don't help anybody. All they do is knock on doors, and bug people."

Good point, I thought. *Gunnar certainly has our number.*

"Yes, them too," Stefan continued, "Think what it must be like to be them. They're young. Like you, they're pushed around. They are told to come to this country, made to wear those suits, knock on doors, stop people on the streets, all the time facing rejection and ridicule."

Wow, damn straight. Where's Stefan been all my life, or at least as long as I'd been in Sweden? In his few words, I felt so understood—and he wasn't even a frigging Mormon!

"Yeah, they're different from us and their ways are different from ours, but 'inasmuch as ye have done it unto one of these the least of these.'"

And then, I couldn't hear another word, not even whispers. No matter, I could finish the passage from the *Book of Matthew* in my head, "inasmuch as ye have done it unto one of these the least of these my brethren, ye have done it unto me." *It's the Golden Rule.*

I finished my bowl of soup while Mike watched. He was being careful about what he ate, not wanting to get sick. He knew how much I had been looking forward to meeting with Stefan.

We hadn't been sitting there too long when Stefan and Gunnar returned.

"It was nice meeting you both," (Det var kul att träffa er) Gunnar said politely. To my surprise, he then offered his hand to shake. There was definitely feeling behind it this time. "See you, hope we meet again" (Vi ses, hoppas att vi träffas igen) he added, using the time honored Swedish good-bye.

I stood, stammering "Yes, uh, er … thank you, I hope to, uh, see you again, too." I could swear Gunnar smiled at me.

As the two walked to the door, I thought about what just happened. I was impressed. Stefan was a remarkable guy. He really connected with people.

"He's a great kid," Stefan said when he returned. "Är ni mätta?" (Are you satisfied?") pointing at my empty bowl. It's another common Swedish expression meaning, "Would you like more?"

"Tack, nej. Det var så gott!" (No thank you. It was so good) I replied.

Sitting down at the table, Stefan told us about Gunnar. "He's had a tough life," he started, "been on the street for years, became a father at 15, got into drugs, been in and out of rehab. The first time I met him was at the train station in Malmö. He was panhandling, bumming cigarettes, drunk out of his mind. Somebody had worked him over pretty good. He looked like he hadn't eaten in days or bathed in a month."

Stefan related how he went by several days in a row, putting money in Gunnar's hat, and talking with him briefly each time. Eventually, Gunnar agreed to make the move to Lund, twenty short kilometers from Malmö. Stefan helped him find a place to live, apply for the generous public benefits available to all Swedish citizens, and later get a job in a bakery. It wasn't all smooth sailing. There'd been setbacks. His shitty childhood left him scarred. Every so often, his past would come back and get the best of him. Still, compared to where he had been, he was light years ahead. In the last few months, he'd even managed to re-connect with his son and get back on friendly terms with the mother.

Once Stefan finished telling us about Gunnar, he got up, put the dishes in the sink, and suggested we go into the living room.

"It's more comfortable in there."

After entering, we rearranged the pillows and sat on the floor.

"Man," I said, "you've got a lot of stuff from Africa."

Stefan explained, "It's tribal art." Simple figures, lots of faces, boobs and erect penises. A couple of them were downright scary looking. One sitting on a table was about two feet high. Three figures stacked on top of each other with huge eyes and grotesque mouths.

"What's that?" I asked.

"Hmm, a representation of the spirit world by the Makonde tribe."

I looked at the object again, "I don't think it's a place I'd want to go."

Mike and Stefan laughed.

"It was a gift ... um, from a family I got to know in Tanzania," he said, pausing briefly before saying, "I love that piece. Looking at it, reminds me of them."

"How long were you there?" Mike asked.

"Oh, uh, about three years," he replied.

"Wow," Mike said, "That's a year longer than us. What'd'ya do there?"

Stefan closed his eyes. It was as though he left the room. Before a minute had passed, his eyes opened. His demeanor was completely different. Serious, real serious. He began talking. A little I'd heard before, when we rode together on the bus. Still, his tale was gripping. Famine. Starvation. Malnourished children, their stomachs bloated. Families ravaged by diseases that, in the Western world, would easily be prevented or cured. People mutilated and dying, ripped apart by both ancient and modern weapons. And in too many places, tribal hatreds, mistrust, and a total absence of human compassion. The suffering he described was unlike anything I could imagine. I'm sure the same was true for Mike.

His voice strained, "We fed and cared for as many as we could ... providing shelter, medicine, setting up camps ... getting people out of 'hot zones' ..."

Then Stefan stopped talking. That was it. He was done. I'd seen this before, whenever I spoke with my Dad about his time in Okinawa as a Navy Corpsman. He'd only say so much and then clam up. No amount of questioning or coaxing could get him to continue.

After that, we sat there, no one saying a word.

Stefan was the first to break the silence. "You want to keep that?" pointing to the newspaper Mike had carried with him from the kitchen.

"Yeah ..."

"I would," I added.

"Pretty important announcement for your Church," Stefan observed, "how do you guys feel about it?"

"Uh, I'm a bit stunned," I replied, Mike nodding in agreement.

"I wish someone had told us," I said sarcastically. Shaking my head from side to side, "And the rest of it ... it's always the same stuff. We sound so weird."

"All churches are weird," Stefan came back, his voice reassuring, "believe weird things, do things, or will do things later, they'll have to live down."

"Well I dunno, I feel kind of happy about this announcement," Mike started, "it proves God is with us, revealing His will to our Prophet ...".

Stefan and I looked at him.

Don't go there, Mike, I thought, shooting him a glance. Unfortunately, he was already pulling out his scriptures, readying for the chase.

"... and the thing of it is, God has always used skin color to separate the righteous from the unrighteous. It's right here." Opening his quad, he turned to the *Book of Moses*, a part of Joseph Smith's "inspired" version of the Bible.

Included is a prologue to the story of the creation and fall of man, plus a revision of the first six chapters of Genesis. Also found are several chapters about an enigmatic Old Testament prophet, named Enoch. While barely mentioned in the version of the Bible known and accepted by most throughout the world, Enoch becomes a major player in Smith's revision, foretelling the restoration of God's true church—the Mormon Church, of course—in the latter days. But, that's not all. These passages also link skin color with sinfulness, a source often cited by LDS members and leaders when justifying the Church's policy regarding people of African origin.

"For behold, the Lord shall curse the land with much heat, and the barrenness thereof shall go forth forever; and there was *a blackness* came upon all the children of Canaan, that they were despised among all people."

I grimaced. *Mike look at me! Hit the off switch. Please. Please.*

"In several places, the scriptures tell us," he continued, "God cursed His people for their wickedness with a *dark* skin." Now, turning to the *Book of Mormon*, "In Alma, Chapter 3, Verses 6 through 9, we are told, 'And the skins of the Lamanites ...'—those are American Indians by the way—'were dark ... which was a curse upon them because of their transgression."'

Mike quickly turned to another section in the *Book of Mormon,* "In second Nephi, Chapter 5, Verse 21, it states, 'because of their iniquity ... the Lord God did cause a skin of *blackness* to come upon them' ..."

At that, I covered my face with my hands. I didn't want to look at him. Yet, through a crack in my fingers, I could see the well-worn and meticulously cross-referenced pages of his scriptures flying, one section to another.

I opened my fingers a bit more. Did he really believe what he was saying or was this just some kind of intellectual exercise, another scripture chase? I wasn't sure. In a way, his approach reminded me of a lawyer, fully aware his client was guilty, but making his best case for the defense.

Stefan was right. As he'd just said, churches believe all kinds of weird stuff. *Who cares what the scriptures say anyway?* God cursing people with a black skin. *It's stupid. Dumb, dumb, dumb.* First Jonah and the Whale, now skin color. Why not slanted eyes, too much body hair? Hell, a Roman nose? *I can't believe this is something God would do. I won't.*

I was just beginning to fantasize about smothering Mike with one of the floor pillows when Stefan gently interrupted, "I'm not really interested in this."

Mike immediately stopped and looked up, his mouth still open. It was like a moment out of TV's most successful courtroom, lawyer show, *Perry Mason,* the judge ruling the defense's arguments, "incompetent, irrelevant, and immaterial."

A long silence followed.

"I know some people find debating these writings, their scriptures, and holy texts exciting, of great importance. But, you know ... I'm just not interested in that, I've never ... I've never found much meaning or joy in it ... I just go about my life, trying to live according to what I believe Christ would do if He were here right now ..."

Of course, I thought, *faith without works is dead.* Together with his earlier comments to Gunnar, Stefan's words made perfect sense. They explained what happened on our way to Lund, when he left the bus to help the accident victims, his kindness toward Gunnar, his work with the raggare. *I get it.* Stefan didn't talk about what he believed. He didn't preach it. He did it.

I found myself reliving a moment that took place the year before my mission. I'm not sure what it was, something about Stefan and what he'd said—his outlook, point of view, his personal "prime directive"—sent me back. I was driving home to California from Brigham Young over the Christmas break. It's a twelve-hour, 900-plus mile drive. Anxious about my traveling alone, Mom and Dad had encouraged me to find someone to take the trip with me, pitch in with the driving and split gas costs. I said I would. I didn't.

About four hours into the journey—just outside of Cedar City, Utah—it started to snow, really snow. Soon, it was a "white-out." I couldn't see a damn thing. As I inched along, following the tail lights of the vehicle ahead, I could feel my car pulling to the right. Within minutes, I was fighting the wheel, trying to stay on the road. Despite my best efforts, I ended up stuck in a drift on the shoulder.

Trucks and other cars rumbled by oblivious to the conditions. Carefully, I got out, looking both ways to make sure I wasn't in some trucker's crosshairs. Walking around the car, I could see the problem. My right front tire was flat. I couldn't believe it. I did have a spare—one of those mini tires about the size of a glazed donut. In this weather, I knew it wouldn't be of much use. Even if I somehow managed to change the tire, my car was still hopelessly stuck.

I ended up walking to a gas station. It took me nearly an hour. By the time I arrived, I was covered in slop and near frozen. I felt relieved; that is, until I saw the place was closed! With the storm in full force, I didn't want to walk back to my car. Not only was it one more hour of freezing my ass off, but also I worried a semi or snow plow would get me this time. *Heck with that.* Lucky for me, there was a phone booth on the lot.

Thumbing through a tattered Yellow Pages®, I found the listing for the Church of Jesus Christ of Latter Day Saints and dialed the number. A couple of rings and the Bishop of the local ward—a person I didn't know from Joseph Smith—answered. Before I knew it, he'd picked me up and took me to his home.

There, I was treated like family. It was great. I could have been their son. The Bishop's wife fixed me something to eat. She also cleaned and dried my clothes. Together with their kids, we sat around the dining room table, playing board games and talking, until it was time to go to bed. In the morning, the Bishop drove me back to the gas station. The owner, also a Mormon, had already been out, found my car, towed it to the station, and fixed the tire!

That's what being a Mormon was like—at least before I'd gone on a mission. We were a family, brothers and sisters all. No matter the circumstance, we had each other's back. Flat tire? No problem. House flooding? The men of the Church will be right there. Hungry? The sisters already have a casserole in the oven.

The fact that we all looked out for each other, I'm sure had something to do with our history. We'd been chased by mobs from New York to Salt Lake, condemned to death in an "extermination order" issued by the governor of Missouri, Lilburn Boggs, in 1838, deprived of our prophet after he was gunned down in his cell (supposedly while in "protective custody"), and invaded by the US Army after trekking with our handcarts across the Great Plains to Utah. On and on, the tales of persecution went, ingrained in all of us. It was part of our identity. Gosh, Boggs' Executive Order 44 wasn't rescinded until 1976, the year I graduated from high school!

As Stefan's words had caused me to leave the room, Mike's now brought me back. Opening his scriptures to the *Book of Matthew*, he began "But what shall it profit a man, if he shall gain the whole world, and lose his own soul?"

Obviously, while touring "Memoryland," I'd missed part of the conversation. It didn't matter. I knew where Mike was going. He was on point, on message, *the message*, the one that counted. As missionaries, we were representatives of the Church of Jesus Christ of Latter Day Saints—trustees of the new covenant, the restored church, God's Church, *the one and only* true church on Earth.

With nothing less than our own salvation on the line, our charge: go into the world, teach the Gospel, convert the gentiles, and make a way for people to return to their Heavenly Father. And the present? Screw it! Who cares about having food in your belly, clothes on your back, or a roof over your head? Eternity—that's what we were about. Yeah, that's our credo. Take care of that first—accept the gospel, join the Church—and everything else will fall into place. And hey, if it doesn't, *then* we'll help you out.

"Don't get me wrong, Mike," Stefan responded softly, "I spend every morning in meditation, in intercession, praying for peace and the welfare of others, in this life and the next. About which church is right, or whose theology is correct? I don't know and, to tell the truth Michael, I don't … I don't care. For me, that's sacred ground, a private matter between man and Maker."

I felt the urge to speak up, say something. Mike and Stefan were on such different planets. Before I could sort my thoughts, Stefan continued, "Every day, I work at understanding my relationship with God. And I've found I feel closest when I'm doing for others, guided by His example, what He did when He was here, when He walked among us. The other stuff, well ... as I said ... I'm just not interested ..."

Mike locked eyes with Stefan. Slowly, he closed his scriptures. This was a first. The chase was over. There was no place for my companion to go. Stefan would not debate. For him, there was nothing to debate. His position? Ask yourself, "What would Christ do?" And if you believe anything written about Him, He treated everyone the same. It didn't matter if they were privileged or poor, healthy or sick, holy or whore, Jew or Gentile. It was all very simple. Love others. Don't discriminate. All are worthy of your time and attention. When you got right down to it, in Christ's club, everyone was already a member.

It was my mouth's turn to hang open. In that moment, my memory of Cedar City took on a new and different meaning. Sure, I'd been treated well. Aside from my experience with Thorsson and his imitators, the Mormons were nice, kind, loving, and thoughtful people. In fact, charity is the currency the Mormon Church runs on. There is no paid ministry. Top to bottom, it's a volunteer effort.

Ask any member, "Are you concerned about people in need?" The resounding answer is, "Yes." It's a central tenet of the faith. Not only that, they'll be able to provide proof of their compassion. Several times a year, most volunteer on Church welfare farms, picking fruit, canning vegetables, and cleaning barn stalls. My family did. Once a month, we fasted and then donated the monies saved to charity. As a young boy, I went from door to Mormon door collecting such offerings. All faithful Mormons pay tithing—10% of their pre-tax income—funds that are used, in part, to help the needy.

For all that good stuff, I now wondered if I would have been treated the same way in Cedar City were I not Mormon? I wasn't so sure. One thing was certain. If I weren't LDS, I wouldn't have called the church office in the first place. Why was that? Well, despite the wonderful way we treat each other, the common perception is that Mormons aren't particularly welcoming of people outside the Church. Polite? You bet. Friendly? Absolutely.

Welcoming? Not really. As much as we try to hide it, we can't get past the fact you're not Mormon.

As Mike and I walked back to our apartment from Stefan's, I railed, "What a bunch of hypocrites!"

The streets were dark. We'd stayed longer and later than we'd planned, well beyond our 9:30 p.m. curfew. Empty buses passed by, the engines belching out the usual smelly exhaust. I myself had a full head of steam.

"While our church—*the one and only true church on Earth,*" my sarcasm echoing off the prefab concrete walls of nearby buildings, "while our leaders were carrying on the grand old tradition of screwing blacks, Stefan was in Africa, in a fucking war zone, actually helping people … bringing them food, digging wells, protecting them …"

"It does say in the *Bible* and *Book of Mormon,*" Mike started, feebly, "that skin color …"

"Do you honestly believe that crap?" interrupting, "The guys who wrote that lived in caves. Sure, you can make a scriptural case for it all night long. Mike, you can make a scriptural case for anything. The Earth is flat. It was created in 6 days. We're the center of the universe. We hung out with dinosaurs. You believe that too? Come on."

"Yeah, well …" he said with a sigh.

"And why the change of heart now? Seems like our government had more moral sense than the Church. What? How long's it been? Fourteen, fifteen years ago, they got their shit together and passed the Civil Rights Act. Us? Huh!"

Mike merely nodded.

"I'm embarrassed. No, ashamed. We should apologize. Justice. There's no justice. And charity? What are we really doing to help people? Anything? Name one?"

"Uh, well, you know," Mike began, stumbling over his words, "We offer … the … the *most* important thing … the possibility of eternal life."

"That's a cop out, Mike—the biggest hypocrisy of them all. Here we are, people in need all around us, and we do nothing. Nothing. We make ourselves different, so different. Our beliefs, our dress, what we do. We wall ourselves off in Salt Lake City and Utah, live white, cushy lives, telling people, 'Come to Zion.' We are God's chosen. We—no one else—have the ticket to eternal salvation. Meanwhile! Meanwhile, families are starving, children dying, people gunned down in the streets. Whole generations wiped out. And the hate. Mike, the hate. Would Christ act like this, us? Would He do what we do? Put on a blue suit, ride a stupid-ass bike handing out pamphlets, pound on doors, use the Bible to justify racism? I'll tell you what he would do! He'd be there. Helping. Healing. Doing the fucking work we should have been doing all along ..."

I paused, catching my breath. Sighing, "I'm done Mike ... I'm done!"

"What do you mean? Are you quitting?" Mike asked, anxiously.

"No. No, that's not it. I'm not leaving, wouldn't do that to my family. But I am going to be more ... more ..." I stopped. *More what?* Then it came to me. More of what I'd promised I'd be, what I decided I'd be on the bus when traveling from Huskvarna to Lund. The stuff I wrote about in my journal. With a confidence and determination that surprised me, "I'm going to be more like Stefan. I'm not sure how ..., but I am."

For the next five minutes or so, Mike and I walked together in silence. I started feeling bad. *Maybe I went too far.* I didn't want to unload on Mike. I liked him. *Heaven knows he has enough troubles of his own without me ripping him a new one.*

With only a couple blocks to go, I was just about to apologize when Mike said, "You know Scott, you are ... you are like Stefan."

"What?"

"You're a great companion, man. You've treated me decent the whole time, better than anyone else so far in the mission ... you spoke up for me, to Thorsson ... that took balls ..., my other companions, they never did anything like that ... they mostly griped about me being sick, our numbers being off ... catching heck from the President and Zone Leaders."

I hesitated. "Thanks for that Mike. I, I guess ... uh, I don't think ... compared to Stefan at least, I don't see myself that way ... don't get me wrong, not that I'm glad you're sick or anything, but I haven't missed the tracting one tiny bit ... and besides that, a few blocks back I dumped on you. I'm, I'm sorry."

Mike responded instantly, "You're doing it again. You're being honest. You apologized. Showing you give a damn *about me* ... around here that's a rare thing. You know that." Now, more serious, "You asked, 'Do I really believe this?' Yeah, well, *I want to.* Like it says in the *Articles of Faith*, 'I hope for all things.' But there's a lot I don't get. You know I love science, and when

the *Doctrine and Covenants* says things like the Earth is only 6000 years old
... 6000 years old? Well ..." he laughed.

"It's just like Stefan said," I replied, and then pointing at Mike's brief case,
"the answers aren't in those scriptures."

"Well, that's not exactly what he said."

"No?"

"No, he said he didn't get much joy from it ... debating and all." With
that, he stopped, thought, "But I do!"

"But racism Mike? Why would you want to debate that? Would you do
the same thing with a geologist who said the Earth is way older than 6000
years?"

Mike came back at me, "Oh you mean more like 4.5 billion years?" smiling. He didn't stop there, "I could debate ... and I would ... if I felt it was
just another attack on Mormons, for being Mormon."

"It's *that* we've gotta stop."

"What? Debating? Defending ourselves?"

"No, being *Mormon*."

As soon as we arrived at the apartment, Mike took his well worn path to
the bathroom. I gathered up the mail and "reklam"—the Swedish word for
the mountain of advertisements pushed through the mail slot each day—
and sat down on my cot. There were a couple of letters for Mike, and a large
envelope addressed to me. It was from Cary Wells. True to his word, he'd
written me. I couldn't wait to open it. Ever since the zone conference in
Malmö, I'd wondered what had happened to him. The return address left no
doubt. He'd gone home.

Tearing the top off, I found a letter, thick stack of papers—most of which
looked like photocopies—and an audio cassette. I went straight to the letter:

Dew!

How are you? I'm home. I guess you probably figured as much.
It's great. I am SO glad to be here instead of there. It's like being
released from prison.

My parents have been cool. It was really hard for them at first,
especially Mom. She cried a lot, didn't leave me alone for a minute.

Thorsson didn't make it easy for them. THE PRICK! You can guess what he did. Pressured them to talk me into staying, telling them I'd be a failure the rest of my life if I quit. He made <u>me</u> pay for the ticket home. No surprise there!

Right now, I'm mostly hanging out. I've got a job for the summer. I'm stocking shelves on the graveyard shift at our grocery store. It ain't much. BUT IT'S BETTER THAN BEING A MORMON MISSIONARY. Ha! Ha!

Got my fingers crossed about getting into Yale in the fall. It's pretty late though at this point. Dad is doing his best to help me get in. He and I haven't talked a whole lot about my coming home. He's more focused on what I'm gonna do next. It's all right.

If I don't get in Yale, no problem. I'll go to UCONN, or maybe University of New Haven for a semester or two. Who knows? I'm <u>not</u> going back to Utah. I don't even want to fly over that state.

I'm done with Mormons and Mormonism. I haven't been to church since I've been back. My parents think it's because of everything that's happened. It's not that. I'm pretty much done with <u>all</u> religion.

Hey, have you read *The Source* by Mitchner? You'd love it. It's amazing how archeology shows what a superstitious crock religion is. Everybody wants to go to heaven, nobody wants to die!

Maybe by now you've had chance to read through the stuff I gave you in Malmö. I'm putting in a bunch more. Most of it is about archeology and the Book of Mormon. Surprise. Surprise. There is none! Wars. Cities. Whole civilizations supposedly living out the stories in that book—and not a lick of evidence ever found anywhere to support it. <u>No buildings</u>. <u>No writings</u>. <u>No artifacts.</u> <u>Period</u>. Good ole Joe made it all up.

I suppose by now you've heard about the BIG REVELATION. Our

exalted leaders spoke to God and blacks are IN! Hallelujah!

Have you heard from Popeye? I sent him a letter too. Wonder how he is doing?

Gotta go. I'll write back as soon as I hear from you. <u>Promise!</u> I've got tickets to see the Ramones next week in New York. You heard of them? Fantastic punk band. Disco's dead. Yeah! I know you're not keeping up with music. Here's a tape of some I like. Tell me what you think.

Hang tight,
Cary

Setting the letter down, I didn't know quite what to feel. I was certainly envious. Cary was getting on with his life, doing the things I loved to do, wanted to do. I also felt sad. I was going to miss him. Plus, I didn't know when or if I would see him again. Mostly, as always, I'd admired Cary. He followed his own path, didn't take any crap from anyone.

When Mike finally came out of the bathroom, I was thumbing through the pile of papers Cary sent. He had a towel wrapped around his waist. Not saying a word, he slowly laid down across his bed, and stared at the ceiling.

I knew something was up. After a moment or two, I asked, "You ok?"

"I think I'm getting worse," he answered. *Gosh,* I thought, *he sounds really beat up.*

"I didn't really even eat anything tonight and I'm crapping my brains out … and the cramps … ugh."

I'd heard him complain about the diarrhea many, many times. This time, something was different. *His face. His color off. He's so pale. And the way he's talking. He's scared.*

"I wonder," he started again, "am I being punished?"

"Punished? For what? What are you talking about?"

"Despair cometh because of iniquity", he replied, citing a well known verse from the *Book of Mormon.*

"What? What iniquity?" wondering what on earth he could be talking about.

"It must be that, that's why I'm sick" he answered, "Our numbers are bad … mine have always been bad … and um, I have doubts … I do."

"You mean like, are you saying, you think God's punishing you?"

"What else could it be? I haven't done what I'm supposed to do, what I was sent here to do."

"Yes you have, Mike. You do everything you can … besides that, you're SICK … you've been sick from the start."

"If I'd done a better job … if I'd had more faith," he continued, "you know the Prophet Ether says, 'If men have faith in the Lord, then He will make weak things become strong.'"

He was quoting the *Book of Mormon* again, a Prophet named Ether who Latter Day Saints believe lived on the American continent around 600 B.C. The section that bears his name contains pages and pages of migrations, murders, and mayhem—a 1500 year time span.

Instantly, I thought of Cary's letter, his comments about archeology. The name "Ether" also reminded me of a quip Cary told me Mark Twain had once made about the *Book of Mormon*. In his opinion, it was nothing less than "chloroform in print," going on to say the real miracle was that Joseph Smith managed to stay awake while writing it.

I wasn't going to get into a scripture chase with Mike. No debates. I simply commanded, "Don't go there Mike. You are one of the most righteous guys I know. You work harder, you're more dedicated, and you're smarter than anyone in this damn mission. You're just sick. That's it. It's not a punishment. It has nothing to do with God, or the Church, or anything else. Something is wrong with your body. That's all."

Mike stood, retrieving a clean set of G's from his makeshift clothesline. "Thanks Scott," acknowledging me with a nod.

I wasn't sure if he was agreeing with me or wanted me to shut up. "It's late," he said, "I think this is the latest I've been up since starting my mission."

I looked over at the clock. It was one in the morning. When I looked back, Mike was on his knees praying, by his bed.

Quietly, I gathered up the letter, tape, and papers and put them back into the envelope. Then, I slid between the sheets of my cot.

Poor guy. He doesn't deserve this.

When he finished, I reached over and turned out the light.

I'm not praying tonight.

~

June 24th, "Midsommarafton." It was the summer solstice, midsummer's day, a national holiday in Sweden, second only in size and scope to Christmas. Two weeks had passed since meeting with Stefan.

Wiggins and I were heading out to take it all in, the festivities. There would be food, dancing, displays of Swedish crafts and traditional clothing, in addition, the raising of the Majstången (May Pole).

I didn't know how long Mike would last. He'd been right. He was getting worse. For too many days, he was down for the count. With his pitiful haircut and gaunt appearance (the man was still losing weight), some days he looked like he could get a side job as a scarecrow.

We spent more and more of our time inside, practicing the language, poring over books borrowed from the library, delving into Swedish culture and history. He even helped me start a filing system for sorting my correspondence and growing number of articles and newspaper clippings. Surfer Scott was turning into scholar Scott.

When I wasn't feeling worried about his condition, I was frankly in awe of Mike. He just kept going, never complaining. "Do your best and then a little more," he would say. How could I argue with that? Had anyone else, particularly the ZL's, peppered me with such simple, homey-sounding advice, I would have told them to piss off. Wiggins had the right. He lived it.

Speaking of the ZL's, Lee and Larson, the Overlords of Lund, had not backed off in any way. "Points and Numbers" was all they ever talked about. So far, during our time together, Wiggins and I had never met our weekly quotas for tracting and "Golden Contacts." Even so, we managed to teach at least 40 discussions, the required minimum. That fact continued to bug the crap out of them. "Frick and Frack" couldn't figure out how we got invited in so often without knocking on doors and stopping people on the streets.

So, how had we pulled it off? I stumbled upon it quite by accident. In every missionary apartment, a mountain of old "Tracting Logs" was stored—pocket sized, spiral-bound notebooks in which Elders record the response they receive when proselytizing. One day, I started going through them. They dated back years. Right there were the addresses of people who'd opened their homes to our predecessors on at least one occasion. Instead of cold-calling, Wiggins and I simply reached out to those people, folks who'd been reported as friendly and welcoming in the past. Wiggins was pleased with my discovery. This was one of the few times the proverbial shoe was on the other foot. I had something to teach Mike. "Nothing succeeds like success," he remarked, "Let's not tell the ZL's our secret!"

Once we left the apartment, we headed up Kyrkogatan (Church street), past Stortorget (Central square) on the way to Stadsparken (City park) where the celebration was taking place. Mike set a brisk pace. At least for the moment, he was feeling all right.

At the corner of Kyrkogatan and Botuffsgatan, we passed by H&M, a men's clothing store, common in Sweden. A few days earlier, I'd been there. I bought a new suit, winter overcoat, and Russian-style fur hat called a mössa ("Mua-saw"). All of it was on sale and conformed to mission regs, although barely.

I used money I'd been saving ever since arriving in country. It had been my "escape fund." Calling it that, I now recognized, was a futile fantasy of a sad and lonely kid. At the rate I'd been going, I would have had to live in Sweden twenty years before accumulating enough money to travel in steerage on a freighter, much less purchase a transatlantic plane ticket. As pointless as the fund was, knowing it was there made me feel better.

Combining a few extra bucks from my parents with money raided from my fund, I decided to treat myself. I was going to change my profile, fit in with the locals. No more idiotic, "Oh look there goes a Mormon Missionary" hat and no more flimsily-lined, freeze-my-ass-off, London Fog® jacket. (Sorry, Mom and Dad).

As for the suit, I badly needed a replacement. Despite Fru Nilsson's repair job back in Huskvarna, with all the praying I'd done, I had nearly worn through the knees. An Italian-made, dark-blue, pin-striped job is what I bought, a definite contrast to the standard-issue, blue polyester from Sears and Roebuck. Mike and I then tore the legs, arms, and pockets off my old one and took pictures of me in it. I sent the photos home to my parents with a note saying I'd been in a terrible fight, but survived. "You should see the other guy," I wrote, then at the end of my letter, "Just kidding. Thanks for the money. I'll send a picture of me in my new suit next time."

We made it to Stadsparken as the Maypole was about to be raised. It resembled a huge Christian cross, about thirty-feet high with a short crossbeam near the top. Large rings hung from each end of the beam. The entire structure was festooned with flowers and ribbons, blue and yellow, celebrating the national colors of Sweden. Hundreds of longer, multicolored ribbons streamed down from the top of the pole, gathering in piles near the base. Nearby, scores of blue-eyed, blond-haired children of all ages stood, ready to grab a ribbon and dance, once the adults hoisted the pole up and secured it in the ground.

The kids were a sight, simply beautiful, as colorful as the ribbons and flowers on the pole. The girls wore lacy white dresses, each of their heads adorned with a garland of flowers. The boys were clad in an old-fashioned "helgdagsskjorta" (Sunday shirt), knee high pants, long stockings, and "kyrkohatt" (Church hat). Wiggins and I perched ourselves on a large rock off to the side, and began taking pictures.

While enjoying the festivities, we remained on alert, keeping an eye out for local members of the Church and the ZL's. We had to. We were out of uniform, dressed in civilian clothes—a serious breach of missionary protocol. I wore a pair of white cords, yellow and pink stripped Ocean Pacific® shirt, and blue Adidas® running shoes. Wiggins chose dark brown cords, orange T-shirt, and loafers. If caught, though we may not have been excommunicated, we certainly risked being sent home. Ultimately, we decided it was a matter of respect. Show up in our blues, and *we* would be the show, the Mormons, intruding once more, making everyone uncomfortable.

In truth, we weren't too worried about the members. Though small in number, the local congregation was young and hip—so unlike the staid and stodgy crowd in Huskvarna and Jönköping. No formal, fancy LDS chapel here either. Services were held on the second floor of an old building, above a dry cleaner. The leader, whose official title was "branch president," was a single, thirty-something guy whose stylish dressing provided, in part, the inspiration for my recent purchase. Shortly after my arrival in Lund, he and a few other members came to our aid, helping us find and move to a new apartment after being kicked out of student housing. How the missionaries scored that location in the first place was a mystery to me. Turns out, they'd sublet the apartment from a student years earlier, the guy having long since graduated!

Adults milled about talking, laughing, drinking beer and "saft," the customary fruit flavored drink. Many were dressed in traditional Swedish folk costumes, folkdräkt ("dreck"). These outfits were striking, distinguished by bright colors and patterns, unique to the wearer's hometown.

Besides all the people, tables and booths—offering a variety of different foods—completed the scene. The usual pickled herring dishes, breads, and cheeses were present, in addition to "korv" (a mild sausage) and "små potatis" (new potatoes). Swedes love "små potatis," regard the little tubers as delicacies.

Screams of joy rose with the Maypole. The children rushed to pick up a ribbon as the adults helped organize them in concentric circles. When ready, a signal was given. A band waiting close at hand picked up their instruments. I thought it was a curious mix: violins, a guitar, tambourine, and accordion. The kids began to dance in step with the music, the innermost ring moving to the right, the next to the left, and so on. As the first song blended into the next, the kids dropped their ribbons, fell to the ground, and started leap-frogging over one another while they sang:

> Små grodorna, små grodorna är lustiga att se.
> (Small Frogs, small frogs are really fun to see)
> Små grodorna, små grodorna är lustiga att se.
> (Small Frogs, small frogs are really fun to see)
> Ej öron, ej öron, ej svansar hava de.
> (No ears, no ears, no tails have they)
> Ej öron, ej öron, ej svansar hava de.
> (No ears, no ears, no tails have they)

I was clapping in time with the music when, out of the corner of my eye, I noticed a woman heading in our direction. She was young, early twenties I guessed, and dressed in traditional folk costume. I thought nothing of it at first. As she continued toward us, however, I grew alarmed.

Who is that? Is she a member? I don't recognize her. What's going on? Are we sitting in a restricted area? Breaking some rule? Is she coming to ask us to dance?

"I thought you looked familiar," she said in English, her accent definitely American.

"Elin?" I said surprised, rising to offer my hand. Taking it, she smiled and pulled me toward her, gently kissing me on the cheek.

A surge of electricity went through me. I never thought I'd see her again.

Seven months had passed since we met at the train station in Borås. What a day that had been, my first in the country. There I was splayed out on the platform, hugging the asphalt. In my haste to make the connection to Huskvarna, I fell exiting the carriage. Elin helped me to my feet and brushed the dirt from my suit. Meeting her was the one nice thing that happened to me that awful day.

She's more beautiful than I remember.

Her blond hair was braided and pinned in buns, Princess Leia style. On her head, she wore a red scarf accented with green and white embroidery. A classic Scandinavian knit sweater covered a billowy white blouse, the cuffs folded back at the wrist. A black and red, ankle-length wool skirt with matching purse completed her outfit.

"Where's your suit?" she asked, taking a step back to size me up. Her tone playful, "Did you quit the Church?!'"

"Quit? No," I said with a laugh, then turned and introduced Mike. "We decided *not* to wear our uniforms today."

"Spectators or participants?" Elin asked.

"What?" I responded, unsure what she meant.

Elin smiled, did a quick twirl, her long skirt swirling about her. Completing the turn, she stopped and studied both our faces, "Are you two going to dance or sit here like two toads on a rock?"

Dancing around the May Pole? That prospect had never occurred to us when Wiggins and I had been planning our adventure into the world of Gentiles.

"Well, uh, er ..." I sputtered.

"Don't be a 'don't be,' be a 'do be,'" she said, giving my cheek a playful pinch.

I recognized the line instantly. It was from the children's early morning T.V. show, *Romper Room*. I hadn't heard that expression in years.

When I looked over at Mike, he was already on his feet. "Let's go!" he said, needing no encouragement.

I wasn't so sure. Next thing I knew, Elin reached down, grabbed my hand, pulled and said, "Come on!"

The second she touched me, I wondered, *what are we doing? Is this how it ends? The next to the last step on the road to hell? First, no suits, then dancing, then ....*

She must have read my mind, "I'm safe," she said holding my hand firmly. Taking Mike's too, Elin led us to the May Pole, first walking then, at her insistence, skipping.

We danced and danced, and danced, and danced some more. First to the right, then to the left, hopping and jumping, laughing and singing. When the band finally took a break, I was spent. Mike was transformed. Just looking at him, how fired up he was, you'd never guess he was so sick.

"You boys hungry?" Elin asked.

"Yeah!" Mike yelled, "Let's get something to eat."

Off to the booths we went. Mike and I went for the korv and småpotatis. Elin chose another classic Swedish dish, "stekt strömming" (pan-fried Baltic herring) served on a bed of mashed potatoes together with "lingon sylt" (cowberry jam). Sitting crossed-legged on a blanket next to one of the many large Beech trees in the park, we ate. Mike devoured his; at one point his mouth so stuffed he looked like a chipmunk.

"Dis is gud" he mumbled, talking while he chewed, "we-ree gud." Or at least that's what I thought he said.

I looked around, taking in everything. It was a beautiful day. I felt positively normal. The sun was out. The temperature was perfect. The park was full of people, all having a great time. Clouds were building up in the northeast. *Hmm, maybe there'll be rain later. Who cares?!*

It was fun being with Mike and Elin. I liked them, liked them both. Mike was happy, carefree even. I'd never seen this side of him before. That strained look nearly always present in his face was gone. And Elin? She was something else, unlike any girl I'd met before. Top to bottom, front to back, inside and out, she was super attractive, so appealing. *What is it about her? She's so … grown up.* I could hear my mother saying, "she's mature for her age." But that wasn't it.

"Hejsan," a voice interrupted. I turned and looked up. Towering over us was a colossus, all decked out in Swedish costume, a beer in each hand.

"Hans!" Elin shouted. In one bound, she was up. In what looked like a well-practiced move, the giant dropped the beers, held out his arms, and caught her as she jumped. Holding him around the neck she kissed him on each cheek, laughing. He returned her kisses, his laughter, full, deep, uninhibited. He looked liked he could easily have accommodated all of us up there if he had a mind to do it.

Once their happy reunion was over, Elin returned to earth.

"Scott, Mike, this is Hans, 'min sambo.'"

Sambo. I knew that word well. It was made up—a slang expression used to describe a very common living situation in Sweden. Thorsson told us about this on my first day in the country. "Sam" meant together, "bo" meant live. Sambo meant live together. Before coming to Sweden, I never knew anyone that lived together. Mormons certainly didn't do it. Among non-Mormons, it was rare and frowned upon.

Hans and Elin live together. Ugh.

The couple joined us on the blanket. "Hejsan," Mike said cheerfully, unexpectedly following the greeting with, "Would you mind terribly if we don't kiss you, Hans?" We all laughed. The "party" did not last very long, however. Once the band resumed, Elin was up, pulling Hans to his feet, leading him to the May pole.

As they danced away, my mood soured. I watched them. *They're having fun, enjoying each other. Here I am. God's mighty messenger in Sweden. I'm the one supposed to be bringing the 'good news,' eternal happiness. But, they're ALREADY happy, feeling great, living together, in love, in bed, having the time of their lives. Me? Compared to them, miserable.*

I continued to brood. *We Mormons are always putting off happiness until later, like when we're dead. And what is it with us and sex anyway? Here, it's just part of life. People aren't hung up about it. They grow up with it. It's perfectly natural—or so it seems. They're just exploring, checking things out, trying life on for size.*

In Mormonism, there is nothing to explore, never any "trying things out." Sex outside of marriage is a capital offense, period. Not assault. Not manslaughter. Murder.

Growing up, I recall several instances of members being excommunicated for fooling around. One image is seared in my mind. *Was I eleven?* Anyway, in front of the entire congregation, the Bishop stood at the podium, struck a serious pose, and solemnly announced that Brother Stevens had been kicked out of the Church. I knew the man's daughter, Olivia. She was in my Sunday School class. And even though I was too young to understand the details at the time, I knew her father had done something really bad. We all knew it.

Later, when I was smack dab in the middle of puberty, all us Mormon kids got the "Rose Lecture." It was delivered at a special meeting for church youth, called a "Fireside." Such get-togethers were usually held on a Sunday evening, following a day's worth of other worship services. Most of the time, they were fun. The kids would all gather at a member's home or the local chapel. Usually a brief, inspirational talk was delivered by some visiting Mormon dignitary. Afterwards, punch and cookies were served and everyone—boys and girls—hung out and talked.

I don't recall the speaker's name, whether he was some Mormon celebrity or local LDS authority. I do remember what happened, vividly. As soon as he started, I could tell it was going to be another "morality" talk—something about his cadence and tone of voice. Plus, these lectures all followed the same formula, starting with "sex is sacred," and adding:

+ *Your body is a temple*
+ *Sex before marriage desecrates the temple*
+ *God and the Spirit cannot inhabit an impure temple*
+ *Temptation is everywhere*
+ *Young people who have sex regret it for the rest of their life*
+ *Forgiveness is possible, but very, Very, VERY difficult*

= *Don't do anything that might result in sex before marriage*

The instruction always ended with the prohibitions, including but not limited to, thinking or fantasizing, looking at pictures, talking with friends, reading books, watching TV programs or movies containing sexually charged content, holding hands, kissing, laying next to or on top of someone of the opposite sex, touching, necking, petting, and the old stand-by, masturbation.

If I had a nickel for every time I'd heard the "sex is sacred" speech, I could have paid for my mission two times over. This time, following a brief introduction, the speaker ditched the standard script and handed out roses to all of us instead.

"O, how much more doth beauty beauteous seem," he began, quoting I later learned, one of Shakespeare's sonnets, "By that sweet ornament which truth doth give." Looking out over the 15 or so youth in attendance, he encouraged us to gaze deeply into and appreciate the beauty of our rose.

He continued, "'The rose looks fair but fairer we it deem, for that sweet odor which doth in it live.' My young brothers and sisters," now speaking to us directly, "put your nose to the rose and breathe in." We all did as told. "Beautiful isn't it? One of the many wondrous and perfect creations God has placed here on Earth for us to enjoy."

He paused, taking time to gaze into our eyes. I looked up from my rose, uncertain where he was going.

"The canker-blooms have full as deep a dye, as the perfumed tincture of the roses", he started in again, requesting that we each touch our rose, encouraging us "to feel and rub the petals."

A few moments passed while we all gave them the once over.

"Smell your fingers," he next asked, "Lovely isn't it? That God would place us in such close proximity to something so exquisite ... we are truly blessed."

I was thinking he was about to connect premarital sex to being pricked by rose thorns, when he surprised me by asking us to pass our rose to the person seated to our left. Back to the sonnet he went, starting at the beginning, "O, how much more doth beauty beauteous seem, by that sweet ornament which truth doth give," and ending with us passing the rose once again. The pattern was repeated until each of us ended up with our original rose.

"Consider your rose," he said. I'd already noticed that mine, like everybody else's I could see, was bruised and wilted, the stem slightly bent.

"Your rose," he continued, "is like your virtue. When you are born, your body, your temple is perfect and clean. As you enter adolescence, you flower, becoming attractive to those around you."

Once again, he paused, making sure he had everyone's attention. When he next spoke, his voice was thunderous, Wizard of Oz like, "Allow yourself to be touched, caressed, passed around, and YOU END UP UNCLEAN, DIRTY, AND ATTRACTIVE TO NO ONE, INCLUDING GOD."

There are two things I remember about this moment. First, spontaneously muttering, "Oh my," to no one in particular. Second, Mary Beth Wilkins standing up and abruptly running out of the room. So much for her rose, I guessed.

Of course, we weren't the only religion that had a hard on against sex. A friend from school, Steve Smith, was Baptist. I don't know if he got something like the "Rose Lecture," but the message he grew up with was the same, sex is bad. Another friend, Robert Newton was a Seventh Day Adventist. He couldn't dance and the girls weren't allowed to wear make-up. In one of my religion classes at BYU, I learned about a group known as the Shakers. They sprang up at the same time the LDS Faith was founded. For them, there was no sex, ever. Not surprisingly, they're no longer with us.

Whether advocating abstinence or free love, it was clear to me that adults were obsessed with sex. Either they were trying to get some for themselves or working like mad to keep me and others my age from getting any.

What did the Prophet Joseph Smith do the minute he had the chance? Shortly after organizing the Church, he secretly began practicing polygamy. He didn't even tell his wife. His first wife! Some of the materials Cary Wells sent me showed that Smith married other men's wives while the men were away serving missions—missions for the Church ordered by none other than Smith himself! Cary's stuff also made clear that the practice did not start, as I'd been taught, as a way of looking after "older, unmarried women." Of Smith's thirty to forty known marriages, many were to teenagers, the largest number falling between the ages of fourteen and twenty. And his were just the beginning. The practice continued following his murder, when the Saints moved to Salt Lake. Even after the Church officially abandoned the practice in 1890, members of the hierarchy took multiple partners in secret.

For Heaven's sakes, why does sex have to be so complicated?

For Elin and Hans, it was part of life. It was as natural as getting up in the morning, sleeping late, going to work, hanging with friends, enjoying a meal, you name it. In contrast, all of my experiences rang the ever-loving life out of it. Somehow the "joy" of sex became the "job" of sex. And, my job for now? Avoid it at all costs. After marriage? Multiply and replenish the Earth.

Is that all there is? It can't be.

Before I could come up with another cheery thought, a low roll of thunder in the distance announced a coming storm. *The party's over.*

As the drops started falling, the dancing slowed down. When it started to pour, everybody ran.

Elin and Hans rushed over, picked up the blanket we'd all been sitting on and covered their heads.

"Nu måste vi sticka" (We've got to split) Elin said. It was the first time she'd ever spoken to me in Swedish. Grabbing my arms, she pulled me toward her, giving me a quick kiss on the cheek.

"Hej då, Scott!" (Good bye Scott), she whispered in my ear, then turned and rushed off with Hans.

"Bye," I said, although I'm sure she didn't hear me.

I never saw her again.

7

SECRETS

∾

"I think a full, free talk is frequently of great use; we want nothing
secret nor underhanded, and I for one want no association with things
that cannot be talked about and will not bear investigation."

JOHN TAYLOR
3RD PROPHET, SEER, AND REVELATOR
CHURCH OF JESUS CHRIST OF LATTER-DAY SAINTS

∾

The Fart. That's what Elder Fissen's last name actually meant when
translated directly into Swedish: the fart. Didn't somebody in Salt
Lake know this when they were making mission assignments? I
don't know how he did it. Getting up each morning at 6 a.m., putting on
his blue suit, donning his gangster hat, going out and knocking on doors,
then boldly announcing, "Hello, I'm Elder Fart. May I come in? I have a very
important message."

Short, and weighing all of 97 pounds, Elder Fissen instantly reminded
me of a kid I knew in junior high: Ned Knipple. What parents would name
their kid Ned if their last name was Knipple? More than that, what parents
wouldn't immediately change their name to Smith or Jones, anything to
spare him the pain and suffering he was in for the first day he showed up at

school? Ned had a bulls-eye painted on his back from the day he was born.

In the locker room, the jocks were always reminding him of just what an unfortunate shit he was. It wasn't his nipples Ned had to worry about, it was getting to third period with his balls intact. The Neanderthals were merciless, forever chasing him around and snapping him with their rolled up towels. And, what about the coaches? Useless, absolutely useless. Whether taking some secret sadistic delight in Ned's torment or hoping that natural selection would eliminate the weak member of the herd, they did nothing to help the boy.

I still cringe whenever I think of Ned. I never did anything to help him. In fact, I'm ashamed to say that I, and the rest of the puny, hairless seventh graders, benefited from his daily run of the gauntlet. He was our ritual sacrifice, sent to appease the gods—the athletes, the pride of Carl Sandburg Junior High.

We'd shadow him as he left the showers, following not too far behind, waiting for him to spring the ambush. As soon as the attack came, we all made a mad dash for our lockers, never looking back, heedless of Ned's screams and the ripping report of snapping towels. Poor Knipple.

My relationship with Fissen started with a phone call from President Thorsson. "Elder Miller," he said, "I have a *special* assignment for you." Then, he swore me to secrecy, insisting, for the good of the mission, what was about to be said remain between us.

By this time, I'd been without a companion for several weeks. I was staying and working with Frick and Frack, the zone Leaders, Lee and Larson, doing the typical missionary stuff: stopping people on the streets, tracting, doing our best to get into their homes. Earlier, Mike was sent home. His body just gave out. When one night he told me he was passing a lot blood with every bowel movement, I took him to the hospital. After a short stay, Thorsson transferred him to the mission office to work as his secretary. I guess the President thought of that as "light duty."

Putting Mike on the train for the four hour trip to Göteborg sucked. We both knew we'd likely never see each other again and, according to mission rules, couldn't talk, write, or communicate in any way. I felt like crying, but pushed it away. I could see Mike was going through something similar. The presence of Lee and Larsen did not help. They were there because once Mike got on the train, I would be alone. That too was forbidden. That too was OP.

Until a replacement could be found, they would be my constant companions.

I helped Mike up the stairs with his bags. Before he went to sit down, he put his arms around me, slapped me on the back, and said, "It's been great. You're great. Do your best …". And that was it.

As I left the train, the goons were waiting at the bottom of the steps. *What are they thinking? I'm going to make a run for it?*

True to form, Lee, the witless wrestler, spoke up, "Oh, how sweet." Turning to Larson, "The girls like each other."

I just looked at him.

"What?!" he asked sarcastically, "You wanna hug me, too? Come on Goldilocks, let's go, we've got work to do."

Within days, Wiggins was re-hospitalized in Göteborg. I found out about this in a letter. Of course, no one in the mission said a word. Mike wrote to me a few weeks after returning to the States. Against his wishes, the doctor insisted he go home, be with his family, and receive specialized care. He was getting it and starting to feel better. Of course, he wanted to stay, do his part, finish his mission and all. That just wasn't in the cards.

I really missed him. It was like losing a brother.

"I'm transferring you to the town of Skövde (Shuv-da)," the President said with great solemnity, "As is true of every district and town in this country, there are many souls there waiting to receive the message of salvation."

I'd heard of the town. Despite the rules about gossiping, missionaries talked, word got around. As far as Skövde was concerned, it wasn't so good. In the 12th century, it was an important city, the burial place of Saint Elin. Legend says she was murdered on the way to a church consecration. In 1164, Pope Alexander III canonized her. For many years afterwards, the devoted made pilgrimages to her grave. That was the last time anything noteworthy happened there. Now, it was just one more featureless industrial center, a place few Swedes would visit let alone choose to live.

The one saving grace about Skövde, if any at all, was the LDS members. Sometime around the "Summer of Love" in 1969, a tight knit group of hippies joined the Church. I'd heard the ten or so families that made up the small, local congregation were living a communal lifestyle of sorts. Although a bit "peculiar," they were active, supportive, and best of all, loved the missionaries.

Thorsson paused. I said nothing. *Where is this going? Why a personal call rather than the usual letter in the mail?*

"There's something more," he added.

What could it be? I hate to admit it, but a small part of me wondered, hoped really, I was being promoted, becoming a member of the mission elite, one of the chosen ones. After all, rank does have its privileges. I'd have a little more freedom to decide what I did from one day to the next. Plus, I could expect more respect, and less abuse from the likes of Lee and Larson. I also thought that I had something to offer. I could contribute, make the mission better, make a difference.

Continuing, the President said, "Your new companion will be Elder Fissen,"

Did I hear that right? The Fart? Oh brother, what a name. Never heard of him.

Getting no response from me, he went on, "Elder Miller, your new companion is a godly, young man. He's been here, working in the Lord's vineyard, for 18 months …".

Eighteen months? Damn, there goes the promotion. I'm still going to be a junior companion.

"… and you will be the Senior Companion," finishing his sentence.

Surprised, I responded, "Senior companion? But, President, *he* has seniority."

"Yes, that's true," Thorsson said, "But Elder Fissen is … *special* …"

Special? Is that what I think it means?

"He struggles with the language … and … he never passed the discussions."

I instantly felt sad for the guy. *Never learned the discussions? Out 18 months and still a junior companion? That's gotta hurt.* Most missionaries passed the discussions within a couple of months and were promoted to Senior, given a "greenie" to break in, at around the 9 to 12 month mark.

"Elder Fissen needs your help, Elder Miller." He paused. Once again, I said nothing. "You have a gift …"

A gift? What is he talking about?

"… the gift of tongues," he answered.

Of course. As different as his use of the expression was from the traditional meaning, I'd heard it before. Where most, including early LDS church members, understood "speaking in tongues" as babbling incomprehensibly when moved by the spirit, modern Mormons were far more pragmatic.

Missionaries serving in foreign countries were said to have the gift when they learned to speak the language.

Thorsson's voice grew louder and a bit distorted, as though he was speaking too close to the mouthpiece of the phone. "An awesome responsibility is being placed on your shoulders Elder Miller. You are now an Area Leader *and* Senior Companion. As our Prophet Joseph Smith once said, 'where much is given, much is expected.' Not only are the people of Skövde depending on you, but *you* are responsible for Elder Fissen. He must pass the discussions. It's your job to see that he does."

He ended, saying, "Elder Miller, I can't emphasize enough the importance of keeping this information to yourself. You are not to discuss this with anyone, under any circumstance. Have I made myself clear?"

He waited.

That was my cue. "Yes ... yes ... President Thorsson, clear ... very clear."

"Good, now give the phone to Elder Lee," he ordered.

I did as I was told. Looking over, I could see that Larson was staring at me, expectantly. He grinned, exposing his array of badly broken teeth. I'd never get used to that.

"What's up?" he asked.

So soon I was put to the test. "Uh, I ... I ... I'm not at liberty to ... say, Elder Larson," feeling strangely satisfied about knowing something he didn't. Larsen's face registered disappointment.

Lee hung up the phone. He hadn't spent more than a minute with Thorsson.

"So, Elder Miller, you are being transferred tomorrow," his tone uncharacteristically friendly.

"Yes," I said, and nothing more.

The three of us just looked at each other. I knew Lee wanted me to fill him in. Not being "in the loop" was killing him. When it was clear I was not going to say another word, he broke the silence. With his usual contempt, he barked, "Better get packing *Sister* Miller. You've got to be on the 8:02 a.m. train tomorrow."

❧

Four hours. That's the time it took to get from Lund to Skövde by train. It was a beautiful journey up the western coast of the country. We would be passing through several seaside towns and villages, before turning east and heading inland between Sweden's two largest lakes, Vänern and Vättern (pronounced, "ven-nurn" and "vet-turn").

Over the last eleven months, I'd been on my own—meaning without a companion—exactly three times, not including my daily visits to the john. All occurred on transfer days: my first day in country, months later when I moved to Lund, and now. Combining these four hours with the three or so it took to get from Gteborg to Huskvarna, and the nine to Lund, I'd been alone a grand total of sixteen hours since the start of my mission.

After boarding the train and stowing my bags, I took out my journal. First line: "Being transferred to Skövde today." Second: "The ticket cost a fucking fortune, a quarter of my monthly allowance." The third: "Send some stuff home!" In addition to my two suitcases, I now had two portable file boxes for my ever growing collection of books, notes, and articles. My bags were heavier than ever, and neither Frick nor Frack offered to help me on the way. Lee marched ahead, turning occasionally to yell, "Hurry up!" Five minutes from the station, I shouted, "Wait! Elders, I've got to rest."

"You're going to miss the train," Lee said, not bothering to look back.

I couldn't move. I was pooped.

"I'll help you," Larsson volunteered. At heart, he was a good guy, just oblivious most of the time.

After that, the trek went faster. Once at the train, I maneuvered my load up the steps, and turned to wave goodbye. Lee and Larson were already twenty paces away, their backs to me. I said, just loud enough for me to hear, "Goodbye. I'll miss you too. Don't forget to write … you fuckheads."

Fourth line: "What a strange conversation with Thorsson." I then wrote as much as I could recall of what he'd said. Setting down my pen, I wondered, *what is up with him?* Picking it up, I added, "Is he really that concerned about Fissen? So the guy is having difficulty with the language, so what? Heck, Lee can't speak Swedish for shit either. What's the big deal about the discussions? Soon after they are learned, everyone forgets them anyway."

I took a breath and let it out with a sigh. *Why all the secrecy? I have a bad feeling about this.*

Thumbing haphazardly through my journal, I came across an entry about the last time I'd been entrusted with a secret. I hadn't felt great about keeping that one either. It was from the first month of my mission, penned while still at the LTM. I'd just returned from the Provo temple, conveniently located a few hundred yards from the training center. We missionaries were encouraged to go as often as our schedules permitted.

Unlike church buildings, which are mere meeting houses, Mormons consider temples the most holy places on Earth. They've been building them from the beginning. In 1832, just two years after the founding of the church, Joseph Smith received a revelation directing the restoration of temple worship in the latter days. After being chased from Ohio to Missouri, and then Missouri to Illinois, the faithful made their first order of business building another "House of the Lord." Then, four days after arriving in Salt Lake City, having trekked half way across the country, they were at it again.

I looked up and out the train window, picturing the Salt Lake City Temple in my mind, the one most familiar to Mormons and gentiles alike. I'd never been inside.

Returning to the journal entry, I read:

P-day. Wrote letters. Did my laundry. Elder Barrett wrecked all of his shirts and G's by washing them together with his socks! Poor guy. Everything came out a light shade of blue. Got another haircut at the BYU "Butcher Shop." Kung Fu Master O'Leary, our glorious District Leader, has been ragging on me, threatening to write me up, so I went. Afterwards, me, Ken, and Cary decided to go to the temple. One of our teachers told us that when it had just finished being built, the Prophet called late one night to tell the security guards to stay out, not go inside to do their usual rounds. He told them Jesus was in the building, "inspecting it." <u>Inspiring and creepy</u>. Anyway, since we've been praying a lot lately, trying to get the spirit and all, we thought that going might help. It didn't, <u>at all</u>! I don't know what we were thinking. That place, the whole endowment ceremony, it's weird, <u>really weird</u>.

"The Endowment." Before going on a mission, or getting married, LDS church members participate in a religious rite they consider the most important of their lives, one they believe necessary to gain entry into Heaven. Like all missionaries-to-be, I went to "take out my endowment," as Mormons refer to the practice, a few weeks before departing for the LTM.

Access to the temple is strictly limited to those who hold a "Temple Recommend"—a pass resembling a driver's license, complete with name, address, expiration date, and serial number. Just like getting a driver's license, a test is required. Forget parallel parking, this is all about staying within the lines of moral worthiness.

No matter where you are on the planet, you get the same twelve question quiz. Most of the time, the examiner is the local Bishop. That was true in my case. I'd met with him a month before entering the LTM—a man I'd known my whole life, whose daughter I'd dated when we were seniors in high school.

I closed the journal, using the index finger of my right hand to keep the place. Shutting my eyes, I tried picturing his face, our meeting. He'd greeted me at the door of his office at the local chapel. He was friendly as usual, asking me to sit down, beginning the meeting with a prayer. After that, the questioning commenced. In order, I was asked:

- Do you have faith in and a testimony of God the Eternal Father, His Son Jesus Christ, and the Holy Ghost?

- Do you have a testimony of the Atonement of Christ and of His role as Savior and Redeemer?

- Do you have a testimony of the restoration of the gospel in these the latter days?

- Do you sustain the President of the Church of Jesus Christ of Latter-day Saints as the Prophet, Seer, and Revelator and as the only person on the earth who possesses and is authorized to exercise all priesthood keys? Do you sustain members of the First Presidency and the Quorum of the Twelve Apostles as prophets, seers, and revelators? Do you sustain the other General Authorities and local authorities of the Church?

- Is there anything in your conduct relating to members of your family that is not in harmony with the teachings of the Church?

- Do you support, affiliate with, or agree with any group or individual whose teachings or practices are contrary to or oppose those accepted by the Church of Jesus Christ of Latter-day Saints?

- Do you strive to keep the covenants you have made, to attend your sacrament and other meetings, and to keep your life in harmony with the laws and commandments of the gospel?

- Are you honest in your dealings with your fellowmen?

- Do you live the law of chastity?

- Are you a full tithe payer? Do you keep the Word of Wisdom?

- Do you have financial or other obligations to a former spouse or children? If yes, are you current in meeting those obligations?

The whole process lasted about an hour. Throughout, his tone was warm and fatherly, qualities I'd come to know and love over the years. He would nod and, every so often, wink at me. As he asked and I answered each question, he smiled broadly, his deep blue eyes sparkling with pride. Yes, I told him, I believed in God, and yes, I believed in the Church and supported its leaders. *Doesn't everyone?* We were Mormons for Heaven's sake!

Smooth is the word I would use to describe the interview; that is, until we got to question number nine. Still smiling, he asked:

"And Brother Miller, what about the law of chastity?"

"Well," I replied, clearing my throat and shifting in my seat, "I've been, … I've had … I, yes, I am keeping the law of chastity …"

"And, in the past?"

When I paused to think, I could see the color begin to drain from his face. Suddenly, things had gotten dicey and awkward. We'd just walked into a minefield. He'd known me most of my life. Our families knew each other. He'd always see us to the door when his daughter, Angela, and I went out.

He reached for a glass of water and took a sip, momentarily looking away.

"Yes, I have broken some rules in that area," I eventually responded, taking care to emphasize that any such indiscretions were in the past.

He sat there, looking at me, unblinking. Haltingly, he proceeded, "To receive forgiveness, Scott, you must make a full confession …"

When our eyes met, I'm sure he knew. Angela was the wildest girl I'd ever met. Diana, my steady non-Mormon girlfriend, the one I dated from the ninth through the eleventh grade, had been tame by comparison. When I asked Angela to go with me to see the movie "Jaws," she suggested we go to a drive-in. Within minutes, we were in the back seat, her hands in my pants, and mine up her tight-fitting tube top.

He closed his eyes, rubbing his temples with the thumb and forefinger of his right hand, as I cataloged all the unchaste activities I could remember. When done, I paused. He looked at me expectantly and waited. I wasn't sure what he wanted at that point. After a moment or two, he asked. "Brother Miller," his voice weak, "have you ever had … sexual intercourse?"

By that point, I'm sure he was desperately worried about my answer.

"No," I responded quickly and truthfully.

Although he tried to hide it, I could see he was relieved. He wanted me to have a temple recommend, not excommunicate me and his daughter.

A smile having returned to his face, the interview proceeded. Even though there was more to confess, the rest of the questions were, by contrast, a breeze:

- Yes, I masturbated, every so often. Yes, I was doing my best to stop;

- Yes, I paid a full tithe;

- No, I did not drink coffee or tea, and no, I did not use tobacco. Ever;

- Yes, I'd used alcohol and marijuana. In fact, his son Wesley, one year older than Angela, was the one who'd introduced me to both! *Did he know that?* This time his face said nothing;

- No, I had no prior spouse or children and, therefore, was not delinquent on any financial obligations.

We both laughed at the last question.

"I have to ask," he said, then winked. His daughter's reputation still intact, his cheery glow had returned.

At the end, he pulled out a small block of paper resembling a physician's prescription pad and began writing. "I'm very proud of you Brother Miller," I remember him saying as he scribbled. He signed the recommend with a flourish, tore it off and handed it to me, "The Lord will be very happy to welcome you into His House. Great blessings await you there."

Honestly, I had no idea what to expect. All I knew was you began wearing garments after visiting the temple your first time. Other than that, no one—not the Bishop, my parents, my best friend Bill who'd left a few months earlier on a mission to Germany—had said a word about what went on inside. It wouldn't have mattered. I wouldn't have believed them anyway.

∽

My stomach growled. I hadn't packed a lunch for the trip. The fridge was empty anyway—not even any pickle juice. Although I knew it would be expensive, I decided to go to the dining car for a bite. More cafeteria than restaurant, it was all self serve. You took a tray, removing the items you wanted from glass display cases.

All the typical items were there: meatballs, hard bread, herring filets, and a variety of sandwiches. It was the räkmacka (pronounced, "wreck mock-ah") that most appealed to me. Small shrimp piled high on top of buttered bread, layered with lettuce, a hard-boiled egg, lemon and a generous squeeze of mayonnaise. I wanted it. I hadn't had shrimp since I'd been in the country.

Glancing at the price, I exclaimed loudly in Swedish, "Oj då," (Oh boy!). *Almost twenty bucks! For a sandwich?! I can't.* Then my stomach growled again, overruling my reluctance.

Finding an empty table, I sat down. Removing the plate and utensils from the tray, I opened my journal and proceeded to stuff my mouth. *Delicious.*

Once more, I read the entry written at the LTM. It was the only one I'd ever made about the temple. I'd wanted to write more, even started a time or two, but stopped. After all, my first time there, I'd pledged, on pain of death, never to reveal what went on inside. It was a secret.

I looked up and out the window of the train. The scenery rushed by as I munched away. Memories of the day I received my "endowment" returned. It was innocuous enough at the start. After showing my "Temple Recommend" at the front desk, I was met by a kindly looking, older man who reminded me of my Grandpa Miller, my Dad's Dad. I guessed he was in his 70's. His hair was grey, his posture a bit stooped, and he was dressed from head to toe in white: white shirt, white coat, white belt, even his shoes were white. I followed him through several doors to an empty room.

"It's your first time, correct?" he asked, his voice warm and friendly.

"Yes," nodding. This is when the whole thing made a sharp left turn into weird.

"Take off all your clothes and put them in one of the lockers," he directed, without a hint of hesitation.

"Take off *all* my clothes?" my voice rising.

"Yes," he said with a gentle smile.

I didn't feel reassured.

"Then put on 'The Shield'," he continued, handing me a cotton sheet with a head-sized hole cut in the center, much like a poncho. Turning to leave the room, "I'll wait for you outside."

Slowly, I began to undress, every few seconds checking to see if the old man was peeking in on me. I didn't like this one bit, caught between escalating fear and attempts to convince myself everything was going to be OK. My thoughts jumped back and forth. *This is creepy, getting naked in the temple. Oh, come on, they're not going to do anything to hurt you. But they want me to get naked, why? Relax, I'm sure there's a good reason.*

By the time I got my underwear off, I thought I had myself under control. My composure lasted until I put on the poncho. *Shit, this thing is open at the sides. There's no button, no zipper. You can see my dick. What if I get a hard on?!*

I stood there, in place, afraid to move. When the old man came back in, I quickly grabbed at the sides of the gown to keep it closed.

"Follow me," he said quietly.

I did as I was told. It wasn't easy. I could hardly walk in the poncho holding the sides as tightly as I was.

Exiting the locker area, I shuffled along in my bare feet down a hallway, past a series of small rooms. They were nothing more than cubicles really, the entrance of each covered by a flimsy curtain. Through a crack in one, I caught a glimpse of a guy about my age, dressed in the same get-up, his ass parked on a solid, white marble slab. To his side stood a temple attendant, another old man also decked out in white.

As we passed other rooms, I strained my neck trying to a look at what was going on. All I could hear was mumbling. *What are they doing to those guys? What are they going to do to me?* I was soon to get my answer. My grey-headed guide stopped and turned to face me. Pulling back the curtain, "Brother Miller, please enter."

Inside, there was yet another old person. "Please be seated," he instructed, pointing to a rectangular piece of white marble in the center of the floor.

As I moved to sit, he pulled at the back flap of my cover, bringing my bare-skinned butt into direct contact with the cold stone. Then, before you could say Brigham Young, it began. Moving along side me, the new guy recited a scripture from the Old Testament about temple work—something about washing, anointing, and clothing. I don't recall the exact words. It was all in a monotone, as though he'd done it a million times before. *Where is this going?*

I snapped to attention when he began touching me. Just before, he'd reached over to a small basin and dipped his fingers in water. He said some words—I guessed it was a blessing— then ran his wet hand across my brow. More words, another dip, another touch, this time my head. The same process continued for my eyes, ears, lips, and neck.

When he got to my shoulders, he moistened his fingers once more and reached *under* the poncho. I was now on full alert. *Damn! Is he going to do what I think he's going to do?*

"Your back …", his tone hypnotic, dragging his wet fingers across my spine, "Your breast …".

OK, that's it. No way am I letting this guy grab my balls. I moved to stand up. With his left hand, he pressed down gently on my shoulder.

"We're almost through," he said in a soothing whisper.

"Your vitals and bowels." That was my stomach. Wipe.

"Your arms and hands." Wipe.

"Your loins." Wipe. *Whoa, that was close!*

"Your legs and feet." Wipe.

Apparently done, he stepped back. I took a deep breath. *Thank God, it's over.* He smiled.

It wasn't.

A second man entered the room, again elderly. Together, they laid their hands on my head to "seal" the washing and anointing, binding the blessings to me in return for my faithfulness, or so I was told afterwards. Following this, I was ushered into an adjoining cubicle. It was just like the first. Here, the entire process was repeated, this time with olive oil instead of water.

When will this end?

"Please stand Brother Miller," one of them directed. The other drew open a curtain opposite my marble stool. Together, they led me into a third room, exactly the same in appearance as the first two, but without the stone cold seat.

"This garment," the second man said, "is to be worn for the rest of your life." He was holding the underwear up, toward me. I'd seen them many times before. My parents wore them. In appearance, they resembled a set of long johns but with short sleeves and ending at the knee instead of ankle. This pair had an elastic neck which the two men stretched open. I stepped in and the temple assistants pulled the garment up and over my shoulders.

The underwear, I remember one saying, was a symbol. It represented the skins given to Adam and Eve after they disobeyed God, ate the fruit of the "Tree of Knowledge of Good and Evil," and became aware of their nakedness. "If you are true and faithful," he continued, "it will be a shield and a protection to you against the power of the Destroyer until you have finished your work on Earth."

Growing up, I'd heard stories about the underwear having magical properties, of protecting wearers from some kind of harm or another. The Prophet Spencer W. Kimball had said as much, at one point writing he was convinced there had "been many cases where there has been, through faith, an actual physical protection." For whatever reason, the tales most often involved fire. "He was burned everywhere on his body EXCEPT where he was covered by his garments!" or so the story usually went.

I never heard anyone in my congregation, or family, make such a claim. Such miracles always seem to happen elsewhere. To me, garments were simply the underwear my parents wore. Putting them on that day was the one thing I knew for a fact would happen at the temple. They felt reassuringly familiar, and I felt proud. Wearing them was proof I was no longer a boy. I was a man. *Yes, I'm a man.* I could feel my mood shift. I wasn't scared anymore. I felt calm, even serene. It filled me with reverence.

Standing opposite me, the two elderly men momentarily paused and smiled, aware of the change in me. "Brother Miller," the attendant to my left started, "With this garment, I give you a new name, which you should always remember and never reveal." There I stood in my G's, still covered with the Poncho, waiting to hear the name. *I've got to remember this. Forget Scott, this is the name God will know me by when I meet Him in Heaven.*

"Your name is," and then he said it.

Ok, ok, that's a pretty unusual name. I need a way to remember it. I've got it. Just remember the name of the band's agent in the Partridge Family. I kept saying it over and over again in my head, along with all the other characters from the T.V. series. *Shirley, Keith, Laurie, Danny. What were names of the two youngest kids on the show?*

The ceremony now over, the man to my right led me back to the locker room. Before leaving, he told me to remove the poncho and dress in my "temple clothes," a complete set of white attire that had been made available to me. "Don't forget the satchel," were his last words as he left the room. Sure enough, on the bench opposite my locker, was a small, white pouch with a fold over top. *What's in it?* I'd know soon enough. *Better get dressed.*

I took off and deposited "The Shield" in a nearby linen basket. As I was dressing to join the men-in-white, I continued to rehearse my name. *What happens if I forget it? Get to the Pearly Gates and can't remember? Do they send you to the back of the line? Or, is that it, my only chance? No entrance for eternity?*

∾

It was at this point that the train came to sudden stop, almost propelling me over the top of the table. My tray and dishes went flying, bouncing off the opposite bench and landing on the floor. An announcement came over the intercom. With a soothing voice, "Ladies and Gentlemen, I'm sorry for this sudden interruption. The track ahead is blocked by several dairy cows. We should be underway shortly."

I stood up, collecting the dishes on the floor and deposited them in the nearby bus tray. Fortunately, none were broken, which made my job easier. With nothing left to eat, I decided to go back to my seat in the passenger car. I'd just sat down when the train lurched forward. With a couple of hours left before I would arrive in Skövde, my mind returned to the endowment ceremony.

My next stop, after leaving the locker room, was a large, richly appointed room, complete with high ceilings and 200 or so seats arranged on either side of a wide, carpeted aisle. Spectacular murals of outer space, shining stars, and a bright sun emerging from colorful clouds adorned the walls. At the front of the room, a silky, white curtain hung from the ceiling to the floor covering the entire wall. Near the center, a velvet-covered altar sat on top of a slightly elevated platform. The place reminded me of a fancy movie theater from the 1950's.

A temple attendant standing near the curtain motioned for us to take seats near the front of the room. By now, a half dozen or so other "initiates" had joined. Everyone was quiet. Several were moving their lips in silence. I assumed, like me, they were doing their best to remember their new names. Our little group was soon joined by a larger one, made up of a dozen or more older men. These, I knew, were going through the same ritual as us, but not for the first time. They were there "taking out endowments" for the dead, serving as proxies for people who had died before converting to the Mormon faith, a ritual necessary for entry into Heaven.

Women were also present but seated across the aisle, on the other side. *Guess we won't be sitting together.*

I leaned over slightly to take a look. Most were, like nearly everyone else I'd met so far, old. The only exception was one girl about my age. *Pretty. Too young to be going on a mission.* Females can go, but not until they are twenty-one. *She must be getting married.* Sitting next to her was a middle-aged woman. Catching my eye, she lowered her brow in disapproval. *Must be her mother.*

I'd just sat back in the seat when the lights dimmed slightly. A voice spoke from overhead, welcoming everyone to the temple and reviewing what had taken place so far. All the while, the man who'd ushered us to our seats, stood silently at the front of the room, hands clasped together over his belt.

"Each of you should have received a New Name...", the voice from beyond continued, bidding anyone who had forgotten it to stand. *Oh my, that would be embarrassing.* I felt a surge of adrenaline.

Uh oh, what is my name?

Somewhere along the way, I'd stopped rehearsing it. *Oh no.* I broke out in a sweat. Thankfully, my mnemonic kicked in and the panic just as quickly subsided.

The voice announced the endowment was about to begin. Soon we'd be learning the secrets required for "getting past the sentinels guarding the gates of Heaven." In exchange for this knowledge, we had to make "solemn promises." Breaking them, the voice warned, would invite the wrath of God—up close and personal. "God will not be mocked!" we were warned. Anyone wanting to leave should do so now.

Gosh, they're not playing around. "Solemn promises?" What could those be? Nobody moved. Taking my cue from everyone else, I stared straight ahead. That's when the room went dark and the curtains parted revealing a screen. *I was right. I am in a theater.* After that, a movie started, recounting the Mormon version of creation, the fall of man, and the one true path to redemption. It starred none other than God, Jesus, the Archangel Michael, Lucifer, Adam, Eve, Peter, James and John. All the players were there.

The epic-length feature progressed, stopping and starting, as we moved from one impressive, thematically painted room to another. We'd begun in the "Creation Room," then moved on to "Paradise": tall trees, lush vegetation, friendly animals and, of course, an apple tree. In the next, we saw a depiction of the earth following mankind's banishment from Eden. The walls showed a lifeless desert scene, said to represent the "lone and dreary world" we now inhabit. The last room reminded me of a ballroom, the kind you would see in an expensive hotel. The colors were soft and muted. Chandeliers hung from the ceiling and fancy wall treatments and other architectural details replaced the murals.

Getting to this point in the endowment had taken at least two hours. I wasn't sure exactly because I didn't have my watch. It was with the rest of my belongings in the locker room. The entire time we did not speak—not a word—except when taking oaths. The movie would stop. The voice would then command us to stand and raise our right arm. Next, the promise we were about to make was recited, followed by an order to bow our heads and, in unison, say "Yes." That was it.

When all was said and done, I had pledged to:

• Obey, without reservation, God and all Church authorities;

• If need be, sacrifice everything I owned, including my life, to sustain and defend the Church;

• Avoid all light mindedness and loud laughter;

• Refrain from criticizing Church authorities;

• Keep the law of chastity; and

• Consecrate myself, time, energy, effort, and all worldly belongings to the Church.

Along with the oath taking, we put on and took off various articles of clothing. That's what I'd had been carrying around in the satchel. By the time we made it to the ballroom, we were attired in a pleated robe, baker's style hat (women wore a veil), disposable booties over our white socks, and a sash. Around our waists, we wore an apron, green in color, embroidered in the style of fig leaves. To say we were a sight doesn't quite capture it. Imagine a cross between the Pillsbury Doughboy and the Swedish Baker from the Muppets.

Despite how truly odd we looked, no one laughed. The mood was dead serious. Mormons are actually buried in this outfit. I knew because I'd been to a number of Mormon funerals, including my Grandpa Daniels, my Mom's dad. The belief was that, on resurrection, we'd be in "appropriate attire" for Heaven.

It was not enough to wear the special clothing or keep our promises. To get into Heaven, one also had to know and use several special handshakes. These we were never to divulge. The penalty was death. To drive the point home, we simulated taking our own lives: cutting our throats, ripping out our hearts, and being disemboweled.

As far as I was concerned, the secrets would be safe with me. *Who was I going to tell?* No person outside the church would ever believe any of this. The clothing, promising to kill myself, the voice of the controller. Even the members don't talk about it. Straight out of the Outer Limits.

And, it still wasn't over.

The curtains in the ballroom parted. Simultaneously, the voice announced, "Brothers and Sisters this is the Veil."

OK, I get it. This represents the boundary between Heaven and Earth. God is on the other side. Our goal is to cross over.

One by one, we were to approach and demonstrate what we had learned. A temple attendant was standing on the other side of the veil playing the role of God. If we did it right, the endowment was over. We were ready to make the trip. The veil would be parted and into "Heaven" we'd go.

Oh my gosh, a test!

I had an immediate flashback to one of the worst dreams I had at B.Y.U. I show up to take the calculus final. I've studied and feel really prepared. The test is passed out. I get it, look at it. I don't recognize anything, not one question. My mind is a complete and total blank. I'm doomed. I'm going to fail this mother and return home in humiliation.

Next thing I know, I'm up at the veil. A temple worker close by hands me a small wooden mallet, motioning for me to knock on a post, letting "God" know I'm there. After a couple of whacks, the man behind the veil, playing the role of God, asks, "What is wanted?"

Even though everything had been reviewed before I got up there, I couldn't rub two thoughts together. I was spent. I'd even forgotten my new name. It was one of the first questions I was asked. I sputtered, "Partridge Family." The worker who'd given me the mallet looked over, his eyes wide with confusion. Quickly regaining his composure, he approached, gently coached me through the process, whispering instructions, reminding me of my temple name and how to do the handshakes.

"You did it," he said warmly, and gave me a fatherly shove through the veil. Stepping past God's stand-in, yet one more old guy, I entered the "Celestial Room." Everything was white: walls, carpet, chairs, and couches. It was rich and luxurious, and represented the Kingdom of Heaven, the place where God and the Faithful will reside.

My fellow initiates, those who'd gone before me, were there. Some were standing, some sitting, others milling about taking in the sights. Nobody was talking. I sat down in one of the plush armchairs and took in the room.

Driving home on the 605 Freeway in my Dad's 65 VW bug, I kept asking myself, *what in the Hell was that about?* Up to that point, nothing in my life could compare to it. The only experience that came close was the induction ceremony for the "Order of the Arrow," a super secret club within the Boy Scouts. Seated around a camp fire, select boys were "tapped" for membership. They were removed from the group, given a new name and special sash, then put through a ritual known as, "The Ordeal." The next day, when the "Arrows" returned to the troop, they wouldn't say one word about what had happened. They'd been sworn to secrecy.

During my time in the Scouts, I was never tapped. Now, I had a fairly good idea about what it meant to go through an ordeal. Maybe that day at the temple should have been a clue to me about what was to come. The beliefs I'd grown up with, knew as a child, bore little or no relationship to what I experienced in the temple. It was light years away from singing the Sunday school song, "Yes, Jesus Loves Me for the Bible tells me so." Getting into Heaven now meant assuming a new name, playing dress up, exchanging secret handshakes and cryptic passwords.

When I finally made it home, my parents and I just looked at each other. Although I was dying to talk over what had happened—get their take on it, have them explain it to me—not a word was said. Given the choice between starting a conversation and being disemboweled, I opted for silence.

～

"Nästa station," (Next station) the conductor calmly announced over the loudspeakers, "Skövde!"

I looked at my watch. Time had really flown by. I put my journal away, stood, retrieved my bags from the overhead rack, and began making my way down the aisle towards the door.

"Exit on the right," the voice advised.

Stepping off, I spotted Fissen in an instant.

My secret mission was about to begin. *Does he know it?* I wondered.

8

ON MY OWN

~

"And when we are asked why we are such a happy people, our answer
is: 'because we have everything—life with all its opportunities, death
without fear, eternal life with endless growth and development.'"

SPENCER W. KIMBALL

12TH PROPHET, SEER, AND REVELATOR

CHURCH OF JESUS CHRIST OF LATTER DAY SAINTS

~

"I can't do it," Fissen whispered, "I'm not gonna pass this one."
"Stop that!" I replied, unable to hide my irritation, "You're always
doing this, talking bad about yourself ...".
"But ...".
"No buts," I interrupted, "There is no but. You're ready. You can do it."
I turned, looking at the line of people ahead of us. We were at the post
office. At my feet were two large boxes. I was following through with the
commitment I'd made to myself on the train ride from Lund to Skövde. I
was sending stuff home—most of it books. During my time with Wiggins,
I'd collected a ton of tracts and small hardbacks put out by the Jehovah's
Witnesses. We'd read and marked them up religiously (ha ha), and used
them like secret weapons when out Bible bashing. The JW's were always

shocked that for one, we had their publications, and even more, could deploy their writings against them in our debates. I was no longer interested in bashing. Tired of lugging them around, but not quite ready to toss the lot, I was shipping them back to the States.

I was also sending nearly everything Cary Wells had sent me since leaving the mission, including the volume on church history he'd given me at the LTM. I'd read and re-read the stuff. I about had it memorized anyway. Plus, nobody here was interested in discussing Mormonism's checkered past. To that, I added a bunch of other LDS publications I'd collected, and the scrap books I'd made since coming to Sweden. I had binders full of train tickets, photos, brochures, newspaper clippings—even napkins from the homes of investigators and members—complete with a reference to the page in my journal where the item and its importance were described.

The last item was my copy of *Catcher in the Rye*. I'd brought it with me from the States, managed to sneak it past the surprise inspection at the Mission Office on my first day, and kept it hidden for the last year in my bag. I hesitated at first. Given the cost of mailing, and my limited budget, I was planning on sending the boxes home "by boat." It took longer—most often six to eight weeks—but was much cheaper than airmail. It was risky though. Through the missionary grapevine, I'd learned that not everything sent this way made it back to the States, or arrived undamaged. Even though I hadn't read *Catcher*, nor removed it from its secret hiding place for months, I didn't want to lose my copy. I valued it, in a way felt protected by it. I'd even named the first volume of my journal after the lead character, "Holden Caulfield, my best friend."

After thumbing through the yellowed pages and reading a passage or two, I placed it inside and sealed up the box.

"Nästa, tack!" (Next please), the agent at the window said loudly.

As the line moved forward, we followed, pushing the boxes ahead with our feet. There were still several people waiting in front of us. Elder Fissen nudged me in the side with his elbow, nervously laughing. Although I was used to it by now, the sound he made reminded me of a donkey—low and grumbling at first, then high pitched. His braying always drew attention.

"You *really* think I can do it?" he asked. His hands were thrust deep in his pockets and he was turning slowly back and forth at the waist.

"Sure man," I said reassuringly, "You've got it down."

Every day since my arrival in Skövde, we'd been practicing. I never said a word about my meeting with Thorsson and my so-called "secret mission." It wasn't so much out of loyalty to the President and his usual bullshit. I just didn't see the point. It would only hurt Fissen's feelings. Plus, the guy got right to work, never a complaint.

Each morning, he'd study and we'd drill, fifteen minutes at a time, sometimes up to a couple of hours. When we were out and about, I'd quiz him. At night, we repeated the same routine. It was working. He already passed off two of the three remaining Discussions in the time we'd been together.

"Test me!" he insisted, then hee-hawed.

I did. He didn't miss a word. I'd start a sentence, he'd finish. I'd direct him to a certain section, he recited it successfully. His accent was terrible, only slightly better than his pronunciation. No Swede would understand a single word of it. But that's not what mattered. He just had to say the right words, in the right order when he met with Elder Beech, the District Leader, at Church the next day.

Leaving the Post Office, we began making our way to our first, and only, appointment. It was with the Mårtanssons (pronounced, "More-tan-sons"). Although I was a bit preoccupied with the cost of sending the packages—fifty bucks out of my $250 monthly allowance—I was really looking forward to this meeting. Kerstin (pronounced, "Cher-sten") Mårtensson was already a member of the Church. She'd joined when all her fellow hippies converted back in 1969. Herr Mårtensson, Stig (pronounced, "Steegh"), was the lone holdout of the group, his only concession to the Mormon faith being that he had agreed to marry Kerstin so she could be baptized. Before, they were, like most Swedes, living together.

The couple resided in a classic, two-story, red and white Swedish home distinguished by its characteristic barn roofline. The house itself was part of a compound of similarly constructed homes, located at the edge of town in a thickly forested area. Although the group had given up the strict communal lifestyle they once followed, and now resided in separate homes, they were still farming together, and helping parent each other's kids. In addition, each household—whether it be selling food items, farm goods, crafts, furniture, or clothing—contributed earnings to support the general community.

This would be our third visit. The first two times we went out, we ate with the entire group in their common dining hall. It was a blast, vegetables straight from the garden, farm raised chicken, freshly baked bread, and homemade "saft" (the fresh fruit drink prepared from concentrate). We listened to music, sang Swedish folk songs, danced, and played games.

Prior to meeting the Mårtenssons, Fissen had filled me in about Stig. Every missionary assigned to Skövde since 1969, had tried to convert him, made him their "pet project." Stig had heard the Discussions so many times, I bet he could teach them himself.

Every trick of the trade had been tried. Of course, the Elders started and ended any visit with a prayer, asking God to open Stig's heart to the truth. They'd left brochures, cited scripture, and sermonized. When that didn't work, they played the guilt card ("Herr Mårtansson, don't you want to live with your family in Heaven, for eternity?"). And then, as I gathered from Fissen, they tried "ass-kissing" (my words, not his), ingratiating themselves, complimenting him, acting as though they were good buddies. Throughout the campaign, Stig apparently met all attempts to convert him with a cheerful composure, but firm refusal. Having met their match, most eventually stopped visiting, turning their attention to greener pastures.

"Bernie," I said, using Fissen's first name, "we're going out there to have fun. That's it. Fun. For the next couple of hours, let's forget we are missionaries." On our second visit, I even suggested we wear our civies.

"Really?" he asked, his mouth wide open.

"Yeah, really," I replied.

Fissen merely nodded. Then, as soon as we sat down on the bus, "Quiz me!"

"No," I objected, "Get out your discussion book and go over it *by yourself …*".

"Ah, c'mon," poking me in the ribs with his elbow.

"… like we do at home. Just pick a random page, point to a spot, cover it with your hand …".

Hee-haw, he laughed, "Oh, all right."

I turned and looked out the window of the bus. It was the last of three we'd ride to get to the Mårtenssons. Then, we'd have to walk a ways—not far, about half a kilometer.

The trees were changing color. Fall was here. Soon there would be snow. I wasn't looking forward to the return of winter. *I can't believe I've been on my mission over a year.*

I watched as a Swedish letter carrier cycled by in the opposite direction, his bright yellow and blue bike catching my eye. *I hope the boxes make it home in one piece.* I went over the contents once again. The JW books were all in Swedish. *I'm never going to read them! Why did I spend money sending them home?*

Again, I thought about my copy of *Catcher in the Rye. I hope it makes it.* Overhead, the bus driver announced the name of the next stop. We had two more to go. *I don't want to carry around that crap anymore.* I was done with it. *If it gets there, it gets there.*

Days earlier I'd re-read the booklets Cary had sent me about the temple. One of them contained a verbatim transcript of the entire endowment. I remember how shocked I was seeing it in print. Somebody had broken their pledge, risking death by writing it all down, spilling everything.

One tract traced the history of the temple ceremony, linking it to Joseph Smith's involvement in Masonry. Turns out, he and his family were members of the organization, with Smith being a "32nd degree Master Mason." According to witnesses, one of the Prophet's last acts on Earth was flashing the secret Masonic hand signal for distress. Apparently, he hoped that a brother member would intervene and stop the angry mob from attacking the jail where he and his brother, Hyrum, were being held on charges of treason. It didn't work. The two were shot to death moments later.

The similarities between the temple ceremony Smith introduced and Masonic symbols and rituals were striking, almost identical, including the assignment of a new name, the crazy clothes, secret handshakes, blood oaths and more—much more. In time, the LDS endowment evolved and modernized. The movie replaced live actors. A promise to avenge the murder of the Prophet was dropped. Best of all, as far as I was concerned, was the elimination of a full body bath in the buff. I'd been lucky. My "washing and anointing" was a just a touch here and wipe there. By comparison, my grandparents undressed completely, got into a tub and had *every* part of their body scrubbed by a temple attendant.

Such changes had not been without controversy. During his lifetime, Joseph Smith asserted that God "set the temple ordinances to be the same forever and ever … [and] ordinances instituted in the heavens … are not to be altered." Critics of the LDS Church never miss an opportunity to cite the Prophet's words when changes to the endowment ceremony are made. "How," they ask, "can Church leaders feel free to tweak it whenever they want?" Of course, I knew how the leadership would respond. I'd heard it from the time I was a kid: "Continuing Revelation." God talks to our current Prophet who, in turn, tells us what we need to know. Simple. That's what they'd said when the Church began admitting blacks to the priesthood. That's what they always said.

"Silly!" That's the word Cary Wells used to characterize his view of the temple. The letter he sent me with the publications was his boldest. And while it frightened me to admit it, I agreed with him. The whole thing seemed silly. God needs a special handshake? Really? If He's omnipotent and omniscient, He'd know what's in my heart, in all our hearts. No password would be required at the Pearly Gates. He'd either say, "Scott, you've lived a good life. Here are the keys to the executive elevator. Come on up, I'll see you in a few," or he'd press the switch to open the trap door.

The bus pulled to the side of the road. We had one more stop before getting off. Glancing over at Fissen I could see he was doing as I'd asked. His nose was buried in the discussions. I was glad because I needed time to think. I wanted to think.

Staring straight ahead, the bald head of the man seated in front of me filled my field of vision. I decided to close my eyes. And with that, Pandora's Box opened. My doubts were out. No longer limited to the endowment ceremony or even Mormonism, I was having reservations about all the world's religions—their rituals, liturgies, baptisms, prayers, protestations and pilgrimages.

Does God really care about this stuff? I didn't believe it. *Did God even exist?* I wasn't so sure anymore.

I thought about the Prophet Joseph Smith. He'd been in a similar place early in his life. That's what Discussion C was all about: the First Vision. It was that time when, full of doubt about which denomination was right, he went into the woods to pray. While there, God told him to start a new church—the one that millions including almost everyone I knew and loved believed to be the one and only true faith on Earth.

How could everyone be so certain? Not just Mormons, but all believers? The JW's, the Catholics, the Pentecostals. Everyone.

Once more, Discussion C came to mind. Joseph Smith had also been deeply puzzled by the "extraordinary scene of religious feelings," the "great love ... [and] zeal manifested" by those of different faiths. It was part of the story, Smith's tireless quest for the Truth. Where he ended up deciding, "The seemingly good feelings of both the priests and the converts were more pretended than real," I now believed no one really knew the answers to the BIG questions. Some were just more confident in their ignorance than others.

Just then the bell chimed overhead. I heard the bus driver announce our stop. Fissen and I stood and exited at the rear, walking briefly down the main street, until turning onto a small, single lane gravel road.

We were soon caught in the headlights of a fast moving vehicle. The horn of the car blared loudly as it approached, the pitch changing as it sped by. All of the passengers, including the driver, had their arms extended, giving us the bird.

"Go home you fucking Americans!" someone screamed in English at the top of their lungs.

"Fan ta Er!" (Fuck you!) I screamed back, instinctively, "Jag älskar det här landet era jävlar!" (I love this country you bastards!).

Fissen stared at me. "You sound like you were born here," he said, adding after a short pause, "I'm not saying nothing tonight."

"What? Why not?"

Continuing to stare, "You sound like you were born here. My Swedish sucks."

I reached over and patted him on the back, "C'mon, you're going to do fine. Do what we've practiced."

As Wiggins had done with me, I'd taken Fissen to the library, had him check out and listen to Swedish language tapes.

"You've got the language, the structure down ... just pay attention to *how* you sound." At least, that was the trick I'd learned. It was the accent that gave you away. We spent a fair bit of time listening to the tapes, mimicking the speaker's intonation.

"If you're uncertain, just say, 'ett ögonblick' (just a second) or 'förlåt?' (I'm sorry?), and they'll repeat what they said. No harm in that."

"OK," he said resigned.

The rest of the time we walked in silence, our pace gradually picking up. It was cold. Before too long, we were standing on the Mårtensson's front stoop. Soon after ringing the bell, Stig opened the door.

"Hallå grabbar!" (Hello guys!) greeting us enthusiastically, "Stig på, stig på" (Come in, come in).

We stepped in, first taking off and hanging our jackets on the hooks lining the wall in the entry way. Slipping off our shoes, I could hear Pink Floyd playing in the background. I recognized it instantly, the track "Us and Them" from the *Dark Side of the Moon* album.

Glorious. How long has it been since I heard that?

Fru Mårtenson, Kerstin, soon joined us. Lightly patting me on the arm, "Sätt er, sätt er," (sit down, sit down), motioning toward chairs in the front room, "koppla av lite" (relax a little).

"Let me turn down the music," Stig said, moving toward the stereo.

"No!" I objected, holding up my hand, "Please don't. I haven't heard Pink Floyd in months."

"You know Pink Floyd?!" Stig responded both surprised and pleased.

"Of course. I even saw them in concert."

"Wow … is that true?" his excitement mounting. Then, the conversation took off. Stig pulled out a bunch of other albums, spreading them on the floor. We sat down together, going through them one by one, pointing out a favorite song, reading a sentence or two from the back covers or liner notes.

I'd seen a lot of the bands live. Jethro Tull, ZZ Top, YES, Emerson Lake, and Palmer, Deep Purple, Black Sabbath, the Eagles—the Who's Who of Rock 'n Roll. A lot of the groups had played at the California Jam during my sophomore year in high school. It had been held at the Ontario Motor Speedway, just fifteen minutes from my home.

Fissen was right there alongside us. I'm not sure he understood much of what was being said, but he joined in as best he could. My suspicions were confirmed when Kerstin leaned over, tapped Bernie on the arm and, in her quick, clipped Göteborg accent asked, "Kan du hjälpa mig I köket?" (Would you help me in the kitchen?).

A look of confusion immediately crossed Fissen's face. It was clear he hadn't understood. To his credit, he did not, as was his habit, break into English. Just as we had practiced, he paused briefly then said, "förlåt?" (Excuse me?) By the time Kerstin repeated her request, he'd figured out what she'd said. The two stood and made their way to the kitchen.

Stig changed the record. I waited in anticipation as he asked, "You know this one?" It was instantly familiar, the title track from Elton John's LP,

Madman Across the Water.

"Of course. Next to *Tumbleweed Connection* it's one of my favorites, before he hit it big, when he started doing pop tunes."

"Hmm," Stig said, sitting back down on the floor.

We listened to the song in silence. After a minute or two, he turned to me, "Can I ask you something?"

"Visst!" (Sure).

"You're the strangest missionary I've ever met!" he said.

"What?!" surprised by his remark, "Why ... why do you say that?"

Looking me directly in the eyes, "This is your third time here ... and you've never brought up the Church ..."

"Yeah, well ..." I said, with a chuckle.

"... you haven't asked me to pray with you, if I want to hear the discussions, left any brochures, nothing. You don't even try to bless the food."

I nodded, looking away, first up at the ceiling then down at my hands. I could hear *Madman* slowly fading out on the stereo.

When the next track, *Indian Sunset*, began to play, Stig continued, "Every missionary that comes here tries to steer the conversation toward the Church ... wants to convert me ..."

I said nothing.

"Why not you?" he asked insistently, "What's with you?"

Oh brother, what do I say? This is not a conversation I'd expected to have with anyone, any time soon.

I looked back at him. Measuring my words carefully, "You and Kerstin invited me into your home. You've treated me nothing but decent, been friendly and super welcoming. It'd be rude for me to come in here and start preaching."

Stig blinked slowly, "So ... what *do* you believe?"

Damn, I don't want to have this conversation. What do I say? How much should I share?

"What do I believe?" buying more time by repeating his question. "Why would I ..." struggling to find the right words, "I know most missionaries think you have to become Mormon before you can ever really be happy ... but look, I'm in *your* home ... it's not my place ... I just think ... you guys are already happy ... enjoying life ... who am I to tell you what the right way to live is ..."

Although I felt satisfied, Stig wasn't going to let me off the hook. "Yeah," he said, "We are happy … thanks … I'm asking what do *you* believe deep down inside?" (Ja men, vad tror du innerst inne?).

I didn't even try to stop myself. It just came out, "I believe that actions are more important than words. I don't care what people believe, or say they believe. It's what they do that matters to me. All the other stuff … who cares?"

"By their fruits, ye shall know them," he replied, citing the familiar passage from *The Book of Matthew*.

I could tell there was more he wanted to say but, before he could, Bernie and Kerstin returned from the kitchen. They were each carrying a tray stocked with fruit, cheese, and tunnbröd (thin bread), a crisp, wafer-thin Swedish hard bread.

"Var så goda," (Help yourselves) Kerstin said, setting the trays on the nearby coffee table.

Among the items was a small saucer of finely chopped purple onion. In all the homes I'd ever visited, I'd never seen it served before.

"Lök?" (Onion?), I asked inquisitively, "Vad skall den användas till?" (What's that for?)

"Ja, du," (Well, my friend) she replied with a smile, "Vi skall äta nått *mycket* speciellt ikväll" (We are going to eat something *very* special tonight).

"Jasså?" (Oh?), I replied and looked over at Bernie. He shook his head from left to right, raising both hands in the air, palms up.

Stig met my glance with a nod. "I doubt you've ever eaten it before," he said, then standing, picked up the trays and disappeared together with Kerstin into the kitchen.

"Stay there," he commanded, and with a laugh added, "No peaking,"

The seventh tune, *Rotten Peaches,* from *Madman* had just started to play when I detected a foul odor. Faint at first, it gradually increased in intensity.

I looked at Fissen. He had a sheepish grin on his face.

"Bernie!" my tone harsh, "Did you cut one?"

"No," his smile quickly giving way to shock, "I thought it was you! Maybe the sewer is backed up."

"What? No," covering my nose, "Phew, it's getting worse."

Emerging from the kitchen, Stig and Kerstin in unison shouted, "Surprise!"

As they approached, the smell became almost unbearable. It was also unmistakable. Cat poop. Imagine burying your face in the litter box right after your cat did its business. It was that bad.

"What is that?" I asked.

"Surströmming!" (Pronounced, sewer-stroom-ing]) Stig replied, his voice full of pride.

Literally translated, the word "surströmming" means "sour herring." Every spring, the small fish native to the Baltic Sea is caught, cleaned, soaked in brine, then canned and allowed to ferment for six or so months before being sold. I'd seen the bright yellow and red containers stacked in baskets at local grocery stores, the lids and bottoms bulging as though infected with botulism.

Unless you wanted your home to stink permanently, the highly pressurized cans were opened outside or in a sink filled with water. One Elder in our mission mailed a can home. As a joke, he told his family that the Swedish tradition was to place it in the center of the dining room table, then join hands and dance in a circle around the table, singing, "O Vad det Luktar" (Oh How Bad this Smells) to the tune of "Happy Birthday." At the end, everyone was supposed to lean over the can while someone opened it. It was Mike Wiggins who told me the story, adding that the Elder was forced to borrow money from the Mission Office when his family stopped sending him letters with his monthly check.

Legend has it that the putrid product originated in the 1600's. As told, Swedish sailors ran out of the salt used at the time for preserving fish. When their cargo began to rot, the sailors conned a group of Finnish islanders— invariably portrayed in jokes and stories as gullible or stupid—into buying the fish, making a fast exit before their ruse could be discovered. When the Swedes eventually returned, they were surprised the islanders wanted to buy more. After trying it themselves, a tradition was born.

For hundreds of years, the fermented fish was a staple of the northern Swedish diet—the area of the country where Stig was raised. The military served it as rations to soldiers during the 30 Years War. After all, it couldn't go bad. Plus, the smell was sure to deter any enemy.

Nowadays, surströmming is considered a delicacy and reserved for special occasions. Most often, it's smothered with onions and eaten between two pieces of tunnbröd. As with most meals, små potatis are served on the side.

"I ate this several times a week growing up," Stig said, setting the plate down on the coffee table. About a dozen or so of the small filets were lined up, side by side on the dish. They looked no different than sardines.

While Stig made the sandwiches, Kerstin poured us each a large glass of the thick, sour milk I'd first tasted at the Tre Kronor Hotel my first day in Sweden. Surprisingly, I'd grown to like the stuff.

"Äkta Norrlänningar," (Real Northerners) he started, "drink sour milk when eating surströmming. Don't let anyone tell you different!" To my amazement, people actually debated what beverage would best compliment the decomposing dish.

We raised our glasses in a toast.

"To friendship," Stig said, "May we always feel free to share our hearts, minds and burdens."

"Skål" (Cheers) everyone replied, taking a gulp.

Setting down my glass, I took in the scene: Stig, Kerstin, Fissen, the music, the food. I felt great. I felt high—warm, happy, comfortable, peaceful—feelings I hadn't experienced for I don't know how long. Despite the wicked smells, I was at home, with the Mårtenssons and with myself.

I took a bite. *Hmm, not bad. Who could believe it?*

Looking over at Fissen, I could see the sandwich was not going to get past his lips. He was holding it like a live grenade, his hand trembling, his face all pasty white. That's when he gagged. Standing abruptly, he blurted out, "Får jag omvÄnda din toalette?" (pronounced, "Four ya ohm-ven-dah dean toy-let?")

At first, no one responded. I'm sure Stig and Kerstin were, like me, surprised by what he'd said. Bernie had misspoken. He'd only mixed up two letters in a single word, but what a difference it made.

He'd been trying to ask if he could use the bathroom. Obviously, the prospect of eating the rotten fish had proved too much. He was about to be sick. In place of the word, "använda" (pronounced, ahn-venda) meaning "to use," he said "omvända" (pronounced, ohm-venda) meaning to convert, in a religious sense.

In short, saying ohm versus ahn, meant he'd asked, "May I convert your toilet?"

Stig soon spoke up, saying in his slow, deliberate Northern Swedish accent, "Well, you can try, but I have talked to it many, many times and it just won't listen!" (Ja, du får väl försöka, men jag har pratat många gånger med den, och den lyssnar inte!").

Bernie looked perplexed then high tailed it down the hall to the bathroom. When the door slammed, we burst into laughter.

Several minutes later, he emerged. His color was back and his composure restored. With confidence, he said in fluent Swedish, "Hey, I must have caught your toilet at a receptive moment, I got at least two of the discussions in ..." and then sat down.

The laughter started again. Bernie hee-hawed, drowning out everyone else.

9

THE LAW OF JANTE

∾

"I have done more to boast of than ever any man had …
Neither Paul, John, Peter,
nor Jesus ever did it. I boast that no man ever did such a work as I."

JOSEPH SMITH
FIRST PROPHET, SEER, AND REVELATOR
CHURCH OF JESUS CHRIST OF LATTER DAY SAINTS

∾

"**C**an you believe this snow?" I asked.

"Otroligt!" (unbelieveable) Fissen responded, his accent near perfect.

Mountains of it had been carried off by truck and stacked two and three stories high in parking lots at the edge of the city. We saw them grow each time we went to visit the Mårtenssons. It was a feat of engineering. They'd start with a large base. Once complete, the trucks would climb a ramp made of snow to the top and begin a new level. Up and down the vehicles went, each dumping their load, until it was no longer possible to go higher.

"It's way more than last year …" I sighed.

"For sure," he laughed, "ha ha ha."

We were sitting together on the bus, heading to the station. It was inspection time again. The District Leaders would meet us there and we'd swap companions.

"Can you move over a bit?" I asked, "You're kind of crowding me."

"Oh, oh, ok," scooting over, "I'm going to miss running tonight."

"Me too," I said. A month earlier, I'd checked out James Fixx's new book, *The Complete Book on Running* from the public library. We bought sweat suits from the "Skövde Idrottsförening" (Sköde Athletic Club) and started running each night. Everything about it was against the rules: running, being out after curfew, not wearing our suits. But I wanted to do something more than just walking to and from our appointments. Heaven knows, it was impossible to ride our bikes in the snow.

"I'm going to miss OP too," he added. OP. That was our cat. Yeah, we had a cat. OP was a perfect name because pets also were strictly "off the program." One night while out running, we found him in a paper sack by the side of the road. Apparently, someone had dumped him there, or tossed him out the car window.

We heard this pitiful cry as we jogged by. Opening the sack, he looked up at us with these big green eyes. He wasn't more than a month old, grey and white in color and adorable. When Fissen reached into the bag, the cat sunk his claws into the sleeve of his running jacket and wouldn't let go. He'd decided, "No way I'm going back in that bag." Walking back to our apartment, he meowed the whole way.

I wasn't really sure what we were going to do with him. We made a bed out of a cardboard box and old towel. He didn't stay there, of course. Soon, he was snuggled up with Bernie in bed. Turns out, it was a bit of a rough night. Having no food, we'd given him milk. It didn't sit well with him. He ended up with diarrhea.

By morning, he was better and we had to decide what to do with him. Bernie said, "Let's keep him!" It didn't take me more than a moment to decide, "Yeah, let's do it."

Now, the apartment was full of cat stuff—cat box, cat litter, cat nip, cat toys, and cat food—all of which we had to hide before the DL's came to do their security sweep. Lucky for us, we'd befriended our next door neighbors, the Erikssons, an elderly couple that had a dog named "Bo" (pronounced, "bow"). Long before getting OP, we'd taken to walking their dog. We did it every evening after coming home. It wasn't strenuous. He was as old as they were and, like them, warm and friendly. Bo took an instant liking to OP. The cat liked to curl up on top of him whenever we came to visit.

Bernie was worried, "I hope the DL's don't find out about OP."

"How are they going to find out?" I asked. That morning the Erikssons, our willing co-conspirators, had happily taken OP and all his stuff into their apartment. If rapid tail wagging was a sign, I'm pretty sure even Bo was excited. "So," I continued, "just don't say anything. Do what you're told …".

"But you know how it goes. He's going to question me …, ask me about you, about what we're doing, the rules …".

Bernie was right. He was going to be questioned, pressured to squeal. It wasn't going to be the "Inquisition". It would start off slow, "How is the work going?" but end with pointed questions aimed at exposing any transgressions.

I answered, "For all I care, just tell the truth … I'll deal with it."

"But, I don't want to get you in trouble … I care about you."

"Thanks," I said, "me too …". Seeing he was still anxious, I then told him, "Bernie, I don't feel like … look, were not doing anything wrong. We're not partying, we're not breaking and entering, we're not having sex, we haven't murdered anybody. What's the big deal? So, if they ask me whether I'm doing anything wrong, I'm going to say no … and I'm not going to feel bad about it."

"You make it sound easy … you think really good on your feet…I'm not as quick as—"

"Bernie!" I interrupted, "Don't let them get to you like that, make you feel bad. It's their job to find something wrong, that's what they do. But they're no better than we are. If, when you're together, Beech says something you agree with like, I don't know, your shoes need shining, well take it in, agree with it, thank him for it. But if you think he's full of shit, tell him to 'stick it,' in your head at least."

Fissen leaned over, putting his head on my shoulder, "Thanks, Scott."

"It's ok, its ok," I said, "Straighten up. Look, we're almost here."

As soon as we stepped off, I could see the DL's standing near the bike rack at the station. Their uniforms made them instantly recognizable. The same old blue coats, black fedoras, and missionary-issue grey brief cases.

"Unbelievable. Along with the Great Wall, we're the only thing visible from space," I muttered.

"Did they ride their bikes?" Fissen asked, equally incredulous.

Shaking my head back and forth, "Idiots."

"Who is that with Beech?" Fissen added.

"Who? What?" taking a closer look. In fact, it wasn't Elder Roberts. It was someone else.

"He must have a new companion," I observed. I sucked in my breath, steeling myself up for what I knew could be a difficult couple of days. As we drew closer, my apprehension gave way to recognition.

"Popeye," I shouted. I could hardly believe my eyes. It was Ken Arnold, one of "Three Musketeers" from the LTM. Suffice it to say, I never thought I'd see him again. The last time we'd been together was with Cary Wells at the Tre Kroner Hotel, our first night in Sweden. We all cried together. The next morning, Ken was the first to be dragged off to the train by Pierce and Payne.

Without thinking, I rushed over and hugged him, "I can't believe it ... man, it's great to see you!"

Nothing.

For all the world, it was like hugging a tree. No movement, whatsoever. He didn't lift his arms, pat me with his hands, reciprocate in any way.

"Elder Miller," he said coolly, "I'm going to be with you the next couple of days for the inspection."

Still striking a familiar tone, "You're the new D.L.? Wow! That's great."

"Where's your hat?" flatly.

"My hat?" reaching up, touching my fur covered mössa, "it's on my head."

Turning to Beech, Arnold asked, "Is that hat regulation?" When Beech nodded, Ken looked back at me and said, "Let's get going. We're burning daylight."

His use of that expression was familiar. It was a favorite quote of his from the John Wayne movie, *The Cowboys*. Before hearing that, I was confused, even hurt, by the way he was acting. Now, I got it, I understood, or so I thought. Ken was acting. He couldn't be his old self in front of Beech. *I can't wait till we're alone.*

"Right, let's go," I said.

～

When we reached the landing, I glanced at the mail slot. It displayed two last names uncommon in Sweden: Sanneving and Lindencrona. *It's got to be a young couple living together.* I knocked. A few moments later, the door swung open. Another pretty, blond, blue-eyed twenty-something greeted me. There were so many here in Sweden. Believe it or not, I'd grown used to it.

"Hej," (Hi [pronounced, "hay"]) she said warmly.

I'm pretty sure we'd woken her. Her hair was tussled and all she was wearing was a knee-length T-shirt.

"Förlåt Fröken ...?" (Excuse me, Miss ...?)

"Sanneving," she said in a lovely voice, "Maria Sanneving."

You could never be sure who was answering whenever two last names were listed on a door. Early on, I'd decided it was more polite to address the person by name rather than launch into our standard missionary pitch. If I timed it right—pausing briefly after mister or miss—most filled in their name for me. That's the way Swedes were.

"Ah, god morgon Fröken Sanneving," (Oh, good morning Miss Sanneving) I continued, "I'm sorry if we've disturbed you."

"No, no, not at all," waving her hand, "would you like to come in?"

I turned to look at Arnold. Slowly, he shook his head back and forth, frowning.

"I just need to put some pants on," Maria added as she began walking back down the hallway of her apartment. It was hard for me not to admire the view.

"IS YOUR HUSBAND HOME?" Ken asked in a voice loud enough for the entire apartment building to hear.

"She's not married, Arnold," I whispered in English, "there are *two* names on the door!"

He didn't respond. I'm sure it was because I was speaking English. Gosh, only yesterday I'd been so happy to see him. When Fissen and Beech rode off on the DL's bikes, Ken and I set off to catch the bus. My plan was to go to the apartment first so he could drop off his bag. I'd scheduled a number of people for us to visit that morning. As we walked, I gave him a friendly, teasing shove, told him how much I was looking forward to catching up.

"Speak your language" is all he said. He didn't even bother to look at me.

I stopped dead in my tracks, "Ken, what's the matter? It's me ... I ... it's

Scott." When he kept going, I called out, "Ken!"

Finally, he stopped, turned around and stared at me. The look on his face, it was like I was a stranger to him, some guy he'd never met. When I didn't move, he asked, "Are you coming? We've got work to do." And that was that.

From then on, I knew whatever we'd had before, whatever we'd meant to each other as friends at the LTM, was gone, over. Arnold had become someone else. Hell, he even looked different. The easy-going Utah farm boy, with his muscular frame and thick arms, had been replaced by an unfeeling, rail thin, mechanical man.

Nothing was said the entire time we were on the bus. In a way, I was glad. I didn't know what I would or should say to him. I was feeling hurt and confused. *Where to begin?* Thank God, the ride didn't last much more than 10 minutes.

When we got off, we ran into two "Gamla gubbar" (old men) Fissen and I had befriended over the last month or so. Despite the weather or time of day, they could almost always be found on the same park bench, smoking cigarettes and swilling beer from a large brown bottle.

Only a few weeks earlier, the two had lashed out at me and Fissen as we walked by.

"Djävla Bondjävlar!" (Fucking Mother Fuckers), they'd screamed. As far as swear words go, they were among the worst in Swedish.

Instead of ignoring them, I went right over, sat down beside them, and struck up a conversation. It turned out to be the first of many. Eventually, the two began waving at us whenever we passed by. Of late, they'd taken to calling us over for a chat. At their request, we soon were using their first names, Bengt and Peter. We got to know who they were. Before the park bench had become their second home, both had worked at the local Volvo factory assembling car engines. Whenever we saw them, they took considerable delight in filling us in about the latest scandal to hit the tabloids, especially if it had happened in the States.

"Äldste Miller!" (Elder Miller!) Bengt yelled, his words slurred, "Come and talk with us!"

"Bengt! Peter!" I returned, walking over to shake their hands, "How nice to see you—"

"Who is this?" Bengt asked, standing to shake Ken's hand.

"This is Elder Arnold, he's visiting for a couple of days."

Standing up, Peter bowed in Ken's direction, "Welcome here, Elder Arnold!" then putting his arm around my shoulder, "You know Elder Miller, eh? He's a good guy, our friend." Before Ken could get a word out, Peter spoke over him, "Fissen is coming back, right?"

"Sure, he'll be back tomorrow", I answered.

"Good", Bengt chimed in, "because we want to talk with you about the Mormon sex slave!"

Laughing, "What?! Sex slave? Come on—"

"Yeah, you know, that missionary, the one in England, who was kidnapped."

"Kidnapped?"

"Yeah, and chained to a bed, then fucked by the beauty queen." Bengt couldn't contain himself. Grabbing Peter, the two fell back onto the park bench and began laughing their asses off.

I read the newspaper almost every day. Never came across any story about a Mormon sex slave. That would have been hard to miss. I didn't know if my two buddies were telling me the truth or yanking my chain, again. They sure loved teasing us.

Turns out, the story was on the level. A Mormon missionary really had been kidnapped. It happened in the U.K., right on the front steps of an LDS Church building. A former Miss Wyoming pulled up, abducted, attempted to seduce, and when that failed, raped the guy. The British tabloids fell all over themselves covering the story with headlines such as "The Manacled Mormon," and the "Mormon Sex in Chains Case."

I wanted to laugh right along with Bengt and Peter, and would have, but was acutely aware of Ken standing off to one side, his disapproval radiating in my direction. When he finally spoke, it was to put an end to the conversation.

"It was a pleasure meeting you both," Ken said, his tone as flat as before, "We'll see you later."

He used the exact same words with Fröken Sanneving. "We'll see you later," adding, as he shut the door, "*when your husband is home*." It was rude beyond words. Swedes, I'd come to appreciate, are a private people. They are friendly, but reserved. It's not common for them to invite strangers in. And what does Ken do the moment one opens her home to us? He shuts the door on her! When he blew off Bengt and Peter, the latter looked at me and asked, "What's with him?" I'm sure it had hurt his feelings. Despite his gruff exterior, he was a proud man.

"You know the rules," Ken said as he turned to knock on the next door, "We can't teach young women alone."

I said nothing. It wouldn't matter anyway if I did. He wasn't in a listening mood. According to him, any time spent with Bengt and Peter was a complete waste. He'd been super critical of the appointments I'd made, the people we met after dropping off his bag at the apartment.

"Not one of them are serious about the Church," he lectured, "you need more prospects and the only way to get those is by tracting."

When I told him I thought knocking on doors was a waste of time and annoyed people, he cut me off, "What? You think you are *smarter* than the Brethren? That you *know* more than them about how to do missionary work?"

The truth was I hadn't been out tracting for months, not since I'd been with Wiggins in Lund, and then only sparingly. I'd avoided it by scheduling appointments back to back most days, well exceeding the established weekly quota for discussions. We were only out now knocking on doors because he'd insisted.

"No," I replied, attempting to sound reasonable, "I don't think I'm *smarter* ... I just think ... it's better ... I've been more successful trying to get to know people."

"You should know better", he interrupted again. "Time to get 'On the Program,' The *Lord's* program". Facing the door, he knocked.

It wasn't the first time he'd so admonished me. The night before, following the appointments, Ken found the cassette tapes Fissen used each morning to study Swedish, the ones I'd checked out of the library. We'd done a good job hiding the evidence of OP the cat, but forgotten about these, as well as a newspaper or two, and a novel I'd been reading.

Ken brought the contraband items into the kitchen. I was fixing a late night snack for the two of us.

"What are these?"

I looked at them. He knew full well what they were. *It's more bullshit from Kenedict Arnold.*

"They're mine," promptly taking the items and setting them on the counter. I went back to fixing the snack.

"I have to report this to the President."

I'd had enough of him, "Yeah, well, knock yourself out *Ken*."

He stood there. I didn't say any more. When he next spoke, "You don't get to write your own program, do what you want ... you're not *special* Miller. Who do you think you are?"

"Funny," I sniggered.

"What'd you say?" losing his cool again.

"I said, 'It's funny.'"

"What?" obviously irritated.

"You telling me I'm not special, accusing me of thinking I'm smarter or know more—"

"How is that funny? I don't get you. How is any of this funny?" his voice growing louder and more stern.

Picking up my novel, the one he'd brought into the kitchen, I said, "because that's what this is about."

A Fugitive Crosses his Tracks (in Swedish, *En Flyktning Krysser sitt Spor)* is a classic of Scandanavian literature. Written in the 1930's by the Danish author, Aksel Sandemose, the book tells the story of 34-year old Espen Arnakke, a sailor from the small, fictional village of Jante in Denmark. It's a deeply personal and disturbing narrative. The lead character talks directly to the reader, reviewing his life and the choices he's made, including a murder he committed in his youth. In an effort to understand himself, he holds nothing back, sharing everything he thinks, feels, and has done.

On one of our visits to the Mårtensson's, Stig told me about *Fugitive*, offered to loan me his copy. "If there's anything that will help you understand the Swedish mindset (Svenskt mentalitet), it's this book." We'd been talking about differences between Swedish and American Culture. "Swedes have been greatly influenced by the Law of Jante" (Jantelagen), adding, "it is this that Espen, the protagonist, describes in rich detail."

Simply put, the Law of Jante states: *You are not to think you're anyone special or that you're better than anyone else.* In sharp contrast to the United States, where the focus is on the individual and competition, Scandinavian culture emphasizes community and collaboration.

Of course, in real life, the "law" has both plusses and minuses. On the positive side, it means that in most areas cooperation (samarbete) is prized over competition. For example, the country has a parliamentary system of government in which many political parties, with often disparate platforms and agendas, must somehow share power. Sweden's welfare policies are another clear demonstration. They insure that every citizen has access to healthcare, food to eat, and a place to live. "Allmänsrätt," (Everyone's Rights) guarantees that all Swedes, regardless of income, class, religion, or race, have equal access to (att njuta) the land. One can drive for miles, for instance, without seeing a fence—not between neighbors and certainly not in the country's abundant forests and lakes. The list goes on and on.

At its worst, Jantelagen has at various times taken on a near Calvinistic spirit. In *Fugitive*, Espen Arnakke felt oppressed by it, linked his identity and the course of his life to its influence. He speaks of ten specific ways the law is applied:

1. You're not to think you are anything special.

2. You're not to think *you* are as good as *us*.

3. You're not to think *you* are smarter than *us*.

4. You're not to convince yourself that *you* are better than *us*.

5. You're not to think *you* know more than *us*.

6. You're not to think *you* are more important than *us*.

7. You're not to think *you* are good at anything.

8. You're not to laugh at *us*.

9. You're not to think anyone cares about *you*.

10. You're not to think *you* can teach *us* anything.

Preached from the pulpit, taught in the schools, and enforced at home, many modern Scandinavians consider Jantelagen responsible for killing individual initiative and achievement. And yet, the ethos remains. To this day, the Swedish word for "brag" sounds terrible: att skryta (pronounced, "aht skree-ta"). It even feels ugly when you say it.

As Stig described "Jantelagen," so much of what had bothered me about what Mormon missionaries did in Sweden made sense. It was like pieces of a puzzle coming together. Suddenly and unexpectedly, I saw what before I'd only felt. *Good grief. Look at how we acted.* We walked around in pairs, wore silly hats and suits, knocked on people's doors any time day or night, constantly pushing ourselves on them and, worst of all, claimed to represent the one and only true church for everyone, living and dead. Gripped by Stig's description, I had to read it for myself, in English. Luckily, the public library had a copy.

"Of all the missionaries I've met," Stig said, "You're the most *Swedish.*" He meant it as a compliment. I thanked him. He went on to repeat what he told me before, the night Fissen asked if he could convert the toilet, "You're the only one that didn't come in here and try to convert me, act like you knew everything, what was best—"

"I don't want to hear it", Arnold barked, "That book is OP". Pointing to the cassette tapes, "Those are OP! You've been here long enough to know that. *Grow up, and get 'On the Program'.*" After that, to my utter amazement, he bore his testimony!

"I know this Church is true, that God talks to the Prophet Spencer W. Kimball, that Joseph Smith was a true prophet and that he restored the fullness of the Gospel ... and if we humble ourselves before our leaders and the LORD ... do what they tell us ...". Blah blah blah.

What a night. It ended as awful as it had started. Now, standing on the landing with Ken, waiting to see if the door he'd knocked on— twice— would open, I could only shrug in resignation. I was in a pickle. Be the missionary that Ken wants and I'm a horse's ass in the eyes of the Swedes. Follow the Law of Jante—be humble and polite, respectful of Swedish culture and tradition— and I'm the poster child for apostasy.

That's when the door opened. Standing before us, was a kindly looking, elderly woman attired in a dark print dress and sweater.

"Hello," he started his pitch, "My companion and I are two representatives of the Church of Jesus Christ of Latter Day Saints. We have an important message. May we come in and talk with you about it?"

"No, thank you," the woman replied, "I'm not interested—"

"If we could have just a moment," Ken said, stepping in between the opened door and frame, "we have a very important message about your salva—"

She cut him off, "I would like to show you something before you go though. Wait here."

I watched as she walked back to an upright piano that stood at the end of the hall. It was covered with pictures in frames. She took one and returned.

"I want to show you this," handing the frame to Ken. I looked too. It appeared to be a photo. I had a hard time making it out. It was all white except for a couple of very small dark spots in the center. We both stared at it then looked up at her. Hell if I knew what it was.

When it was apparent neither of us had anything to say, she continued in her warm grandmotherly voice. "See those two black dots here?" pointing. We looked again. "That's two of you boys, you Mormon missionaries. I took this picture from my front window during a snow storm. Whenever I get down, or feel sad, I look at that picture and think, 'I guess I don't have it so bad.'" Taking the frame from Ken, she smiled, said, "Good day," and closed the door.

I think Ken was stunned. He looked like he was stunned, he didn't move a muscle. Without raising her voice or taking on airs, she politely put him in his place. Ken came out of his stupor when the door to Fröken Sanneving's apartment opened. She was fully dressed. She still looked great.

"Aren't you coming in?" in that same lovely voice.

"I'm sorry," I said, "We have to go. Maybe another time?"

"Oh, oh, ok …".

When she closed her door, I turned to Ken, "I'm done".

It didn't take long to get back to the apartment, fifteen or twenty minutes is all. As soon as I opened the door, I could see the mail had been delivered. It was all over the floor. Thank God it was lunch time. There'd be no more tracting today—and if I could help it, for the rest of my mission. Like the day before, I'd booked appointments one after another for the time Ken and I had left together.

I walked into the main room, mindlessly sorting through the letters.

"Are you going to make lunch?" Ken asked.

"Sure …" noticing what looked like a wedding announcement addressed to me.

Pointing to his watch, "We don't have much time." *True to form.* I was breaking another rule: going through the mail on a work day.

I set all the other letters on the desk, and walked toward the kitchen, the one gilded envelope still in hand. The postmark was from Provo, Utah, where BYU is located. *Who could this be from?* I didn't really know any guys of marriageable age living in "Happy Valley," as the locals referred to the town. *Must be one of the girls I'd met my freshman year.*

Opening the neatly folded and engraved parchment paper, I was surprised to see the face of my former college girlfriend, Katie Barrett. She was as beautiful as I remembered, long blond hair, crystal blue eyes, and amazing smile. I looked at the guy who had his arms wrapped tightly around her. I didn't know him. *Wait a minute, his name is Scott Miller!* No shit. Scott Miller. What were the chances of that?

Setting the invitation on the counter, I opened the fridge. I was going to cook "pigs in a blanket." The night before, after Ken had worked me over for the book, tape, and bad attitude, I'd stayed in the kitchen a while, and made bread dough. As I took it and the package of hotdogs out, my mood darkened. At first, I wasn't sure why. Katie and I had ended our relationship before the end of the school year. I didn't think about her much anymore and never thought about us getting back together. When it ended, that was it. It was over. Still, seeing her made me think of what had been and, more, everything I was missing because I was here. And what was I doing here? Doing stuff to people who did not want me doing it to them, for people who didn't even like me.

The phone rang. An extension hung on the wall just outside the kitchen. I reached around and picked it up. It was Elder Beech and he wanted to speak with Ken. I handed him the phone and made my way into the kitchen to finish making lunch. *Soon this day will be over.* Tonight we'd be switching back. I couldn't wait. *I hope that's what Beech is calling about.*

I didn't have to wait long to find out what was up. Soon, Ken poked his head through the kitchen door, "Put your jacket back on," he said, "We've gotta go."

"What?" surprised, "No lunch?"

"Elder Fissen is in the hospital."

Between walking and waiting for buses, it took us about an hour to get to the hospital. At the front desk, we were told Beech and Fissen were still in the emergency room (Akuten) and we should go there to meet them. The place wasn't very big; it wasn't hard to find.

When we walked in, the nurse at the front desk merely pointed in the direction of a small enclosure. Once again, our clothing gave us away, made it easy to tell who we were there to visit. I pulled back the curtain to find Fissen lying on a hospital style bed, wires emerging from the smock he was wearing. Beech was standing next to him on the other side, smiling.

Catching Bernie's eye, *did he just wink at me?*

"What happened?" Ken asked, using his Mormon voice of authority.

"We'd been out tracting all morning," Beech started, "I told Elder Fissen it was his door. He reached out to knock and 'bam,' that's when it happened. He got all wobbly and passed out." Pointing to a bandage wrapped around Bernie's head, "He hit his head when he fell."

Arnold turned away and looked down the hallway, "What are the doctors saying?"

"His head? It's OK, just a bump and a scratch. They're also running some tests to find out why he fainted."

I looked at Fissen again. This time he looked down at his hands. He busied himself with a small piece of plastic, something I'm sure had come off one of those wires connected to his chest.

This wasn't the first time Bernie had been at this hospital or fainted. He'd passed out a time or two in the beginning of our companionship. One time, we'd just left the apartment. The other, we were far from home. Each time it was snowing and we were on our way to an appointment. On both occasions, I was quizzing him about the language, making him repeat words over and over until he got the accent right.

The first time, I helped him up, took him back to the apartment and then called the Mission Office. *Not another sick companion,* I thought. President Thorsson told us not to fool around. We were to go directly to the hospital and have it checked out. We did. The doctors found nothing.

The second time he went down, I just stood there and looked at him lying on the ground. He was breathing. I'm not sure what came over me. For some reason, I got the feeling that this was all bogus. It just seemed fishy because both times he fainted I'd been challenging him to try harder with the language. I wasn't being mean, but I was pushing.

After thirty or so seconds, I kicked his foot and demanded, "GET UP BERNIE!" Instantly, he opened his eyes, stood, and brushed himself off. He didn't say anything and neither did I. We simply went on as though nothing out of the ordinary had happened. And until now, there'd been no further incidents.

"I'm sure I'm OK," Fissen spoke up, "Elder Beech gave me a blessing."

"A blessing?" I asked, my tone just this side of sarcastic.

"It's amazing," Elder Beech chimed in, "It was like a reflex or something. I got down on my knees, whipped out my keychain, opened my vial of consecrated oil, dropped some on his head, laid my hands on him, and ... commanded in the name of Jesus Christ for him to be healed—"

I looked at Bernie. He was grinning, a kind of cat–who-ate-the-canary type of smile. Turning toward Ken, I could see that he was entranced. His eyes were wide open and fixed on Beech.

"... and, as soon as I said 'Amen,'" he opened his eyes and stood up!"

Ken shook his head back and forth. Looking my direction, "The power of the priesthood—"

"Oj," (Oh my), the doctor exclaimed when she drew back the curtain and entered the enclosure, "There are a lot of you!"

"Hi," I replied, and extended my hand, "My name is Miller, Elder Fissen is my companion. How's he doing?"

After confirming with Bernie that it was all right to discuss his health with the three of us, she flipped the aluminum cover of his medical chart open and declared, "Well, we can't find a thing wrong" (Ja väl, vi kan inte hitta något fel).

I watched as Beech and Arnold exchanged a knowing smile. I'm sure they were both thinking they'd just witnessed a miracle.

And who knows? Maybe they did. After all, who was I to say?

∾

"This crazy cat. Bern! Can you play with him for a minute?"

I was recording a tape to send home along with the photos I'd taken over the last couple of months. Adding narration to each picture was another thing I'd picked up from Wiggins. My Mom and Dad loved it. I'd tell them about each picture, naming the people and describing the occasion or location. To signal that I was moving on to the next photo, I'd strike a pencil against an empty glass jar to make a clinking noise. The sound was like a homing beacon to OP. He'd been pacing back and forth across the table, batting at my photos with his paws, loudly meowing ever since I'd gotten started.

"I only got a few left to do."

Grabbing OP, Bernie asked, "Then we'll go running?"

"Sure," I answered, "Gimme five minutes."

I picked up the next picture. Without having to think, I knew exactly when and where it had been taken: 6 a.m., December 13th, in our apartment. The photo was dark; most of the ones left on the stack were. I hadn't had time to connect the flash to my Canon SLR camera so I just opened the aperture wide and snapped away.

December 13th is Santa Lucia Day, one of the few saints days celebrated in Sweden. As the legend goes, Lucy, a Sicilian girl, had been praying for her mother, who was deathly ill. In answer to her plea, an angel appeared. Soon afterward, Lucy converted to Christianity. Although pledged in marriage, she embraced a chaste life, renouncing sexual intercourse. Her husband, apparently taking considerable umbrage at this development, turned her over to Roman authorities. Unfortunately for her, this was the time of the "Great Persecution" ordered by the Roman Emperor Diocletian. Christians were subjected to wholesale slaughter. The faithful young virgin Lucy was burned at the stake, and after that, beheaded.

Although it's now a religious holiday, the celebration of December 13th predates Christianity in Scandinavia by many centuries. It's tied to both pagan traditions and Scandinavian folklore. Locals mistakenly believed the date to be the shortest of the year, the winter solstice. Starting that night and continuing through the midwinter festival known as "Yule," a female demon known as "Lussi" took to the skies in search of misbehaving children. Down through the chimney she'd come to steal them away. To protect themselves from these and other evil spirits, including trolls, families held vigils, helping each other stay awake until the next morning.

Fissen and I were fast asleep on December 13th when a knock came.

"Who is it?" I asked, groggily.

The reply came in Swedish, "Elder Miller? This is Brother Mårtensson. Can you let me in?"

BROTHER Mårtensson? Why is he here? And why is he calling himself Brother? Something must be wrong.

"Herre Gud," (Oh my God!) I exclaimed in Swedish. Fumbling in the dark to release the lock, "Is everything all right?"

Cracking open the door, I peeked out. It was Stig and he wasn't alone.

Standing in a line behind him in the hallway was every female, young and old, from the Skövde congregation. Each was clad in a floor length white dress and carrying a candle. At the head of the procession—directly behind Stig—stood 20-year-old Tove Dahlberg, wearing an entire crown of lit candles!

As I was only wearing my G's, I quickly ran back to my bed, grabbing the camera from the table on the way. Stig pulled open the door and the group began filing in one after the other while singing (in Swedish):

> Night walks with a heavy step
> Round yard and hearth,
> As the sun departs from earth,
> Shadows are brooding.
> There in our dark house,
> Walking with lit candles,
> Santa Lucia, Santa Lucia!
>
> Night walks grand, yet silent,
> Now hear its gentle wings,
> In every room so hushed,
> Whispering like wings.
> Look, at our threshold stands,
> White-clad with light in her hair,
> Santa Lucia, Santa Lucia!
>
> Darkness shall take flight soon,
> From earth's valleys.
> So she speaks
> Wonderful words to us:
> A new day will rise again
> From the rosy sky ...
> Santa Lucia, Santa Lucia!

If you didn't already know, one would be hard pressed to tell the song is about the young Sicilian girl martyred for her faith. Only the refrain at the end of each verse mentions her name! The rest of the song is about darkness and light, an important subject for a people that contend with so little daylight for six or more months per year. Visit a Swedish home during winter and they will "tända ett ljus" (light a candle). It's not a romantic gesture. It's deeply symbolic, even spiritual. On the flip side, as soon as the longer days of spring arrive, Swedes sit outside faces turned up toward and moving in unison with the sun.

"I can't describe how beautiful their voices sounded," speaking into the microphone of my cassette recorder.

Clinking the glass, "Look at the next picture, number 32. See the girl in front with all the candles in her hair? That's Tove Dahlberg. We met at the grocery store. When she saw us, she came right up, introduced herself. Her mom is married to an American guy who originally moved to Sweden to avoid the draft. We started meeting, going over to her parents' house. Her dad's nice, plays in a rock band that's pretty big here. She likes talking about music and movies, the States. Now, she's coming to Church."

I continued adding narration to the remaining pictures. Most of them were from *Julafton* (Christmas Eve). We'd spent the day with the members—the former hippies—hanging out, singing, dancing and of course, eating. They'd done up the communal dining room and kitchen in traditional Christmas colors and decorations. It was a Sunday, so earlier we'd been at Church. A few members had dressed up and put on a Christmas play, re-enacting the nativity.

Clink. "Number 36. This is called the 'Yulbord.' Like Grandma Daniels, the Swedes eat their big meal and open gifts on December 24th. Look at all the food! On the left, at the edge of the table in the different colored crocks, is 'sil,' the pickled herring I've told you about before. It's fantastic. I can eat it every day. We had mustard, tomato, salt and pepper, and sour cream, I think. Right next to that is smoked fish. Dad, you'd die. They had a bunch of different kinds: salmon, halibut, mackerel. Next to that, all the vegetables you see are grown in their garden."

Clink. "OK, move on to number 37, the casserole dish. It may be hard to make out, but that white gooey junk is 'Lutfisk.' It's a very traditional Christmas dish made out of dried cod. It's from the olden days, when all of the fish was preserved with salt. Starting in November, you can see pieces of it hanging from strings in the grocery store. One of the sisters told me that to eat it, you first have to soak it in lye for several days. LYE, can you believe it? After that, you soak it in water. Then you steam it in a pot. It

has a really strong smell, I can't describe it, sort of like old fish and Comet®
mixed together. Think fish flavored jello."

Clink. "38. This is another traditional dish, a casserole called 'Jansson's
frestelse.' The first word, 'Jansson' is a Swedish last name, and 'frestelse,'
means, temptation. So: Jansson's temptation. Mom, it's kind of like your
scalloped potatoes, but made with anchovies! They love it here. They love
anything with fish here. I think the Swedes would put fish in chocolate cake
if they ate chocolate cake. They don't. I ate it. It was pretty good but I won't
be bringing the recipe home!"

Clink. "Moving on, 39. I hope this isn't boring, all these pictures of the
table, and what they eat on Christmas Eve. This one is the meats. Like us, they
do a ham. In the blue bowl are meatballs, and, next to those, the long, round,
red things are called, 'korv,' kind of like a fancy hotdog. The short, skinny guy
standing there, loading up his plate, is my companion, Elder Fissen."

Clink. "Next picture please, number 40. This is me—and no, Mom, I'm
not losing weight. Please don't worry. We're just 'on the go' a lot. As you can
see, when we're with the members, they feed us well! The item I'm holding up, between my fingers in my hand, is an almond. See the bowl in my
lap? That white stuff is called 'risgrynsgröt.' That's rice porridge, a dessert
eaten on Christmas Eve. Basically, its rice cooked with milk. It's kind of like
cream of wheat. The brown stuff sprinkled on top is cinnamon. I'm smiling
because I got the almond. The cook puts one in the pot as it's being cooked.
The tradition here is that the person who gets the almond will be the next
one to marry! Everyone clapped when they saw I got it. I don't know for
sure, but I think it might have been a set up."

Clink. "Next, number 41. We're all in a line, holding hands. That's me
off to the left. I'm holding hands with Agneta, to the right, and Björn, on
the left, the Carlsson's kids. My goodness, they're cute. You should hear
them talk. At Church that day, Björn was practicing his 'r's'. In certain
words, Swedes roll them. They make a snare drum kind of sound with their
tongues. At Church, he sat on my lap because his Mom and Dad were in
the play. Right in the middle of it all, he starts saying, 'teag-gerrrrrr-rah,'
the Swedish word for Tiger, over and over again. No one said anything. It
was really funny. You can learn a lot about the language by listening to kids,
how they talk. Anyway, the picture is a bit blurry 'cause we're in motion.
We're dancing around the Christmas tree, singing. It's another tradition

here. Brother Mårtensson, the man I told you about before, you remember, his wife is a member? He was at the head of the line. Because there were so many of us, he lead us around the tree, up and down the stairs, into the cellar and out again. We're singing a song I'd not heard before, 'Nu har vi ljus här i vårt hus.' It means, 'Now we've lit candles in our house.' As you can see, the tree in the background is decorated with lit candles!"

I had so much fun. I didn't want it to end. It was so much better than last year. You remember? In Huskvarna? Elder Church insisted we go out and tract. Knock on people's doors on Christmas Eve! No one let us in. Later, we went to a member's house for dinner, then sat there and watched while they opened their presents. It was one of the worst days of my life."

Clink. "Moving on, almost done, number 42 ...". Clink. "43 ...". Clink. Clink. Clink. Pounce!

"Meow," OP cried out, scurrying across the table, sending my photos flying in different directions.

"OK, ok," I said, picking him up and holding him tight to my chest. "Vad är det med dig?" (What is it with you?) I asked in a baby voice. "Vad är det?" (What is it?)

As I ran my hand over his fur, he pushed his head into my palm, purring loudly.

Looking over at Bernie, "You ready to go, man?"

"Yep," he responded, standing. "Glad to be back with you partner," he said for the umpteenth time. On his way to the door, he patted me on the back.

"We'll be back soon," giving OP one last pet. Still talking baby talk, "Don't worry, we're just going out for a run. We'll be right back". As I locked the door, I could hear him complaining. He hated being alone.

Off we went into the night. It was pitch black and so cold my breath froze, forming an iceberg on the scarf I had wrapped about my face and neck. The streets were packed deep with snow, at least two feet if not more. I could tell the snow plows had been out recently. The top layer of newly fallen snow had been cleared off, and a fresh layer of sand and gravel put down. Fissen and I ran side-by-side down this road and that, past apartment buildings and houses, saying nothing. Here and there, a family could be seen, seated together around their dining room table, eating or talking. An electric candle was displayed in the windows of most homes. From some, a shifting blue-grey hue made clear the TV set was on.

We'd only been back in the apartment a few minutes when the phone rang. I looked at the clock. It was 9:35 pm. Mission rules were clear. We had to be in by 9:30 p.m., no exceptions. We'd timed the run just right. Too early and we couldn't answer the phone. It might be the DL's calling to check on us. Come in before 9:30 pm and we'd get yelled at for being slackers. Come in after and we'd be in trouble for being late. Several times, back in Huskvarna with Robbie the Redemmer, he'd made us stand outside the door of our apartment until the exact minute.

"This is Elder Miller," I answered.

The voice on the other end was instantly familiar, "Elder Miller, Stig." He was kind of whispering.

"Hello, everything all right?"

"Yeah, yeah, fine", he responded, his voice still quiet, "do you have a minute?"

Sitting down, "Of course!" OP jumped up on the desk and began batting the mail around with his paw. The wedding invitation from Katie Barrett spun in a circle toward the edge and fell to the floor. Watching it, *why did she send an invitation to me? And Scott Miller! Please.* Fissen had disappeared into the kitchen to fix us a bite, so I picked up the cat and put him in my lap.

As I petted OP, Stig continued, "I'm ready."

"Ready?"

"I'm ready to join the Church, be baptized."

"What?!" responding much louder than intended, my volume causing OP to flee from my lap and Bernie to poke his head through the kitchen doorway. I waved him off, mouthing, "It's ok."

"Yeah, Kerstin's birthday is coming up you know, and I thought it would be a nice present for her, for me to get baptized."

I was floored. "Well, you know ..." I started, simultaneously trying to collect my thoughts. "But you ... I thought ... you never—"

Interrupting, "I know, I know ... but I think it's time (in Swedish, "Nu är det dags").

"But ..." is all I managed to say before falling silent.

"Would you? Do it? I mean baptize me?" he asked.

I felt a rush of adrenaline, my heart beating hard in my chest. *Baptize him? Me? Mr. Full-of-Doubts? Him? Be baptized?*

"Uh, I'm honored but, are you sure?"

"I am. Actually, I've known for a while."

"You have? But you never—"

"I know—"

"… and getting baptized for Kerstin … it's not the right reason … you won't pass the interview … with the District Leaders … they have to approve …".

"I'll pass," he responded assertively, "I'll pass. Don't worry about that."

"Well, uhh—"

"It will make Kerstin so happy … and it would make me happy to have you do it—"

"Not one of the other men? The guys, your gang?"

"I want *you*," he said sincerely.

"Well, uh, OK," I said, pleased, "I'll do it."

I hung up the phone and stared at the wall. Stig was a friend. I liked him, cared about him. Obviously, he liked and cared about me. *I should feel honored he asked me to perform the ceremony but I don't. I feel like a hypocrite. I don't believe in this stuff.* I needed a couple of minutes to think.

Yelling toward the kitchen, "Bern, I'm jumping in the shower. Be out in a bit and we can eat."

"Fint" (Fine) Bernie shouted back. I barely heard him. I was already in the john, door shut, stripping off my sweat suit and G's.

For as long as I can remember, the shower has been a refuge. The hot water. The steam. The quiet. It was a place I could think, relax. Sad or happy, fantasizing or brooding, I could go in, sit down, and let my mind wander. For much of my mission, our apartments didn't have showers. They had tubs; if we were lucky, one with a spray wand. This apartment had a tub and a shower—a real shower, one with a shower head mounted on the wall. After so much time without, having one was heavenly.

Reaching past the curtain, I felt the water. It was perfect. I stepped in, letting it's spray hit me directly in the face. Adjusting the temperature a bit, I sat down, and let out a sigh. The water poured over me. *What was I thinking? How could I say yes?*

"I just don't believe this stuff," I said out loud, blowing water out of my mouth.

Leaning back, I extended my legs, filling up the length of the tub. *No,*

I thought to myself, *it's more than that. It's not just that I don't believe. I reject the entire premise. What's the point in going around claiming you* <u>don't</u> *believe in something—fairies, trolls, bigfoot, aliens from outer space, or Santa Claus. How about the tooth fairy or Easter Bunny? They don't exist. Period. There's no need to hedge about it. It's all a sham. The same with gold plates, visits from angels, secret handshakes and passwords, the whole thing.*

I stood up, turned around, and backed into the water. Closing my eyes, I could hear the water pelting my head. *What am I going to do? I can't back out now. Stig will be bummed if I say no. Isn't that the right thing to do though? Say no? He's a reasonable guy. He knows how I feel. He'll understand, I'm sure.*

I tried to reason it out. *Is there any chance that me doing this could* <u>hurt</u> *Stig? Heaven knows, Kerstin will be overjoyed. If this whole Church thing is* <u>not</u> *true— if it's a sham—well, what does it matter? It's what Stig wants. HE asked me. It's important to him.*

But what if I'm wrong? What if it turns out, that everything the Church says is true. What then? Will God hold a grudge against Stig?

I picked up the bar of soap, rubbed it on a cloth, and began washing my face. Turning into the water, I rinsed off. My eyes still closed, I heard the shower curtain slide open. I immediately turned and saw Bernie stepping into the tub. *Jesus Christ!* He was completely naked, his free hand barely covering his privates.

Startled, I blurted out, "WHAT ARE YOU DOING?!"

Standing in the tub inches away, he answered, "I just thought, I—"

"Get out of here," I demanded, shouting "NOW!"

When he reached for the curtain to exit, I could see he had an erection. *What the fuck?* My heart racing, I turned off the water and stood there. *What was he doing? Jesus, he had a hard on. He was coming in to screw me!*

Grabbing a towel off the rack, I dried off. By now, I was enraged. Even though I'd never been in a fist fight in my life, I felt like running in there and beating the ever living shit out of him. He only weighed 98 pounds. It wouldn't last long.

I didn't. Instead, I pulled the shower curtain to one side and sat down on the edge of the tub. *What in the Hell am I going to do? This is crazy. I can't believe he did that.*

Instantly, I was transported back to my first childhood home. Not the one my family lived in now, but the one before, on the other side of town. I lived there until I was eleven. On our block there was an older kid, James Lange. He must have been 15 or 16 at the time. I'd never told anyone that he fondled me. I felt so guilty. He'd invited me into his house, told me he'd give me a Matchbox® car if I'd come in. I loved those little toy cars, had a whole collection of them, so I went.

What happened next was like a dream. No, it was a nightmare. Within a minute, he had his pants off. He told me to remove mine or he'd tell my parents I'd touched him. When I protested, he said they'd believe him because he was older. Not knowing what to do, I froze. I didn't want to get into trouble. Plus, my parents had told me many times not to go inside the Lange house. They weren't Mormons and the kids were older. More, the parents frequently threw wild parties. In fact, the police had been over several times. I knew, because my younger brother Marc and I watched the action from our bedroom window.

Despite my parents' warnings, I wanted the toy, so I went in the house anyway. Feeling ashamed and scared, I pulled down my pants.

"The underwear," he insisted, "take them off too." I slowly pulled them down to my ankles. "Gimme 'em," he demanded. Holding them up in front of me, "Tell anyone about this and I'll show them these! They'll know what you did." After that, he started touching me, stroking and pulling at my penis. When I got hard, he took my hand and placed it on his. "Rub it!" he said.

I'd never done anything like this, had never touched another kid. I hadn't even touched myself. Holding my hand, he showed me, "like this … faster … not so tight … keep going …" After he came, he gave me the toy car and told me to get out. I put my pants back on—no underwear he still had them—and ran home, throwing the car in the ivy hedge bordering our front yard.

I never told anyone what happened. My parents didn't pick up on anything, and my Mom never mentioned the missing underwear. Even so, for several years, I worried about James Lange showing up unexpectedly at our house waving my little briefs, come to tell on me.

I stood, slipped on a fresh set of G's and sat back down on the edge of the tub. *Fissen is no James Lange.* I'd been with him for a long time. *I knew him. He wasn't like that. So, what gives? And what am I going to do?!*

From outside the door, I could hear OP; over that, the sound of crying. I opened the bathroom door and went into the main room. Fissen was sitting crossed-legged on his bed, head in hands, sobbing.

"I'm sorry ... I'm sorry ...", he blubbered, "I didn't mean anything ..."

OP ran over, hopped on the bed, and then up into Fissen's lap.

Sitting down on my bed, across from him, I asked, "What were you thinking?" I was still rattled, furious.

"I don't know ...", he said softly, followed by deep sobs.

"You just got in the shower with me ... and your ... and you have, you know ... and you don't know why you did it? That's it? That's all you can say? 'I don't know?'"

Slowly, Bernie stopped crying. Wiping his nose with a tissue, he turned to look at me, "I like you".

I answered, "Yeah, well, Bernie ... I like you too, but ...".

"No," he said, cutting me off, "I *really* like you".

Oh shit! It took me a moment to absorb what he was saying, "You mean, you *like me*, like me?"

He nodded his head up and down, sniffling. The next thing I said was the first thing that came to my mind, "YOU HAVE A GIRLFRIEND!"

We talked—a long time. I wouldn't have believed what he told me had he not said it himself. I'd never met a guy who liked guys—or at least would admit it. I didn't know shit about homosexuality, except that the Prophet Spencer W. Kimball said it was caused by masturbating. That had to be nuts because whacking off had never had that effect on me. Growing up, in elementary school, I remember some of the boys cutting up about the milk cartons we got at lunch time. On the side, written in bold letters, it said: HOMO MILK. I laughed right along with them, though I honestly had no idea what was so funny.

"I like girls, Bernie!" I told him. "Get that in your head. Whatever kind of feelings you have, you've got to keep them to yourself. No touching me, no trying to do that stuff with me."

He promised. "I could get excommunicated. Please, please don't tell anyone."

"Who am I going to tell? The DL's? Thorsson?" I asked, "It's not like I'm buddies with them."

"Please," he begged.

"I won't say anything."

"I keep praying ..." he offered, "but nothing happens."

I just looked at him. I knew the feeling.

When we finally turned out the light to sleep, it was super late. I laid there, eyes wide open. I was still creeped out. I wasn't scared of Fissen trying to do something again. I was actually feeling sorry for the guy. A lot of what he'd done before, now made sense: always touching me, sitting too close to me at Church and on the bus, putting his head on my shoulder.

What a day.

10

IN THE END

∼

"Most missionaries will say that their missions were the best two years
of their lives ..."

LOWELL M. DURHAM, JR.
ASSOCIATE EDITOR, *NEW ERA MAGAZINE*

∼

"What are you going to do when you get home?" Carl-Erik asked.
We were all seated around his dining room table eating Middle
Eastern food. Ali Baba's was the latest ethnic restaurant to open
in Kristianstad. He'd wanted to try it for weeks. I'd never had this kind of
food before.

"I've still got three months to go", I said dismissively, "don't count me
out yet".

My companion, Elder Milton Johnson, dipped a piece of pita bread into
the hummus and took a bite. "Two digit midget", he said with a swallow,
"You're short, man; less than 99 days left of 'the best two years of your life!'"

"Best two years my a ...", I grumbled, stopping short. Munching some
shawarma, "Wow, this is delicious".

Johnson continued, teasingly, "Its official. Today, you're a two-digit
midget. Don't get yourself killed before you get to go home."

Carl-Erik set down his fork, a piece of falafel still speared on the tines. "What? Don't get killed?" Turning to me, "What's he mean?"

"Ah, he's just joking," I said, with a laugh, "It's an expression from Vietnam. Short-timers, guys that were close to finishing their tour of duty were afraid of getting waxed before going home." Looking back at my companion, "I'm being careful, man. I already sold my bike and we're taking the bus everywhere we go."

Johnson smiled widely.

"Plus," I added, "I'm looking both ways before I cross the street."

Carl-Erik asked again, "So, what are you going to do when you get home?"

I didn't mind his question. I liked him. He was a member. We met in Church the first Sunday after I was transferred from Skövde to Kristianstad—a city in southern Sweden, and my latest and probably, last assignment. That day, he played the hymns on the piano and, man, could he play. Most congregations in the country were so small, members sang without accompaniment. Carl-Erik burned the keys. It was more like a concert than a church service.

Actually, Carl-Erik was a graduate of the Royal College of Music in Stockholm. He commuted to Göteborg, where he was the pianist for the city's symphony orchestra. Next to the dining room table, in front of a large window, sat his Steinway baby grand. We'd already been to his home several times and, on each occasion, as we approached the front door, we heard him going at it with a passion. I loved listening to him play, even brought my cassette recorder along so I could capture him playing and listen later. In a few weeks time, I learned more about classical music than I had my entire life.

There wasn't any doubt about my post mission plans. "I'm going back to school. I'm already registered, have my classes picked out. I start two weeks after I get home …".

"To BYU?"

I nodded. Although I'd considered applying elsewhere, reality changed my mind. I was like the guy who hated his job, but was fully vested in the company's retirement plan. BYU had a fantastic language program. Take a few classes and pass a test, and I'd not only earn a minor in Swedish but enough college credits to make up for the two years I'd been away.

"What *is* this stuff?" Johnson asked, ignoring the topic of conversation.

Tearing the receipt off the delivery bag, and reading slowly, "it must be the … baba ganoush."

"Like that helps …", Johnson joked, "What I meant was, what is it?"

In the lottery of mission companions, this time I'd been fortunate. He was a good guy. By that, I mean, he was easy going. Almost from the first moment we met, I knew I could trust him. He had neither the stern, "no joy allowed" manner or the "I drank the kool-aid" beatific smile of so many I'd encountered over the last 20 months. On our first day, as we walked from the railway station to the apartment, I could tell he was sizing me up, wondering what sort I was.

"Is it true?" he'd eventually asked breaking the silence, "that you have the scriptures memorized?" He was referring to the method Wiggins had taught me for locating scriptures. It had caught on, spreading throughout the mission. Because of that, I'd gotten something of a reputation.

"Not all of them, only the *Doctrine and Covenants*," I said, with a chuckle, "Just joking … amazing isn't it? What some people will believe?"

"Whew," he responded, wiping his hand across his forehead in an exaggerated fashion, "I was worried they were sending me another prima donna."

We both laughed. "You OK calling me Scott? Or Dew? That's my nickname."

"Sure," he said.

"And you? I'll call you Elder Johnson if you want, but …?"

"Just don't call me Milton. J.J. works. James is my middle name." From then on our companionship was stress-free. J.J. was from Northern California. He'd completed his freshman year at Stanford. Needless to say, he was one bright guy. We spent hours and hours talking about every subject except Mormonism: history, economics, politics, philosophy. He immediately warmed up to reading the newspaper every day, and signed up for a library card when I went to get one. Although his accent wasn't the best, his grammar was near perfect. Long and lean with jet black hair, J.J. was easily the tallest companion I'd ever had, standing six and a half feet tall. In all ways, he made an impression.

Responding to J.J.'s question, Carl-Erik reached in the take-out bag and retrieved the menu. "Says here baba ganoush is … pureed eggplant with Asian spices."

Apparently satisfied with the answer, Johnson hefted a double portion of the green stuff onto his pita and put it in his mouth.

"I've even got a job," I said, returning to Carl-Erik's question, "I'm going to be a resident assistant in the dorms. I get my room and board, plus a little spending money." On this score, I'd lucked out. During my freshman year, I'd gotten close with the dorm mother, Francis Horton. I'd written to her off and on throughout my mission. Months earlier, I asked her what the chances were of getting a position in the residence halls. To my surprise, she offered me a job.

"Cushy," Johnson editorialized, "Will you think of me when you're gone? Between classes and co-eds?"

"Is someone waiting for you back home?" Carl-Erik asked, curious.

Nodding my head back and forth, "Nah. Had a girlfriend, but we broke up before I came to Sweden. She's married now, nearly two months."

"Probably pregnant, too," Johnson interjected, making a political pun, "Just as in the Presidency of the United States, those first hundred days in a Mormon marriage are mighty important. Gotta start that eternal family!"

"Geez," I responded, feigning anger, "what are you on anyway? No more baba-whatever-it-is for you." Looking back at Carl-Erik, "I do have a couple of girls I've been writing to. It's picked up a bit now that I'm short. One girl is from my home town, the other is the sister of a guy I knew from the dorms my first year."

I reached into my suit pocket and removed my Day-Timer®. I'd become addicted to the little organizer when I was with Wiggins. He had one. After seeing him use it for a while, I had to have one too. I kept everything in it: my money, ID, calendar, contacts, to do list, plans for the future, and photos.

"This is Jaime Lee, the one from Glendora," turning the page, "and this is Allison."

Carl-Erik tapped the picture with his finger, "Allison, hmm. SHE's pretty."

"I barely know her, met her once when she came to visit her brother. Suddenly six months ago, we're writing each other, sending tapes back and forth. Weird how intense it's gotten."

Johnson couldn't resist commenting. He chimed in, "Mill-dew is gonna be an RM, returned missionary, big man on campus, have to beat them off with a stick. Got the 'Celestial Smile' and the right qualifications after his name: RM, *Really Marvelous, Raw Meat, Ready-for-Marriage* ... a Mormon chick magnet."

"Yeah, well," I said, spooning a couple falafel balls onto my plate, "I've got a lot of stuff to do, and getting married is not one of them." Changing subjects, "My Mom and Dad are coming to Sweden to pick me up. So, right now, I'm planning their trip. We're going to tour around the country a bit."

"Will you be coming to Kristianstad?" Carl-Erik asked.

I fell silent. Caught up in the moment, I realized I'd already said too much.

Carl-Erik instantly sensed a problem. "What?!" he inquired, "Is there something wrong?"

Once a missionary completed his mission, it was OP to return to the places he'd formerly worked. Thank you, President Thorsson. He'd informed me about this policy at the last zone conference when I made the mistake of telling him about my parents' plans.

"They are welcome of course," he began, "but …," his voice assuming the imperial tone I'd come to know, "… they need to understand that you must first leave the country for at least a week. After that, you may return to Sweden, BUT you may not visit any areas in the Sweden Göteborg Mission."

I nodded my head in agreement while thinking, *yeah, yeah, absolutely. Watch me.*

Until now, I'd told no one else about my plans, or what Thorsson had said—not even my parents. "I'll take care of the arrangements here," I'd written to them, "all you need to do is tell me when you are arriving and when you'd like to go home." I'd already sent letters to and received responses from several tourist bureaus within my mission. My Mom loved crystal, collected it. I was bound and determined to take her to where it was made regardless of Thorsson's bullshit. In fact, I'd already made a hotel reservation in a town near the two most famous factories, Orrefors and Kosta Boda, both within the boundaries of the mission.

"It's against the rules for me to visit areas within the mission," I said, throwing caution to the wind.

"But why?" Carl-Erik asked, genuinely puzzled, "I'd love to meet your parents."

If it were only that simple. Most members were clueless about missionary life, what it was really like. Carl-Erik was no different.

"I know they'd love to meet you, too. I'm sure the President has his reasons, but at the end of this, when I'm done, he doesn't get to tell me what to do anymore."

Carl-Erik squinted, obviously confused.

Johnson spoke up, this time all in English, "Free at last. Free at last. Thank God Almighty, you'll be free at last."

～

It wasn't a big surprise when we found the transfer notices among the letters splayed about the floor opposite the mail slot. In fact, we'd been expecting them. Fissen and I had been out shopping, hunting for a couple more souvenirs that he could take home to his family.

Like a lot of other missionaries, he wanted a giant Swedish flag to use for a bed spread. He also picked up a number of brightly painted, carved wooden handicrafts, including several traditional candle holders (in Swedish, "ljustacke") and an assortment of the iconic Dala horse statues (in Swedish, "Dalahäst"), from the Dalarna region of Sweden. Added to the items he'd already collected—colorful, hand knitted mittens from the village of Lovikke (pronounced, "low-veak-ah) for every member of his family and a near life-sized baby goat made of straw traditionally displayed at Christmas—he had to buy an additional, third bag to carry it all home.

Setting the packages down, I picked up the mail, including the two letters from the mission office.

"Don't you want to know what's going to happen?" Fissen asked, "If you're going to stay or go?"

"Nah," I answered, "You hungry?"

"Yeah, starving."

"I'll make us something to eat. You go ahead and pack. We know where *you're* going. You've got the 'Golden Ticket.'"

Bernie laughed loudly then inhaled sharply, making that hee-haw donkey sound. I hadn't heard that in a long time.

"Quit rubbing it in," I shouted from the kitchen.

In return, Fissen started singing Simon and Garfunkle's, *Homeward Bound*.

"… Home, I wish I was, homeward bound. Home …"

Popping his head through the kitchen door, he handed me the letter, demanding, "Open it!"

Waving him off, "I've been here over six months. I'm gonna die here." My comments weren't without reason. Most missionaries were transferred to a new area every three months, four at the outside. It kept Elders on their toes, prevented them from becoming too familiar with one other. I had to face facts; Thorsson was sending me a message. I'd been banished to the "Mormon Island for Misfit Boys," Skövde. Hell, I never heard a peep from him following my disastrous visit with Ken Arnold—and I'm sure my former friend had given him a blow-by-blow report of my numerous failings.

"Come on, open it", he pleaded, "I wanna know—"

"You open it then." I placed slices of cheese onto freshly cut pieces of bread. On the stove, I was heating up "svamp soppa," some mushroom soup one of the members had given us.

I don't know why I felt bugged. Maybe it was just envy, me wishing I was the one going home. After all, Skövde wasn't a bad spot. The members were great. During our time here, two people had joined the church, Stig Mårtensson and Tove Dahlberg. Compared to the mission average this was a miracle. Most missionaries in Sweden never baptized anyone.

I'm sure I didn't help my reputation with Thorsson when I asked him not to report our two baptisms in the mission newsletter, the *Harvester*. I'd written to him in our weekly report explaining how I didn't like the way the statistics were used, pitting zone against zone, turning the work into some kind of competition. He didn't answer back and, not unexpectedly, my request was ignored. Our names and the numbers were listed in the monthly rag, pushing our zone to the top.

Despite Thorsson's indifference to my concerns, and the reservations I had about baptizing Stig, the day was a real high. Because the church in Skövde had no baptismal font, we were forced to travel 45 miles south to Jönköping for the service. It was there, one of the few Mormon chapels in Sweden stood—the one I'd attended on Sundays, when I'd been stationed in nearby Huskvarna with Elder Church over a year earlier.

Stig, Tove, me and Bernie all dressed in white, wearing clothing borrowed from the local congregation. After an opening prayer and hymn, I stepped into the water followed by Stig. It went fast. Down and up he went. Wiping water from his eyes, he looked for Kerstin. She was crying. We exited, and Bernie and Tove entered. It was his first baptism. Although anxious, he pulled it off, in Swedish, without a hitch. At the end, before heading home, the Mårtenssons took everyone out to a fancy dinner.

Fissen returned to the kitchen door, cat in hand, "If you're leaving, we've gotta drop off OP".

Knowing there was a chance I'd be shipping out, we'd already made arrangements for our furry companion. We talked to our neighbors first, the one whose dog we walked. They declined, worrying they were too old to care for such a young animal. One of the street kids we'd befriended, Annica, agreed to give him a home. She and her gang of girls lived in our apartment complex. They spent hours perched on the benches in the common area, talking, chain smoking, and slowly getting stoned on "mellan öl" (near beer). The beer was cheap and had little alcohol but teenagers could buy it. To get a buzz, they had to drink a lot.

Like Bengt and Peter, they jeered us the first time our paths crossed, hurling epithets, calling us names. "Fucking CIA spies" or "Haven och Halven" (Laurel and Hardy) were the most common. I don't recall what we'd been doing before meeting Annica and her gang. We dropped our briefcases in the apartment, grabbed OP, and went right back out. Maybe it was the cat. Almost immediately, the rough-around-the-edges "ragara" melted into a group of high-pitched, baby-talking wannabe moms, fighting over who got to hold OP.

After that encounter, we looked out for each other. Their acceptance, willingness to talk to the "guys in blue," changed how others in the building related to us. You could feel it. Increasingly, people met us with their eyes, even said hello, didn't cross to the other side of the walkway to avoid us. For our part, we acted like older brothers: listening, gossiping, offering advice and, on occasion, helping one of the drunken teenagers get to their apartment and avoid freezing to death. Most of the time, we were simply kind and interested.

If I was leaving Skövde, I would really miss OP. I felt good knowing Annica would be looking out for him. Of all the kids, she struck me as the most level-headed and responsible. Recently, she'd dumped her dead-end boyfriend, an older guy, who never warmed up to either me or Bernie. Her ex was a real dick, pushed her around, and cheated on her.

Annica had dropped out of school a year after getting pregnant. The government provided her with an apartment and small monthly allowance. Her mother looked after the baby most of the time when he wasn't at "Dagis" (public day care). Although I only met him once, Joakim was adorable. He had her mouth and thick, wavy brown hair.

Annica and I talked at length about school. I told her about my plans to become a veterinarian. She wanted to become a beautician and someday have her own salon. I learned she'd even talked with her case worker at social services about applying to the local cosmetology school.

Spooning the soup into bowls, I yielded, "OK, ok. I give up. Go ahead and open it."

"Cool!" Fissen responded excitedly, putting OP on the floor.

Moving toward the table in the main room, "Grab the bread first. Let's eat."

He ignored me. Tearing open the envelope, Fissen yelled from the kitchen, "PACK YOUR BAGS BUCKO, you're going to … beautiful … Kritianstad?!"

"Back to Skåne," ("Sco-nah") I replied.

"Where?"

"Skåne. South, not far from Lund. At least it will be warmer."

"Your companion is … Elder Johnson. You know him?"

"Nope."

Fissen set the bread and cheese on the table. Taking his seat opposite me, "Says you're gonna be co-area leaders with him."

No matter how I felt about my mission and Mormonism, I felt a twinge of disappointment. Call it pride. My last city and I wasn't even a senior companion. I can't say I was surprised, and yet it still stung a bit. For an "old timer" like me, the assignment summed up Thorsson's opinion of me: "whatever you think *you* have to offer, guess what, we're not interested." No doubt about it, I would be ending my mission a buck private.

I ate in silence.

Apparently sensing my change in mood, Fissen broke in, "You've been a great companion …"

"Thanks Bern," I responded with a shrug.

"You really helped me a lot," he persisted, "A lot. I never would've passed the discussions … become a co-area leader with you, er … had a baptism … *You* did that."

"Thanks Bern," I said again, this time meaning it.

We finished up, then started planning how we'd spend the next three days. We had tons to do: pack, clean the apartment, and put in a change of address at the post office. We also had to say goodbye to OP, Bo the dog and his owners, the Erikssons, the members, and the friends we'd made on the streets.

I thought Bengt was going to cry when we told him we were leaving. He hugged us both, slapping each of us on the back. Peter, the quieter of the two, slipped something into my palm when we shook hands goodbye. It was a polished worry stone. The size of a 50 cent piece, it was brown and flat with an indentation in the center. You laid it against your fingers and rubbed it with your thumb. When I thanked him, he responded, "Det var så litet"—a classic Swedish "you're welcome" that translates to, "It's so very little."

On one of the evenings left, the Erikssons invited us over for dinner. Mr. Eriksson gave me the name and number of his son, who was the chef at a well known hotel in Göteborg. "Call him," he advised, "he'll make sure you and your parents are treated well." For dinner, Mrs. Eriksson made lasagna. I'll never forget it. First, the dish isn't common in Sweden. I'd never heard of it being served, or even seen the ingredients in a grocery store—and believe me, missionaries would have made it because it's cheap and filling. Second, the pasta was full of dog hair! Cutting into my piece with a fork, Bo's long black mane curled up on the plate, mixed in with the cheese and tomato sauce. It was sickening. I was sure it wasn't intentional. The apartment was littered with dog hair and Mrs. Erikson's eyesight was more than bad. It didn't matter; I couldn't eat it. I snuck each piece from the table into a napkin on my lap and later flushed the lot down the toilet. Unfortunately, I wasn't able to warn Bernie. He wasted no time wolfing down his piece and promptly asked for seconds!

On the way back to the apartment, he commented, "Man, what a treat."

I didn't have the heart to tell him. All I could say was, "Never had anything quite like it." As we entered the apartment, I had a fantasy of him coughing up a hair ball that night.

On our last night in Skövde, the members surprised us with a going away party. It's the only one I'd had or even heard about. Usually, missionaries simply disappear and are replaced by another guy in a blue suit. Anyway, Fissen and I were coming back to our flat after giving OP to Annica. Everybody, including the cat, cried. When we opened our door, we were greeted with a loud, "Surprise!" Kerstin Mårtensson had organized food and drinks. For a little over an hour, we ate, talked, and exchanged promises to stay in touch. When everyone left, it was eerily quiet. It felt so final. I'd grown to love these people, would miss them.

The next morning, I called a cab to take us to the train station. No way was I walking. We had so much junk, including my stupid bike. We locked up the apartment, sliding the keys through the mail slot before making our way down the stairs. Our replacements would have to talk with the building superintendent to gain entry.

The taxi ride there took all of 5 minutes. We unloaded and found a place to sit down in the "Väntasal" (Waiting Area). I took out my journal and pen and began writing, catching up on the last few days. Fissen did the same.

We hadn't been sitting there long when the DL's, Beech and Arnold entered the building. Both had their bags in tow. They, too, were being transferred. Seeing us, they walked in our direction.

"Good morning Elders," Beech said, in Swedish, his tone formal.

I looked up, nodded, and went back to writing. They didn't move. I didn't want to make nice with them. My personal feelings aside, I had a good excuse: it was against the rules to talk to other missionaries on transfer days. That didn't deter Fissen, however. Cheerfully, he asked, "Leaving town?"

I looked up from my journal momentarily. Beech and Arnold were both wearing serious expressions, more stone-faced than usual, if that were even possible.

"Because I am," Bernie proceeded, excitedly, "I'm going home!" He snorted, making his donkey sound, "I'm done. Finito. Bon voyage buddies!"

"We better head to the tracks," Arnold said to Beech, ignoring Bernie's question and commentary.

"Hej då," (Good bye) Ken said dispassionately. I nodded once again, saying nothing. As they turned to walk away, a folder Arnold had been holding under his arm fell to the floor. Papers flew everywhere. Without thinking, I set down my journal and got up to help.

I'd picked up several pieces when I noticed that one was Ken's transfer letter. Although I shouldn't have, I read it. Ken was being sent to Helsingfors, a city on the east coast. It also said he'd been promoted to Zone Leader. Now I understood their solemn expressions, and I couldn't help but think, *If a guy like Arnold can get promoted, God has left the building.* The next thing I know Arnold is standing in front of me, "I'll take that Elder Miller. It's private."

After they left, I put my journal away and walked over to the station kiosk. I bought a couple of candy bars and two soft drinks. One, "Sockerdricka," was Bernie's favorite, and the one I liked, "Pommac." They're hard to describe, and there's nothing like them in the States. Fissen's tasted like carbonated rock candy (the name actually means, sugar drink), mine like an unsweetened ginger ale.

Giving Bernie his drink and a candy bar, I said, "Time to go, man." We grabbed our bags and headed for the platforms. As he was leaving first, I walked across the tracks to the other side and waited with him. When the train pulled in, I helped him on with his luggage, placing the piece I'd carried on the overhead rack.

"Thanks, Scott."

"No problem," I replied, "Well," rubbing my hands together, "I guess that's it."

"Yeah...".

"I should go," checking my watch, "my train leaves in four minutes." Stepping off the train onto the platform, I turned to wave.

He was standing in the door, "I wanted to give you this."

"What is it?"

"Nothing ... just a little gift." A chime sounded, signaling the doors were about to close. "Thanks for everything," he said, as I took the small package from his hands.

"All aboard!" the conductor hollered. I stepped back and the train began pulling away. Putting the parcel under my arm, I lifted my bags and walked toward my track.

In the train, after stowing my gear, I sat down and unwrapped Bernie's gift. It was a book with a bright yellow cover, titled, "I'm OK, You're OK," written by Thomas Harris. I'd never heard of it. The back cover described it as a breakthrough in psychology, a book that could help readers transform their lives and the lives of others.

I was left to wonder where Fissen had come across it. I'd never seen him with it, or anything similar. Opening the book, I found an inscription inside the front cover:

Dear Scott—

Over six months together. We had some good times and some bad times. I can't believe we survived it!

Thanks for all your help and support. Thanks for understanding, you know what for.

I'm going home a different and better person because of you. You're O.K.

I hope you like this book. I think you'd be good at this stuff.

Your friend,
Elder Bernard L. Fissen

∾

The phone rang. Opening my eyes, I could see it was light outside. *Crap! We've slept in again.* "J.J., get up, we're late!" I shouted.

"What? Huh?" Johnson responded, groggily.

Stumbling toward the phone, "We've slept in! Damn it, get up!"

"Hello, this is Elder Miller," I said, trying to sound awake.

"Scott?" the voice on the other end asked. From all the scratchiness on the line, I could tell it was a long distance call.

J.J. brought his little, portable clock over to where I was standing and pointed to the time. It was only 5:30 a.m. We had not slept in. We weren't due up for another half hour. The displeasure showed on his face. Furrowing his brow, he tossed the clock onto my bed and flopped back down on his.

Nearly two years in the country and I still wasn't used to the shifting daylight. For the second time on my mission, we were approaching the summer solstice—in this part of the country that meant twenty or more hours of light per day.

"Dad?" I asked, "Is that you?" My heart rate quickening, "Is everyone ok?"

The quality of telephone calls between the United States and Sweden really varied. Sometimes, they were crystal clear; others were full of static and prone to delays. That meant if you didn't time it right, the parties often ended up speaking simultaneously, cancelling out what the other said. This was one of those calls.

I was only getting bits and pieces, "Yes ... it's Dad ... every ... ok. ...m calling ... bout Steph ... from high ... scho ..., remember? She's been ...

England … for … stud … nursing … well … homesick … visit …"

I waited for the line to go silent before speaking, "Dad, this call is terrible. Don't talk until you hear me say 'over,' ok? OVER".

Speaking as though we were using walkie-talkies, we eventually managed to communicate. Dad was calling because a girl I'd grown up with in Glendora, Stephanie De Luca, was in Sweden. I'd known Steph most of my life, had a big crush on her from about sixth grade on. Although we were friendly, I never acted on my feelings. Steph and I ran in different crowds. She wasn't LDS, not that it would have made any difference. More important, she was way out of my league—or so I thought. In high school, she was the head cheerleader. Her steady was the quarterback of the football team.

There was more to Stephanie than her looks. She danced, sang, and played the violin. She was also smart; the girl voted most likely to succeed by her classmates and our class valedictorian. After high school, I had not heard anything about her and most of the kids from my home town. Extra credits earned at summer school had enabled me to graduate early. That's when I got the job delivering flour to tortillerias. I did that for six months before moving to Provo and attending BYU.

Anyway, Dad told me that Steph was attending a conference in Malmö, about an hour away. She'd been living in the U.K., completing some advanced training in nursing. It was a temporary arrangement. The program was based in London and lasted six months. She'd been there for three weeks and was homesick.

Apparently, Steph's parents knew I was in Sweden. How? I don't know. Maybe, Dad told them. Our families knew one another. Mr. de Luca owned a shoe store in town that my family shopped at for years. Steph, along with me, attended La Fetra Elementary School, where my father had been the principal. Whatever the case, everyone thought that meeting me—seeing a familiar face—might cheer Steph up, and somehow help her stay. She'd been calling home, threatening to return to the States before completing the training.

"Do you think you could see her? OVER," Dad asked.

It was odd, my father calling. He knew the rules and we'd abided by them throughout my mission. Since I'd been in Sweden, we'd talked exactly six times. The first three were right after I arrived in the country and was so homesick. After that, we talked on Christmas day, and my birthday. They did have my telephone number—I always sent it—in case of an emergency.

In Dad's mind this somehow qualified as urgent.

"Sure, where's she staying? OVER"

I wrote down the name and number of the hotel. We chatted for a minute or two longer about nothing in particular when my father said, "This is expensive. Write and tell us what happens, ok? We love you. OVER."

Hanging up the phone, I looked over at Johnson. He was lying face down on the bed, the pillow wrapped tightly around his head. Our apartment was small, one room with a hot plate and mini-refrigerator. With no place to go, I sat in the one chair by our tiny desk, doodling, and more. I felt mad. I'd only talked with my family a handful of times in nearly two years—and they *never* called me. The first time they do, it's about someone else, a person I hardly knew anymore. *He's worried about her being homesick. What about me?* When I was having such a hard time in Huskvarna, miserable as hell, it barely seemed to register. He pretty much ordered me to stay. I kept doodling, brooding, until the point on the pencil broke.

What to do about Steph?

We couldn't go to Malmö. It was out of our zone. The risk of getting caught was high. The ZL's there lived in the middle of town. I knew because I'd been in that zone, when I lived in Lund. That's where I'd met Cary Wells, last—when he told me and Thorsson he was going home. Get caught, and I'd be excommunicated and kicked off my mission.

I'm too short for that. No, Steph will have to come here, to Kristianstad. What about J.J.?

He was a good guy. Incredibly tolerant of me. We already bent the rules a fair bit. When we first met, I told him how I liked to work. First, that I would not go tracting or stop people on the streets. Second, I used old tracting logs to identify "friendlies" and spend time with them. But this— inviting a friend, and a girl to boot, to meet us—was pushing the limits to the max. I knew it. How could I ask him to agree to this?

When I got around to telling him what was up, he responded, "Be willing to have it so", quoting one of his favorite philosophers, American psychologist, William James.

I thanked him, commenting, "I hope it'll be ok."

"What could happen?" he asked rhetorically.

"You mean *besides* getting caught?" I came back. Getting caught was one worry. But that wasn't the whole story. In reality, I felt anxious about meeting Stephanie. What would she think of me and how I'd spent the last two years? Gosh, she was already a nurse working on an advanced degree. What had I accomplished?

"We have to live today by what truth we can get today and be ready tomorrow to call it falsehood," Johnson continued, adding another quote from James.

"You're awfully philosophical today. I like that one though. Where's it from?"

"*Essays in Pragmatism*, one of my faves," he answered, as I picked up the phone and dialed the number my father had provided.

"Hotel Tunneln," a man answered. I'd heard of it before, come across it while researching places to stay for my parents' trip. It was one of the oldest, finest, and most expensive in Malmö.

"Hejsan, jag söker Stephanie de Luca, hon stannar i hotellet. Tack," (Hello, would you please connect me with Stephanie de Luca, she's staying at the hotel. Thank you).

I waited as the phone rang. It was early yet. I hoped she was still in her room. I didn't know how many days she would be in Sweden.

On the third ring, she picked up. I recognized her voice instantly. It was warm and friendly, although I could tell she'd been crying—either that or she had a cold. I bet it was the former. "I'm so glad you let me know you were here," I said, "How are you?"

"I'm good", she lied.

"It's been a long time—"

"Three years," she replied, rapidly. Clearly, she'd been doing some thinking about the old days.

"You want to get together?" I asked, "My Dad filled me in a bit …".

Although not intended, my words triggered the waterworks. I listened as she sobbed, telling me how homesick she was and why. Mostly it was about her boyfriend, a doctor she'd been living with for the last six months. When the opportunity came up to go to England, he hadn't wanted her to go, told her he couldn't promise he'd be there when she came home. She went anyway, always the super achiever. His lack of commitment was driving her crazy. For what they'd spent calling each other, she could have commuted from the U.S. weekly!

The conference, she told me, wasn't important. She'd only decided to attend because there was a chance of meeting me. I told her about my situation, the mission rules regarding travel, and she agreed to take the train to Kristianstad the following day.

J.J. and I were waiting on the platform when Steph stepped off the train. Seeing me, she ran up, threw her arms around me, and hugged me for the longest time.

Stepping back, she eyed me from head to toe, "It's so great to see you. My God, you're all grown up!"

Steph was as attractive and stylish as I remembered, only now a woman. Five-foot six, shoulder length blond hair, blue eyes, and a fabulous body. She could have been born in Sweden. Feeling ridiculous standing there in my blue suit, and name tag, I found myself at a sudden loss for words.

"And, think of all you've done," she went on, "living here, being on your own ... wow ... I'm such a big baby," she said with a laugh. Steph had a way about her. Despite "having it all"—looks, brains, popularity— she made you feel good about yourself. She'd always been that way. You couldn't help but like her. I did.

After introducing J.J., we crossed the street to the main boulevard on our way to Kong Christian, a restaurant in the center of town. Aside from the breakfast I'd shared with Wells and Arnold my first day in Sweden, I'd not eaten out a single time on my mission. Either we prepared our own food or ate at a member's or investigators' home.

Figuring this was a special occasion, I'd made a reservation. I was anxious to try eel, a house specialty and dish famous in this part of the country. Carl-Erik had told me about it the night we ate Middle Eastern food at his home. According to him, it was a bit early for the fish. The prime harvest season, "Ålamörkret" (Eel Darkness), wasn't for another three months, when the daylight grows short, and the rivers swell with eels fattened up for their journey to the Sargasso Sea. The darkness makes it easier to catch the usually crafty creatures because they are not able to see the fishing nets. When I called to make sure they were available, the manager assured me we'd be able to order the eel served ten different ways.

By the end of lunch, we'd eaten eel smoked, baked and grilled, in salad, with a variety of sauces, and plain. Together with the bread, vegetables, and små potatis, it was a feast. Treating Steph and J.J. also cost a fortune, or at least that's what I thought. Then again, what did I know? I hadn't been out lately! What can be said is that it took every last "öre" (penny) I had on hand to pay the bill!

Having the chance to catch up with Steph made it all worthwhile. She knew everything about everyone from home. Most of the kids we went to school with were still living in town and, as she put it, "doing little with their lives." The class president, for example, who shared the honor of being voted "most likely to succeed," was working behind the counter at the local drug store. There were a couple of shockers. My old girlfriend, Diana, was living in Hollywood with a big time movie producer. Steph's ex, the star of the football team, was in prison serving a life sentence. He murdered the husband of an older woman with whom he'd been having an affair.

After we finished eating, we walked around the town, taking in the sights. We ended up across from the train station at *Heliga Trefaldighetskyrkan* (Holy Trinity Church). It was one of the tourist attractions in the city. The massive, red-brick structure was built in the 1600's by Christian IV, the king of Denmark, who founded Kristianstad. At that time, much of Sweden was under Danish rule.

Designed by a Flemish-Danish architect, it's widely considered the finest Renaissance church in all of Scandinavia. The exterior resembles churches more often seen in Holland than Sweden, especially the scalloped roof lines and tall steeple. The interior also stands out. Massive dark, granite pillars support a ceiling of star-shaped, cross vaults reminiscent of those found in St. Peter's Basilica in Rome. Opposite the Sanctuary, above the nave, sits an enormous gilded Baroque pipe organ. Though it was OP, J.J. and I had attended a concert held in the church a couple of Saturdays earlier. It was packed, which is saying something, as the church seats 1400!

Stephanie was impressed. We took turns taking pictures of each other in front of the Altar. J.J., always the joker, removed a barrier and climbed up the stairs of the pulpit, an amazing structure made entirely of marble. A brochure we picked up at the door stated that the canopy alone weighed over a ton.

I snapped a shot and ordered him to come down, "Someone might see you!"

Ignoring me, he began exploring his surroundings, "Hey, there are a lot of buttons up here, wonder what they do?"

Before I could say, "Don't touch anything," the bells in the tower began ringing. "Oh my God", I exclaimed, panic gripping me.

In a flash, J.J. was down the stairs, standing next to Steph and me. "I didn't do anything," he said, huffing and puffing from having run so quickly, "It just started ringing."

As quickly as they'd started, they stopped. J.J. had not set the ringing in motion. The tower was merely signaling the time. It was three o'clock.

Relieved, we decided to mill about a few more minutes to look at the artwork. Like everything in the place, it was impressive.

As we were about to leave, a voice spoke from behind us. It sounded like the Swedish baker from the Muppets, except in English.

"U keds wand ah reel sperience, du ya?"

An older gentleman, in dark pants and shirt shuffled toward us. From the logo on his breast pocket and large ring of keys, I could see he worked for the local security company, *Securitas*. He was doing his rounds. I gathered he must have heard us speaking to each other in English and assumed we were tourists. I switched over to Swedish.

"Ja så," (I see) he responded, "du snacker Svensk?" (you speak Swedish?). His dialect was instantly recognizable. Called "Skånska" (Scanian), it's unique to the southern part of the country. In terms of sound, it's similar to Swedish spoken with a Boston accent. Many Swedes find it difficult to understand, and hold it in the same low regard as some Americans do a southern drawl.

"What did you have in mind?" I asked.

"The bell tower is open," he answered, "though it's not for the faint of heart! Up a spiral staircase sixty meters high," he said, his arm slowly rising in the air, index finger extended.

I did the math in my head. Sixty meters was about one hundred eighty feet. Steep, indeed.

Steph watched, her eyes shifting between me and the man, as though following the conversation.

The guard's voice shuddered, "Near the top, the handrail disappears. To get into the tower, you must step across the gap between the last stair and the wooden ledge in front of the door. The 'leap of faith' I call it."

He paused, looking at me expectantly. Reaching into his pocket, he removed a rusty, old skeleton key on a string, "If you want to go, you'll need this. Stick it in the keyhole at the top and turn it twice. Nudge the door with your shoulder and it'll open. The view is one you'll never forget. You can see for miles on a day like this."

I took a moment to translate for Stephanie. Johnson listened attentively. I'm sure he wondered, like me, if she'd be game. I was nervous myself. I wasn't one for heights.

"What do you think?" she asked.

"Nothing ventured, nothing gained," I replied, acting braver than I felt, "and we can always come back down."

We looked into each other's eyes. I was waiting for her to say no when Steph spoke up, "Let's do it."

Holding out my hand, the man dropped the key in my palm and pointed the way. We entered the stairwell through a door near the main entrance. On the wall inside, I found the now familiar glowing red orb light switch. How long the lights would remain on was anyone's guess. I pushed the button and checked the sweep hand on my watch, explaining to Stephanie how the device operated. When ten minutes passed and the lights were still on, I figured we had enough time to make it to the top.

I looked up, "Oh." It was all I could muster. In that moment, my legs felt like the eels I'd just eaten. A drab, grey metal spiral staircase shot up from the floor. It looked like a giant drill bit that someone had used to core a hole through the steeple of the church. Near the top, it disappeared completely into the darkness.

"Oh my," Steph remarked.

Looking up, J.J. completed the thought, "Oh my Lord."

"Ready?" I asked, pushing the button again. The ticking re-started.

Handing Johnson the key, he started up the stairs. I took up the rear behind Stephanie. Together, the three of us climbed the first hundred feet or so fairly quickly. It took more time after that because the staircase began to shimmy and squeak with each step we took. The image of plunging to our deaths kept coming to mind. By the time we were nearing the top, the whole structure was really wobbly, tipping right, left, then back again.

I caught a glimpse of Stephanie's expression when she glanced over her shoulder at me. She was scared. So was I.

Thank goodness the lights have stayed on. I can't imagine doing this in the dark.

Slowing her pace, "I don't think I can go any further."

"There's not much more to go ... " I said, exhaling loudly. Putting on my best superhero voice, "If the view is anything like this climb ..."

"Yeah ..." she said, moving a bit faster.

Around the last bend, the situation went from bad to worse. Just as the security guard had warned, no more handrail. The steps continued to jut out from the steel pole in the center, but now without a rail, there was nothing to grab onto. We were left with a foot-wide gap between the stairs and surrounding wall for the rest of the ascent. Johnson hunched over and began crawling on all fours. Stephanie sat down facing me, perspiration glistening on her forehead, visible even in the dim light.

Wiping her brow, and almost whispering, "I'm scared, Scott ... this is ... I don't think I can do this."

Looking beyond her, I could see that the center pole we were both holding onto for dear life ended, leaving one to stand on the last steps without support on either side. An electric shock shot through my legs and stomach as I imagined myself standing there. Forget the eels, now I felt like I didn't have any legs at all.

I could see Steph was starting to breathe rapidly. "Look at me," I said, patting her gently on the foot, "I'm scared too. Let's take a deep breath. We can do this ... stay focused on the step in front of you. NOTHING MORE."

She nodded, turned back around. I wondered where these words had come from. Who just said that? It couldn't be me, because I was about to wet my pants.

Both of us slowly crawled up the remaining stairs on our hands and knees, following J.J.'s example.

"Almost there," he said from above. I didn't see him step onto the wooden ledge or unlock the door to the belfry. All I knew is that when Stephanie and I reached the top, he was already inside, offering his hand to us.

"Oh my god!" she screamed as she made the leap.

I half expected to see her rush by, plummeting the entire distance to the floor. She didn't. That possibility now awaited me. Standing on the top stair, I paused, dizziness competing with what remained of my wits. *Don't pass out for Heaven's sake.*

"What are you doing?" J.J. barked, "Take my hand."

It took several moments for my eyes to adjust after stepping inside. Blinding bright sunlight was pouring in through the belfry's large rectangular openings. My sense of smell was intact, however. Bird crap—a lot of it, and everywhere. As I stepped forward, it crunched underfoot. All around me, I could hear pigeons cooing, the wings of the little devils fluttering as they moved to get out of my way.

Stephanie met me, taking my hand, "Come here, you've got to see this!"

Looking out, I squeezed her hand, "Wow. It's beautiful, isn't it?"

"Yeah, amazing," she said.

To the side of us, Johnson was slowly moving from one spot to the next, taking in each view. Stephanie let go of my hand and pointed to a large body of water in the distance, "What is that?"

"Hammarsjön— a lake," I answered, pointing, "and just beyond that, the Baltic Sea. Keep going and you end up in Poland!"

Stephanie laughed. Moving to the right, "and that way?"

"Germany," I said, "And over there? That's Denmark."

She looked up at me, "You really know this place."

I looked away and out the window, saying nothing. Spread before us were the red, tile roofs of the city. Tarnished copper turrets outlined the town, lending the impression of a fortress. In the distance, farmland, flat and green.

We stood there together taking in the view.

Steph broke the silence. "Are you glad you went?" she asked, "On a mission, I mean?" Remarkably, Steph was the first person to have asked me this question—and she wasn't even a Mormon! From day one, I'd wondered why I'd gone. *Am I glad now that I stuck it out?*

"That's a hard one to answer 'yes' or 'no'," I responded, shaking my head back and forth, "It's certainly the hardest thing I've ever done. Am I glad I went? Well, I am glad about everything I've learned; like you said, a language and being on my own and all. And from this vantage point, now, here, with just six weeks to go, well, I'm glad I stayed. But in the beginning? Two years away from home, and my family and friends? I'd have given anything to get out of here, *anything*."

Steph nodded, "I know that feeling."

"I haven't had much fun. I mean … that's not the right word. There've been moments, you know, when it's been ok. I've met some really great people, really great. And I have learned a lot. But a lot of it, I could've lived without. It's hard to put in to words, Steph. I wasn't prepared for this," my voice rising, "for how mean and petty people could be, for what I'd be asked to do, *told* to do … *be.*"

I could feel Steph's hand on the small of my back, "Gosh, Scott, I'm sorry."

I paused for a moment to think, "I mean, I, … I was … this forced me to decide what I believe and don't believe in."

"That sounds like a good thing," she said matter-of-factly.

"Huh," I responded, her comment striking home. Up to this point, I really hadn't thought about it that way. I'd been so preoccupied with what I felt I lost—up to my eyeballs feeling homesick, pushed around, bored, bullied, beaten down, deprived, ignored, forgotten, judged, condemned—I hadn't considered, much less recognized what I might have gained.

I looked out the portal, once again taking in the landscape. Hearing a train whistle in the distance, "We've got to get you to the station."

"Is it time already?"

Glancing at my watch, "We don't need to hurry, but yeah, we do need to start heading that way."

Stephanie leaned over and kissed me on the cheek. "This has been a lot of fun, Scott," she said, "Thanks for hanging out with me."

11

LOOKING BACK

∼

"An angel of God never has wings."

JOSEPH SMITH JR.
FIRST PROPHET, SEER, AND REVELATOR
THE CHURCH OF JESUS CHRIST OF LATTER DAY SAINTS

∼

A lifetime has passed since I was "honorably discharged" from the Sweden Göteborg Mission and returned home. I'd served my time, completed my tour of duty. Despite the many years, I can honestly say that my experience as an LDS missionary remains a profound and significant part of my life. Often, I'm reminded of a person or event from that period. Nothing before or after—save the birth of my children—has had a greater impact on me as a person or the course my life has taken.

I'd long thought about writing a book, had even started a time or two. I had copious amounts of reference material to guide me, to jog my memory. By the end of my mission, my journal—the one I refer to in the book—filled six volumes, each one containing detailed, day-by-day entries. I'd also saved every letter I'd sent and received—a dozen three-ring binders –as well as a packing box full of audio tapes and photographs.

Regardless of all that I'd kept from those years, life intruded and foiled my early attempts. There was college and graduate school, marriage and a divorce, moves across the country, re-marriage, children, and a busy professional career involving extensive travel. Moreover, to be truthful, early on I simply wanted to forget much of what had happened, put it behind me, and move on with my life. Why stir the pot? At the time, I could not see what would be accomplished.

Keeping those two years in check meant I did not stay in contact with anyone I met during my mission, Mormon or otherwise. Within weeks of getting back to the States, I received a wedding invitation from Mike Wiggins, my companion in Lund, the one with Crohn's disease. In a photo engraved on the invitation, he looked happy and healthy. I sent him a letter and gift. Later, he responded with a thank you note. We promised to stay in touch. We did not.

At BYU, I ran into a couple of the Elders I knew, including my last companion, Milton "J.J." Johnson. He was the same, solid, easy-going guy I'd known. His first week back at school, he looked me up and invited me to his apartment to catch up. I went. We spent the evening talking about our time together in Kristianstad, including what happened after I left. He filled me in about his last year, his assignments and companions.

He had a juicy piece of gossip about Elder O'Leary, the pious, red-haired, freckle-faced, kung fu master from my LTM days. I'd not seen O'Leary since our first day in Sweden, when he was kissing ass as usual. Through the grapevine, I heard he made zone leader. According to J.J., O'Leary returned to Sweden within weeks of going home to marry a Swedish member. Many Elders I knew had a crush on this particular young woman. She was from a prominent LDS family; more than that, word was she was strikingly good looking. She was also seventeen years old, sixteen when they met. The two married and promptly moved back to the States. So much for OP! J.J. had run into him on campus. No time wasted, they already had a kid!

J.J. also told me what did and did not change when Thorsson was replaced. We knew he was on his way out. In his classic fashion, he'd sent a letter. It came about a week after Stephanie's visit. In his missive, he announced his "time in the Lord's vineyard" was over. To the new leader, he was "passing the baton." Once more, he asserted his unshakeable love for us, expressed his appreciation for our "sacrifices," and pledged he would continue to "pray for our success in bringing the Gospel to a nation in need of salvation." He ended, imploring us to "be obedient and carry on." While preparing this book, I spent an evening on the net looking up people from my mission. I found the former president. From what I could gather, he worked in sales for several years before taking another job with the Church.

Incidentally, Stephanie de Luca chose not to stay in England to complete her training. Shortly after meeting me in Kristianstad, she went home. Just days before I returned to the States, I received a letter from her thanking me for our shared adventure. She also wrote she was too homesick to stay and wanted to be with her boyfriend. At my ten-year high school reunion, I looked for her. She didn't show. I was disappointed. I still don't know what happened to her.

I'd like to say something memorable took place during the final days of my mission. Nothing did. J.J. and I continued our routine, meeting members, seeking out people who'd been friendly toward the missionaries in the past, and helping out the "ragara." We also kept up our habit of reading books and the newspaper, doing our best to stay current with events taking place in Sweden and the rest of the world. Mostly, we talked and talked, about anything and everything. During our one and only visit at BYU, he claimed that after I left, he missed our conversations the most. He even admitted crying as he watched my train pull away. After that pleasant evening in Provo, I made no effort to reach out to him. Curiously, he didn't either.

My first year back at BYU, I did meet one other Elder from the mission. I was already a couple of months into my job as a resident assistant. I'd just parked my car in the dorm lot and was unloading my bike from the trunk. My Grandmother Christina, who lived in a nearby town, let me store the bike in her basement while I was in Sweden. I was so glad to see her when I got back to the States. For the entire two years away, I worried she would be gone before I got back. The reunion was happy for both of us. Just before I left, she put a fifty cent piece in my palm and said, "Get something nice for yourself." I hugged her. I never spent it. It sits on my desk in an old baking soda can I took from her home after she died. Throughout the depression, that's where she kept her money. I look at it every day.

As I was setting the kickstand, I heard someone shouting, excitedly, "Elder Miller!" I hadn't been called "Elder" for some time; it had to be somebody from Sweden. Looking over my shoulder, I immediately recognized the short, stocky fellow coming toward me. It was Lee, the ZL from

Lund—the one who'd tyrannized Wiggins and me about our numbers, called us girls when we embraced at the station during our goodbye, and took particular delight in making himself our nemesis.

I watched as he approached. I'd fantasized many times about just such a moment while on my mission— what I would do if I ever ran into one of my tormentors again. There were two versions of my revenge. One, I would punch him in the nose; the other, get up in his face and, in no uncertain terms, tell him what I really thought of him.

Drawing closer, I could see he was smiling, as though he were delighted to see me. About a yard away, he opened his arms to hug me, saying, "Elder Miller, Scott, it's so good to see you!"

I couldn't believe it. In fact, I was stunned. How could he act like this? Had he forgotten how he'd treated me and Mike? What a dick he'd been?

So, what did I do? I didn't say anything. I ignored him. I just got on my bike and rode away, leaving him standing there.

∾

I can't describe the joy I felt on seeing my parents. I was on the balcony overlooking the baggage claim area at Landvetter airport in Göteberg— the place I'd landed twenty-one months earlier. Standing next to me was Thorsson's replacement. For the last hour, we'd been saying goodbye to the other missionaries heading home.

The new mission president struck me as a really nice man, older and grandfatherly. We'd spent an hour together the prior day following my arrival from Kristianstad. He'd been so complimentary it was uncomfortable; and yet, he was completely sincere. Several times he told me how much he admired my command of the language. He also praised the work I'd done in Sweden. Besides Fru Nilsson and Stig Mårtensson, I'd baptized more than any other missionary in my cohort from the LTM. He wondered if I had any advice to share. It was a bittersweet moment. How different might it have been had he served as President from the very beginning.

I met my folks on the ground floor just outside customs. It was their first trip together abroad. Although they'd been in transit nearly twenty-four hours (Los Angeles to Chicago, Chicago to Copenhagen, Copenhagen to Göteborg), they both looked great. My mother's hair had a tinge of grey that hadn't been there when I'd started my mission. My father had put on a few pounds and was sporting a moustache.

We embraced for a long time. I'd anticipated this moment for many months—from the outset of my mission, actually. Over and over, my mother told me how much she had missed me, how glad she was to be together again. My father kept patting me on the back and saying, "We're so proud of you."

After that, we drove back to the President's home. There, we snacked and talked about our plans. He knew we'd be visiting areas within the mission. I'd informed him the day before, during my exit interview. It didn't seem to faze him. In fact, he wished us an enjoyable time.

That night, we stayed at a hotel in Göteborg arranged by the Ericssons, the elderly couple from Skövde. We were served a gourmet meal prepared by their son, the head chef—no dog hair!—and put up in a deluxe suite, our room overlooking the waterways.

We did have one interesting experience following dinner. We were getting ready for bed, Dad was in the shower, Mom and I were in the main room. Suddenly the lights went out, plunging us into darkness. Finding my way to the door, I opened it, discovering the entire floor was without electricity. There was no emergency lighting. I could hear people in the hallway talking, anxiously discussing what was going on and what they should do.

Right then, I caught a whiff of smoke coming from our room. It smelled like burning electrical wire.

"I hope *I* didn't do this," I heard my mother say.

As it happened, she was responsible for the blackout. Mother and her coffee. She'd plugged a small percolator she'd brought with her from the States directly into the wall, blowing the floor's main fuse. Eventually, the hotel staff managed to get the lights back on. Years later, we laughed about the incident. At the time, Mom was mortified. I remember thinking how little they'd changed while I was away.

Over the next two weeks, my parents and I traveled around Scandinavia. First, by train, to Oslo, Norway. While in the country, we took a ferry to a nearby island to visit the Thor Hyerdahl's Kon Tiki museum. On another day, we spent several hours strolling along the main drag, Karl Johan's Gata, watching the street performers: jugglers, fire eaters, musicians, and magicians. The entertainers are a summer staple in many large European cities.

I'd never seen anything like them before.

After Oslo, our next stop was Stockholm. I was looking forward to touring Sweden's capital city. I'd not had a chance to visit before as it was outside the Göteborg mission boundaries. The weather was perfect when we arrived, 75 degrees and sunny.

Carl-Erik, the concert pianist I'd befriended in Kristianstad, had arranged for his sister to meet us, take us around, and see the sights. We walked the streets of "Old Town," visited the royal castle in nearby Drottningholm, saw the crown jewels, and took a boat tour of the Stockholm archipelago. We spent our last day at Skansen park, an outdoor museum of Swedish history and culture, featuring exhibits with live, period actors. The combination of history, parks, and waterways thrilled my parents. Each night, we returned to the hotel exhausted.

Three days later, we boarded a train bound for Kristianstad. Carl-Erik spent two days with us, leading a tour of the area's castles located just beyond the city limits. Although I'd lived in the town for months, I didn't know the elegant, old structures existed. I would have visited for sure. One even had a moat! On our last afternoon together, he packed a picnic lunch and we ate by a local waterfall. The next morning, he put us on a train headed for Kalmar, a beautiful coastal city near Sweden's famous crystal factories.

Touring Orefors and Kosta Boda—the two largest manufacturers—was a dream come true for Mom. We watched the artisans work, turning molten glass into masterpieces. My parents shipped home enough candle holders, goblets, and sculptures to open an entire outlet store of their own. I still have a beautiful set of crystal dishes Mom bought that day, enough dinner and salad plates, serving platters and bowls for twelve people. We use them on special occasions, birthdays and holidays.

An experience at the Orefors factory has stayed with me for years. While completing the sale, I was speaking Swedish, translating back and forth between my parents and the clerk. At some point in the process, the woman leaned forward and in a whisper asked who the two nice people were that I was helping. When I told her they were my parents, she screwed up her face in confusion, asking, "Can't they speak Swedish?" Bewilderment followed when I answered, "No," adding that they were from the United States. Later, my parents beamed with pride as I related the incident, telling how the clerk could not understand how my parents and I could come from two different countries.

From Kalmar and the crystal factories, we went by train, then boat, to Copenhagen. We spent a few days in the city, seeing the sights, including Tivoli amusement park, and the famous copper statue in the bay, "The Little Mermaid." I think my folks could have stayed longer. Mother wanted to visit Aarhus, her father's ancestral home, but we ran out of time. I was also ready to go. School was starting in a few weeks. I was looking forward to visiting with friends from my hometown before having to pack up my belongings and move away again.

Looking out the window as the plane lifted off the runway at Copenhagen's Kastrup airport, I remember wondering if I'd ever return to Scandinavia.

∽

I imagine many people who know me will be surprised to learn I was raised Mormon and served a mission. With rare exception, it's not something I talk about. During my first few years home, on occasion, I did try to speak with others. In all instances, it was disappointing. Either I was met with skepticism—people questioning the truthfulness of my account—or told my faith, or "testimony," was weak.

One afternoon shortly after arriving home, my best friend from childhood, Bill, and I were swimming in his family's pool. He was my co-conspirator, the one who rocketed out of the room after we tried to learn the meaning of masturbation from our Seminary teacher. We'd been inseparable as kids. Not surprisingly, as we swam, we started talking about our missions. It was soon apparent our experiences were vastly different. More, our views about the Church and beliefs were far apart.

After listening to my account, he responded, "Well, your mission is what *you* make of it. How it turns out is *your* responsibility." His voice was cold, any warmth gone. Somehow, it felt like our conversation had turned into a trial. I was on the stand and he the prosecutor making his case against me. I countered, it was not so simple. He insisted it *was*. "Straight is the gate, and narrow is the way, which leadeth unto life," he lectured, emphasizing the last words, "*and few there be that find it*". In invoking this line of scripture, he reminded me of a Mormon maxim, a basic tenet of faith: only a few make it to Heaven and if you don't, you only have yourself to blame. Our friendship never recovered.

Sometime later, I wrote an article for *Sunstone*, a scholarly magazine about Mormon history and culture, examining the mission experience from a psychological perspective. It was a main feature in that issue and my first publication. By this time, I'd switched majors at BYU, abandoning accounting in favor of psychology. The parting gift Elder Fissen had given me—Thomas Harris' book, *I'm OK, You're OK*—and his inscription on the inside cover had started me thinking. I signed up for a couple psychology classes and fell in love with the subject. My relationships with two professors in particular, Drs. Michael J. Lambert and Harold L. Miller, Jr., eventually led me to choose psychology as a profession. They were scholarly, inquisitive, and accepting. When I was with them, no question was off limits. More important, they were committed to understanding people. They inspired me. I wanted to be like them.

That same year, I gave a presentation based on my article at the annual *Sunstone* conference held in Salt Lake City. I don't know how, but PBS film maker Bobbi Berleffi came across a copy and asked me to appear in a documentary she was producing. It was called, *Mormons: Missionaries to the World.* It followed several Elders over the course of their missions. Participating in the movie and the symposium was the first time I met others with stories matching mine.

Having felt heard and understood, I returned to the *Sunstone Symposium* the following year. This time, however, my reaction was altogether different. The same people were there talking about the very same stuff. I did not want to make rehashing or reliving the past a regular part of my life. Neither did I feel any desire to stay connected to the Church. For reasons of their own, some felt the pressure to do so.

While at BYU, finishing my bachelor's degree, I only went to church services enough to avoid popping up on the "Office of Standards" moral radar. Created during the 1960's, the job of this department was to enforce the University's "Honor Code," which, naturally, included church attendance. As soon as I graduated, I stopped going altogether. I recognized Mormonism had not changed, I had. The only times I've been in a Mormon Church since was for my parents' funerals.

∼

In July 2011, I lost my father. He'd been seriously ill for several years, suffering from an incurable blood disorder. Six years earlier, Mom passed away. He was by her side from the moment they learned she was dying. Their faith sustained them, throughout. They held hands, cried and prayed together, and looked forward to reuniting on the other side.

After Dad's funeral, I met my two brothers, Marc and Doug, in Glendora to sort through our parents' possessions and prepare their home for sale. In our hands, we held all they had saved over the years, deciding what to keep and throw away. Like many who grew up in the Great Depression, they kept everything. We found all our old school papers and pictures, bags of used Christmas bows, even 50 years worth of tax documents. Everything.

In the garage, set high on the rafters, I found the memorabilia from my mission. I'd forgotten just how much I'd collected. That stack of Jehovah's Witness books I'd dispatched from Sweden and a two-by-three foot cardboard advertisement for Burger King® were there. The latter I'd taken from a bus window, the one I rode with Cary Wells in Malmö on his last day in the mission field. I don't know what I was thinking at the time. Perhaps because the sign was in Swedish, and I thought it was cool. Maybe I was going to hang it in my dorm room. Who knows?

Anyway, I threw away the sign and JW books—along with a bunch of other junk—and then carefully packed away the rest and mailed it home to Chicago. A few items I carried with me on the return flight: my journals, the letters my parents and I exchanged, and my worn and dusty copy of *Catcher in the Rye.*

The year Dad died was eventful. With both of my parents gone, any real connection with the Church or its members ended. Until then, my father would faithfully forward my name to the Bishop of the local congregation whenever I moved. Rarely did they contact me. On the few occasions they did, I always told whoever called that they were welcome to visit but I really wasn't interested.

Around this same time, Mormonism was in the headlines. The Church's role in supporting the passage of California's anti-gay marriage "Proposition 8" was the subject of intense media attention. It came out that LDS leaders and members worked behind the scenes donating time and money, organizing the campaign. After the news came out, protesters infuriated with the Church's involvement picketed outside the Los Angeles temple.

Once more, a Mormon was running for President. Like his father, George, and the Prophet Joseph Smith, Mitt Romney was making a bid. Stories about the candidate almost always mentioned his religion and mission to France. While some reports commented on his G's or questioned the Church's controversial history, the overall tone was remarkably tolerant. It made it seem as though there was a very real chance a Mormon could be living in the White House, running the country.

Most surprising, a new musical appeared on Broadway about Mormons and missionary life! It was a runaway hit, playing to packed houses. I couldn't fathom why anyone who wasn't LDS would feel drawn to a performance called, *The Book of Mormon*. When I was a missionary, we couldn't give that book away, much less get past the front door. All of a sudden people are shelling out $300 to $500 a pop to see this thing. Sure, I'd heard the music and dancing were great, and the show was wickedly funny. But come on, an entire Broadway performance about a peculiar religious sect most people did their best to avoid? What could they possibly see in it?

When I got back from the funeral, I began looking up books about missions. Surprisingly, very few existed. Shortly thereafter, I began talking with my long time colleague, Mark Hubble. Also a close friend, he knew I'd been raised in the Church and served a mission. He urged me to write. Offered to do the book with me.

My biggest hesitation was I'd be rejected. I believed people, on hearing I'd been raised Mormon and served a mission, would judge me harshly, just as I had been when I was a missionary. Instead of taking the time to get to know me, I'd be reduced to another blue-suit-wearing, true-believer knocking at their door. Moreover, I didn't want to have to explain myself or the Church. People were going to ask, "Why did you go?" Facing facts, other than "going along with the crowd," I'd had no good reason.

Embarrassment was another factor. Despite being disaffected with the Church, I felt responsible for the choices I'd made, being a representative for an organization, much of whose history, beliefs and practices I came to view as objectionable, in some cases, morally repugnant. Particularly the long time discrimination against people of African origin, the active campaign against equal rights for women and gays, the practice of polygamy and polyandry, and the relentless demand for absolute obedience to authority. The Church's failure to acknowledge its mistakes, historic and recent, only compounded my feelings of shame. Mormon practices and policies were clear, had always been so. In the end, I felt I had only myself to blame. After all, no one forced me to go. Plus, I didn't have a sound reason for having chosen to stay.

I am not saying the LDS Church is unique in its hubris or hypocrisy. Plenty of that exists in the world to go around. Mormons are, in most ways, the same as everybody else. I once heard a story about an old man who dies and goes to Heaven. He's walking up a gold-paved street when he notices a building set behind tall walls, topped with barbed wire. When he inquires about the structure, St. Peter answers, "Shhh, those are the Mormons. They think they're the only ones in here." As funny as the story is, it's an old joke. I've heard it told using Jews, Catholics, Fundamentalists, even Republicans and Democrats for the punch line.

In short, no matter who we are or what we believe, each of us is capable of exhibiting the same love and hate, humility and pride, tolerance and prejudice, kindness and cruelty, truth and error, as anyone else. When we forget how similar we are, come to see ourselves as somehow different, better, even unique, the stage is set for the mistreatment of others. From world wars to bullying in the schools, life is replete with examples of what happens when we set ourselves apart, above others.

So, I decided finally to write the book. No more hedging. No more avoidance. I was raised Mormon. And, yes, I served an LDS mission. In case there is any doubt, admitting this is as much for me as it is for anyone else.

As must be obvious, my time in Sweden was not "the best two years of my life." This assessment is not born of bitterness. Looking back, re-reading my journals, I found myself feeling empathy for the young man I was. As Mark and I talked and wrote, several times arose when Mark expressed shock and anger at what I endured in the name of serving God faithfully. In short, much of what we missionaries had been compelled to do was simply wrong. Additionally, the way we were treated by those in authority was unnecessary, hurtful, and cruel. In that time in my life, separated from home and family, alone and scared, Mark marveled at the absence of what forms the core of Christian faith. Such feelings gave way to sadness as we recognized the opportunity for compassion, consideration, respect, and thoughtful guidance was lost, and with it, my childhood faith and innocence.

Am I sorry I went? Although it pains me to say, the answer is, no. For many years, I found it difficult to acknowledge this fact without feeling I was somehow giving tacit approval to some of what took place. I see things differently now. Sure, I wish a large part of it had been different. The way I was treated was wrong. Inasmuch as the same practices continue, it remains wrong. No one, especially an organization which claims to be the only true, Christian church on Earth, has the right to violate the basic tenet of that faith, *The Golden Rule*. The church exists to serve its members—particularly, its most vulnerable, children—not the other way around. Ultimately, that's why I left.

Still, despite the hardships, I am who I am today because of the time I served. I am a more careful and thoughtful decision-maker—no more going along with the crowd, bending to social pressure. I learned to live on my own, face adversity, and get along with others. I became more studious and disciplined—a hard worker capable of overcoming challenges, and setting and achieving long-term goals. Regularly being confronted with ridicule and scorn, in time hardened me, made it easier to put myself out there, meet people, speak in public, and accept criticism. Most important of all, I came to know what I stand for, my values and beliefs. In this, I was helped by most everyone I met. A handful, Thorsson and the like, showed me how not to act. Many others—Stefan, Elin, Harris, Wiggins, Fissen, the street kids, the members in Skövde, Bengt and Peter—provided examples of kindness, compassion, and tolerance I strive to emulate even today.

BOOK OF A MORMON
"READY REFERENCE"

<u>Cast of Characters</u>: (in order of appearance)

<u>Chapter One:</u>

Spencer W. Kimball, *the 12ᵗʰ Prophet, Seer, and Revelator of the Church of Jesus Christ of Latter Day Saints, famous for commanding that all male members of the faith serve missions and eliminating the Church's ban on blacks holding the priesthood.*

Elder Ken Arnold, aka, *Popeye. One of Scott's two companions at the Language Training Mission.*

Elder Cary Wells, *one of Scott's two companions at the Language Training Mission. A relative of his was among the "Eight Witnesses" to see and handle the gold plates from which Joseph Smith translated the* Book of Mormon.

Oscar Thorsson, *the president of the Sweden Göteborg Mission during the majority of Scott's time in the country.*

Mary Bowen, *Scott's great-great-paternal grandmother who died while emigrating from Wales to the United States after joining the LDS Church.*

David Bowen, *Scott's great-great-paternal grandfather who, together with his son Morgan, traveled by Schuttler wagon to Salt Lake City following the death of his wife and daughter.*

Orson Pratt, *early Church leader and close confidant of the Prophet Joseph Smith who cheated Scott's great, great paternal grandfather, David Bowen, out of wages earned while emigrating by ship from Wales to the United States.*

Joseph Smith, *the charismatic and controversial founder of the Church of Jesus Christ of Latter Day Saints*

Paul B. Miller, *Scott's father.*

Darlene (Daniels) Miller, *Scott's Mother.*

Zerah Pulsipher, Darlene Miller's great-great-great-grandfather. An early member of the Church who was present at most major events during the Church's early days. He baptized Wilford Woodruff, the fourth president of the LDS Church, responsible for the abolition of polygamy.

Doug Miller, *Scott's older brother. His wife's name is Liz. Their son, Tylor, was born days after Scott departed California headed for the Language Training Mission.*

Marc Miller, *Scott's younger brother.*

Elder O'Leary, *the diminutive, super pious, red-haired, freckle-faced Idahoan and Kung Fu master who served as District Leader to Scott's cohort at the Language Training Mission.*

Thomas S. Monson, *one of the "Twelve Apostles" of the Church of Jesus Christ of Latter Day Saints. Shortly before Scott arrived in the country, Monson had visited and rededicated the country to intensive missionary work.*

Elder Pierce, *one of the two "AP's," or Assistants to the President, Scott meets at the mission office on his first day in Sweden.*

Elder Payne, *one of the two "AP's," or Assistants to the President, Scott meets at the mission office on his first day in Sweden.*

Bishop Murphy, *the lay ecclesiastical leader of Scott's congregation in Glendora, California who, on weekdays, managed a frozen food company.*

Doctor Oakes, *the lay ecclesiastical leader of Scott's congregation in Glendora, California who led services when Bishop Murphy was not available. Dr. Oakes was also the Miller family physician.*

Elder Hedger, *a missionary Scott met at the Language Training Mission who cried at night about missing his girlfriend Laurie. On the first day in the country, mission leaders confiscated all of the pictures of her he'd brought with him.*

Sister Thorsson, *wife of the mission president, and pregnant mother of five who prepares a welcome dinner of spaghetti and meatballs on Scott's first day in the country.*

Lilburn Boggs, *Governor of Missouri who, in 1838, issued "Executive Order 44" authorizing the extermination of LDS Church members.*

Christina Daniels, *Scott's Scandinavian maternal grandmother.*

Katie Barrett, *Scott's girlfriend his freshman year at Brigham Young University.*

Wesley Murphy, *the popular son of Scott's local ecclesiastical leader, Bishop Murphy.*

Peter Blake, *a childhood friend of Scott's who played the drums in their on-and-off rock band.*

Bill Price, *Scott's best friend from childhood.*

Chapter Two:

Ezra Taft Benson, *13th Prophet, Seer, and Revelator of the Church of Jesus Christ of Latter Day Saints. Served as Secretary of Agriculture under Eisenhower.*

Elin Olin, *a former exchange student in the U.S. that Scott meets while he's traveling by train to his first mission assignment in Huskvarna.*

Elder Robert Church, *Scott's first missionary companion in Huskvarna, Sweden.*

Dean Ander, *an investigator in Huskvarna that fails to keep his appointment on Scott's first day in Huskvarna.*

Fru Nilsson, *a kind, elderly investigator Scott meets on his first day. She mends the knee of his torn trousers while he and his companion teach her one of the missionary discussions.*

Chapter Three:

Brother Dick Heurtz, *Scott's 9th grade LDS Seminary teacher. The teacher told him, and his best friend, Bill Price, that masturbation was "doing bad things with one's bodily fluids."*

Mr. Kindrick, *neighbor of the Miller Family who told Scott he'd put a special chemical in their pool that turned red on contact with urine.*

Mark E. Petersen, *one of the LDS Church's Twelve Apostles and author of a pamphlet advising that boys tie their hands to the bed to avoid masturbation.*

Sister Cox, *Scott's Sunday School teacher who taught him the story of Jonah and the Whale.*

Elder Pyle, *one of the two ZL's in Jönköping, the city near Scott's first assignment in Huskvarna. He served pickle juice for dinner.*

Elder Chris Harris, *one of the two ZL's in Jönköping, the city near Scott's first assignment in Huskvarna. He helps Scott deal with his homesickness, telling him to remember, "this too shall pass."*

Agnetha Fältskog, *the blond-haired, female singer in the Swedish pop group, ABBA.*

Lars, *a street kid that steals Scott's missionary hat during a confrontation at the bus station in Jönköping.*

Princess Victoria, *the Crown Princess of Sweden*

Brother Seikkula and family, *a Swedish-speaking, LDS, Finnish family that invite Scott and Elder Harris to dinner.*

Chapter Four:

Elder Mike Wiggins, *Scott's companion in Lund who is ill with colitis. He helps Scott master the language, shows him how to mark his scriptures for bashes with Jehovah's Witnesses, and get a library card.*

Stefan Petersson, *a Lutheran minister Scott meets on the bus while traveling from Huskvarna to Lund. Stefan served as a missionary in Africa and works with street kids.*

Brigham Young, *the second Prophet, Seer, and revelator of the Church of Jesus Christ of Latter Day Saints. Young became the head of the church when Joseph Smith was murdered. He directed the migration westward.*

Woodie Strode, *an actor and member of Scott's LDS congregation in Glendora, California.*

Joakim, a third-year physics major at Lund University who asks Scott and his companion to teach him the discussions but ends up debating them about the virgin birth of Jesus.

Elders Lee and Larson, *the zone leaders in Lund. Lee, a former state champion wrestler, constantly harasses Elders Miller and Wiggins about their performance. Larsson is a friendly sort. His teeth were dark and broken due to an accident occurring shortly before leaving on his mission.*

Chapter Five:

Elder Burr, *Cary Wells's companion at the time Scott meets him in Malmö.*

Elder Smith, *the AP, Assistant to the President, who succeeded Elder Payne.*

Elder George P. Lee, *the first Native American member of the Church hierarchy. His ascension was important because Mormons from Joseph Smith on believed the American Indians are descendants of* Book of Mormon *peoples called Laminites. In 1989, he was excommunicated for "apostasy and other conduct unbecoming a member of the Church." Later, he pled guilty to attempted sexual abuse of a child. He died in 2010.*

Elder Simms, *a slim missionary Scott meets briefly at a zone conference held in Malmö.*

Sister Morrow, *a member of Scott's congregation in Glendora, California who always broke into tears whenever sharing her belief in the Mormon Church at the special LDS service known as "Fast and Testimony meeting.*

Lise-Marie Lindfeldt, *a 20-year-old college student Scott and his companion Mike Wiggins met and taught in Lund. She'd been an exchange student in the States and was hosted by an LDS family.*

Lu Lu, daughter of the family that hosted Swedish exchange student

Lise-Marie Lindfeldt. Scott and his companion Mike Wiggins meet her in Lund. She's in the country visiting Lise-Marie.

Chapter Six:

Gunnar, *a young man rescued from a life on the streets by the Lutheran minister Stefan.*

Hans, *Elin Olin's live-in boyfriend.*

Russell Ballard, *one of the LDS Church's Twelve Apostles.*

Brother Wright, *a member of Scott's congregation in Glendora, California that was found guilty of adultery and excommunicated from the Church.*

Mary Beth Wilkins, *a young female member of Scott's congregation in Glendora, California who abruptly left a church meeting during a lesson about remaining "sexually clean."*

Steve Smith, *a friend of Scott's from high school that was raised in the Baptist faith.*

Robert Neufield, *a friend of Scott's from high school that was raised in the Seventh Day Adventist faith.*

Chapter Seven:

Elder Bernie Fissen, *the Elder Scott is assigned to work with in Skövde.*

Ned Knipple, *a classmate of Scott's at Carl Sandburg Junior High School who was bullied by the athletes.*

Angela Murphy, *the Bishop's daughter Scott dated during his senior year in high school.*

Elder Barrett, *missionary at the LTM who washes his white dress shirts together with blue socks turning all his shirts into light blue.*

Diana, *Scott's steady, non-Mormon girlfriend his freshman, sophomore, and junior years in high school.*

Elder Beech, *one of the DL's in Skövde. Elder Fissen meets with him to pass off the discussions.*

Kerstin Mårtansson, *wife of Stig Mårtansson, former Hippie, and member of the Church in Skövde*

Stig Mårtansson, *former Hippie and non-Mormon husband of Kerstin, who all missionaries try to convert.*

Clarence Daniels, *Scott's Scandinavian maternal grandfather.*

<u>Chapter 8:</u>

O.P., *a stray cat adopted by Scott and his companion Elder Bernie Fissen while living in Skövde.*

Elder Roberts, *the DL in Skövde that is replaced by Ken Arnold, Scott's friend and one of the Three Musketeers from the LTM.*

Bengt and Peter, *two retired men who sit on a park bench in the town square in Skövde. Scott and his companion, Bernie Fissen befriend them.*

Aksel Sandemose, *Danish author of* A Fugitive Crosses his Tracks *(in Swedish,* En Flyktning Krysser sitt Spor*), a classic of Scandanavian literature.*

Tove Dahlberg, *the daughter of a Swedish mom who is married to an American draft dodger. She starts coming to Church after introducing herself to Scott and his companion Bernie Fissen in a grocery store.*

Agneta and Björn Carlsson, *two young children whose parents are members of the LDS Church in Skövde. Scott dances with them on Christmas Eve.*

James Lange, *an adolescent neighbor who lures a prepubescent Scott into his home for nefarious purposes.*

<u>Chapter 9:</u>

Carl-Erik Dahlberg, *concert pianist and member of the Church Scott meets while stationed in Kristianstad.*

Milton "J.J." Johnson, *Scott's companion in Kristianstad.*

Francis Horton, *the Dorm Mother that offered Scott a job as a resident assistant when he came home from his mission.*

Jaime Lee, a member of Scott's congregation in Glendora who begins to correspond with Scott as he nears the end of his mission.

Allison, the sister of a friend from the dorms who begins to correspond with Scott as he nears the end of his mission.

Annica, *one of the raggare in Skövde who adopts O.P. the cat when Scott and his companion are transferred out of the area.*

Stephanie de Luca, *a friend of Scott's from High School who comes to Krisitianstad for a visit.*

THE LATTER DAY SAINT SCRIPTURAL CANON:

The Holy Bible (King James Version), *containing the Old and New Testaments.*

The Book of Mormon, a book Joseph Smith claimed he translated from a set of "gold plates" found hidden in a hill near his home in Palmyra, New York. It is said to contain a historical record of God's dealings with the ancient inhabitants of the Americas.

The Doctrine and Covenants, an abridged selection of revelations received by Joseph Smith and some of his successors.

The Pearl of Great Price, a book LDS Church members revere as scripture, equal in standing to the *Holy Bible* and *Book of Mormon.* The slim volume contains five sections: (1) the official account of Joseph Smith's First Vision and other early events in Church history; (2) Smith's translation of Egyptian papyri he said contained the writings of the Biblical Abraham and autograph of Moses; (3) Smith's revision of the first six chapters of Genesis and a prologue to the creation story called, *The Book of Moses;* (4) Smith's revision of the *Book of Matthew;* and (5) A list of the fundamental doctrines of Mormonism known as, *The Articles of Faith.*

The Uniform System for Teaching the Gospel, aka The Discussions, a structured set of lessons for teaching prospective converts about the LDS Church. For many years, missionaries were required to memorize and repeat the content verbatim, including a step-by-step process for securing commitment from prospective converts to be baptized.

Made in the USA
Columbia, SC
29 March 2019